OETRY

A Longman Pocket Anthology
Second Edition

R. S. Gwynn
Lamar University

 LONGMAN

An Imprint of Addison Wesley Longman, Inc.

New York • Reading, Massachusetts • Menlo Park, California • Harlow, England
Don Mills, Ontario • Sydney • Mexico City • Madrid • Amsterdam

Jacket illustration by Stephen Alcorn • The Alcorn Studio and Gallery •
Cambridge, NY

Senior Editor: Lisa Moore
Developmental Editor: Marlane Agriesti Miriello
Text Design: David Munger/DTC
Electronic Page Makeup: Karen Milholland/DTC
Printer and Binder: RR Donnelley & Sons Company
Cover Printer: Coral Graphic Services, Inc.

For permission to use copyrighted material, grateful acknowledgement is
made to the copyright holders on pages 350–353, which are hereby made
part of the copyright page.

Library of Congress Cataloging-in-Publication Data

Poetry / [compiled by] R.S. Gwynn. — [2nd ed.]
    p. cm. — (A Longman pocket anthology)
    Includes index.
    ISBN 0-321-01113-9
    1. Poetry–Collections. I. Gwynn, R. S. II. Series.
PN6101.P52   1997
821.008–dc21   97-16030
                                              CIP

ISBN 0-321-01113-9

45678910-DOC-009998

CONTENTS

Poetry **35**

BEN JONSON (1573–1637)

    On My First Son   55
    Slow, Slow, Fresh Fount   55

ROBERT HERRICK (1591–1674)

    To the Virgins, to Make Much of Time   56

GEORGE HERBERT (1593–1633)

    Easter Wings   57
    Love (III)   57
    The Pulley   58
    Redemption   58

EDMUND WALLER (1606–1687)

    Song   59

JOHN MILTON (1608–1674)

    How Soon Hath Time   60
    On the Late Massacre in Piedmont   60
    When I Consider How My Light Is Spent   61

ANNE BRADSTREET (1612–1672)

    The Author to Her Book   62
    To My Dear and Loving Husband   62

RICHARD LOVELACE (1618–1658)

    To Lucasta, Going to the Wars   63

ANDREW MARVELL (1621–1678)

    To His Coy Mistress   63

JOHN DRYDEN (1631–1700)

    To the Memory of Mr. Oldham   65
    Epigram on Milton   66

EDWARD TAYLOR (1642–1729)

    Housewifery   66

JONATHAN SWIFT (1667–1745)

    A Description of a City Shower   67

ALEXANDER POPE (1688–1744)

    from An Essay on Criticism   69
    Ode on Solitude   70

THOMAS GRAY (1716–1771)

    Elegy Written in a Country Churchyard   71

FOREWORD

The Longman Pocket Anthology series was born of a need we hear almost daily for brief, inexpensive anthologies. Professors tell us they are concerned that anthologies seem to grow larger and larger, and that their students feel cheated when less than a third of the selections are actually taught in the course. To meet this demand, we have published FICTION: A Longman Pocket Anthology and POETRY: A Longman Pocket Anthology, now both in their second editions. FICTION and POETRY can be used individually for courses that focus specifically on one of the genres, or together in an introduction to literature course in combination with selected plays, novels, or collections of works by single authors.

These brief, inexpensive anthologies can easily be carried to class and offer students real value at a reasonable price. They are designed to offer the most essential information on each genre so that our pages are primarily devoted to providing a wide choice for your teaching purposes. To determine which selections to include—and whether this idea would hit a responsive chord among professors—we surveyed numerous professors to ask what they want in an anthology. Our survey helped us determine which poems professors want to teach, and we have made a special effort to broaden the canon. For example, many newly appreciated voices, like Elinor Wylie, Louise Bogan, and Pattiann Rogers, are now included. The suggestions from those professors we surveyed were critical in determining the final shape of the book, with its range of classic and modern writers from around the world.

It is our hope that these books respond to the needs of students and professors who are looking for comprehensive, but affordable, alternatives to the big-book anthology. We particularly want to thank R. S. Gwynn, whose teaching experience and knowledge of literature are the foundation for the Longman Pocket Anthologies. We are also grateful to all those poetry and introductory literature professors whose advice guided us in making selections and putting together the essential introductory material that their students would find useful for the second edition of POETRY: A Longman Pocket Anthology: Shireen Carroll, Davidson College; Tracy Case, Yakima Valley Community College; Bill Clemente, Peru State College;

Michel de Benedictis, Miami Dade Community College; Allen Kupser, Nassau Community College; Dwight McCawley, West Chester University of Pennsylvania; Robert L. McDonald, Virginia Military Institute; Jim Papworth, Ricks College; Frank Rooney, Wentworth Institute of Technology; John Ruszkiewicz, University of Texas; Charles Schuster, University of Wisconsin-Milwaukee; Deborah Sutton, Jefferson College; John Walsh, Saint Peter's College; and David Williams, San Francisco State University.

We are also grateful to the professors who commented on the first edition: Marsha Aldrich, Michigan State University; Herman L. Asarnow, University of Portland; Lea Baechler, Columbia University; Paul Bodmer, Bismark State College; Peggy F. Broder, Cleveland State University; William Covino, University of Chicago; Dwight Eddins, University of Alabama; Wil Gehne, State University of New York, Binghamton; Cheryl Glenn, Oregon State University; Julia Hamilton, Inver Hills Community College; Jennie Harrison, North Harris College; Mary Hojnacki, University of Massachusetts, Lowell; Jim Holte, East Carolina University; Aija Hoover, Odessa College; John Morris, Cameron University; Lee Patterson, Duke University; Marco Portales, Texas A & M University; Lawrence Rainey, Yale University; Kim Roberts, University of Maryland; Danny Robinson, Bloomsburg University; Pam Schirmeister, New York University; James Schuttemeyer, Thomas More College; Shirley Simpson, Nicholls State University; Michael Steinman, Nassau Community College; Kathleen Thornton, State University of New York, Albany; and Clifford Dale Whitman, Southern Arkansas University.

Lisa Moore
Literature Editor

INTRODUCTION

An Anecdote: Where Poetry Starts

The room is not particularly grand, a large lecture hall in one of the old buildings on the college campus, and the small group of first-year students whose literature class has been dismissed so that they can attend the poetry reading have taken seats near the back of the room. They have been encouraged to come for several weeks by their instructor, and when she enters she looks around the room and nods in their direction, smiling.

The seats gradually fill. The crowd is a mixed one—several men and women known by sight as senior faculty members; a scattering of other older visitors, many of them apparently from the community; a large contingent of instructors and graduate students from the English Department sitting in the front rows; and small clusters of undergraduates scattered throughout the room.

One of the students scans the crowd, wondering aloud which is the poet. On the walk to the reading, the class's consensus has been that the poet, a cadaverous grey-haired man wrapped in a black cloak, would recite his poems in a resonant monotone, preferably with a strong breeze tossing his hair. Speculating on how the wind effect might be managed inside a lecture hall made them laugh.

Now the crowd grows quiet as their instructor steps to the podium and adjusts the microphone. She makes a few complimentary remarks about the strong turnout and thanks several benefactors for their financial support of poetry at the university. Then she introduces the guest. Her students know most of this information, for they have studied several of his poems in class that week, but they are still slightly surprised when he rises to polite applause and takes the lectern. The balding middle-aged man wearing a chambray shirt and knit tie could be taken for an associate professor in any campus department, and when he adjusts his glasses and clears his throat, blinking at the audience, there is little about him that would fit anyone's romantic stereotype of the poet.

Surprisingly, he does not begin with a poem. Instead, in a relaxed voice he tells an anecdote about his younger daughter and an overdue science project. When he moves from the background story into the poem itself, there is little change in his volume level, and his tone remains conversational. The students find that the poem, which they had discussed in class only a couple of days before, takes on new meaning when its origins are explained by the poet himself. They find themselves listening attentively to his words, even laughing out loud several times. The hour goes quickly, and at its end their applause, like that of the rest of the audience, is long and sincere.

At the next class meeting the instructor asks for reactions on the reading. While some of the class members are slightly critical, faulting the speaker for his informal manner and his failure to maintain eye contact with the room, most of the remarks are positive. The comments that surface most often have to do with how much more meaningful the poems in the textbook become when the poet explains how he came to write them, how one poem is actually spoken in the voice of his dead father, how another is addressed to a friend who was paralyzed in an automobile accident. While these things could perhaps be inferred from the poems alone, the students are unanimous that knowing the details beforehand adds a great deal to the first impression a poem makes. As one student puts it, "It's just that a poem makes a lot more sense when you know who's talking and when and where it's supposed to be taking place."

"It always helps to know where poetry starts," adds one of her classmates.

Speaker, Listener, and Context

The situation described above is hardly unique. Instructors have long been encouraging, even begging, their students to attend events like this one, and the college poetry reading has become, for many Americans, the closest encounter they will have with this complex and often perplexing art form. But what students often find at such readings, sometimes to their amazement, is that poetry need not be intimidating or obscure, providing a gentle reminder that the roots of poetry, like those of all literature, were originally part of the **oral tradition**, stories and poems that were passed down from generation to generation in ancient societies and were recited for audiences that included all members of the tribe—from the wizened elders to the youngest children. For most of its long history poetry has been a popular art form aimed at *audiences* (remember that the word means "hearers"), and it is only recently that its most visible signs of life are to be found on college campuses. The reasons for this academic retreat are too complicated to go into here, but it is perhaps worth noting that we are daily exposed to a great deal of poetry in oral form, primarily through the medium of recorded song lyrics, and that the unique qualities of poetry throughout the ages—its ability to tell stories or summarize complicated emotions in a few well-chosen words—are demonstrated whenever we memorize the lines of a popular song and sing them to ourselves.

Of course, poetry written primarily for the page is usually more demanding than song lyrics. Writers of popular songs aim at a wide commercial audience, and this simple fact of economics, added to the fact that the lyrics are not intended primarily for publication but for being recorded with all the resources of studio technology, tends to make many song lyrics relatively uninteresting when they appear in print. A poem, on the other hand, will primarily exist as a printed text, though certainly its effect may be enhanced greatly through a skillful oral performance in which the poet can also explain the background of the poem, its setting and speaker, and the circumstances under which it was written. In general, these details, so crucial to understanding a poem yet so often only implied when the poem appears in print, are called the **dramatic situation** of a poem. Reduced to its simplest formulation, dramatic situation can be summed up in a question: *Who is speaking to whom under what circumstances?* If the poet fails to provide us with clues or if we are careless in picking up the information that is provided, then we may begin reading with no sense of reference and, thus, may go far astray. Even such words as "on," "upon," or "to" in titles can be crucial to our understanding of dramatic situation, telling us something about an event or object that provided the stimulus for the poem or about the identity of the "you" addressed in the poem.

An illustration may be helpful. Suppose we look at what is unquestionably the most widely known poem ever written by an American. It is a poem which virtually all Americans can recite in part and, in fact, do so by the millions every week. Yet if we were told that this poem is unusual in that its best-known section is a long, unanswered question addressed by the speaker to a companion about whether or not the object named in the title even exists, then it is likely that most of us would be confused. Before going further, let's look at the poem.

The Star-Spangled Banner

O say, can you see, by the dawn's early light,
    What so proudly we hailed at the twilight's last gleaming?
Whose broad stripes and bright stars thro' the perilous fight,
    O'er the ramparts we watched, were so gallantly streaming!
And the rockets' red glare, the bombs bursting in air,
    Gave proof through the night that our flag was still there:
O say, does that star-spangled banner yet wave
    O'er the land of the free and the home of the brave?

On the shore, dimly seen thro' the mists of the deep,
    Where the foe's haughty host in dread silence reposes,
What is that which the breeze, o'er the towering steep,
    As it fitfully blows, now conceals, now discloses?
Now it catches the gleam of the morning's first beam,
    In full glory reflected now shines on the stream:
'Tis the star-spangled banner! O long may it wave
    O'er the land of the free and the home of the brave!

And where is that band who so vauntingly swore
    That the havoc of war and the battle's confusion

A home and a country should leave us no more?
   Their blood has washed out their foul footsteps' pollution.
No refuge could save the hireling and slave
   From the terror of flight, or the gloom of the grave:
And the star-spangled banner in triumph doth wave
   O'er the land of the free and the home of the brave!

Oh! thus be it ever, when freemen shall stand
   Between their loved homes and the war's desolation!
Blest with victory and peace, may the heaven-rescued land
   Praise the Power that hath made and preserved us a nation.
Then conquer we must, when our cause it is just,
   And this be our motto: "In God is our trust."
And the star-spangled banner in triumph shall wave
   O'er the land of the free and the home of the brave!

"Now wait a minute!" you may be wondering. "'The Star-Spangled Banner' is a *song*, not a poem. And what's this question business? Don't we always sing it while facing the flag? Besides, it's just a patriotic song. Nobody really worries about what it *means*."

In answer to the first comment, "The Star-Spangled Banner" *was* in fact written as a poem and set to music only after its composition. Most of us will probably agree that the words are not particularly well suited to the melody (which was taken, curiously, from a popular British barroom ballad) and the song remains notoriously difficult to sing, even for professional performers. Garth Brooks, the popular country singer, once remarked before attempting it at a Super Bowl that it "is one of the hardest songs to sing," implying that the audience at such an event always seems ready to witness a failure. In its original form, "The Star-Spangled Banner" (or "The Defense of Fort McHenry," the title under which it was first published) is an example of **occasional verse**, a poem that is written about or for an important event (or occasion), sometimes private but usually of some public significance. While poems of this type are not often printed on the front pages of newspapers as they once were, they are still being written. Enough poems appeared after the assassination of President John F. Kennedy in 1963 to fill a book, *Of Poetry and Power*, and the *Challenger* disaster of 1985 stimulated a similar outpouring of occasional poems, one of them by Howard Nemerov, who served as poet laureate of the United States. Most recently, Maya Angelou recited "On the Pulse of Morning" at the inauguration of President Clinton. The author of "The Star-Spangled Banner," Francis Scott Key (1779-1843), wrote poetry as an avocation. Yet like many men and women who are not professional writers, Key was so deeply moved by an event that he witnessed that occasional poetry was the only medium through which he could express his feelings.

Now let's go back to our question about dramatic situation, taking it one part at a time: *Who is speaking?* A technical word that is often used to designate the speaker of a poem is **persona** (plural: **personae**), a word that meant "mask" in ancient Greek. Even though the persona of "The Star-Spangled Banner" never uses the word "I" in the poem, the speaker seems to be Key himself, a fact that can be verified by biographical research. Still, it is probably safer to look at poems carefully to see if they give any evidence that the speaker is someone other than the poet. Poems like "Ulysses" by Alfred, Lord Tennyson or "Porphyria's Lover" by Robert Browning have titles that identify personae who are, respectively, a character from ancient epic poetry and a unnamed man who is confessing the murder of his lover, Porphyria. In neither case is the persona to be identified with the poet himself. Other poems may be somewhat more problematical. Edgar Allan Poe's "The Raven," like many of Poe's short stories, is spoken by a persona who is not to be identified with the author, even though he shares many of the same morbid preoccupations of Poe's other characters; even Sylvia Plath, a poet usually associated with an extremely candid form of autobiographical poetry known as **confessional poetry**, identified the persona of her masterpiece "Daddy" as an invented character, "a girl with an Electra complex." Sometimes poems have more than one persona, which is the case with Thomas Hardy's "The Ruined Maid" and Robert Frost's "Home Burial," two poems which consist almost entirely of dialogue. In other poems, the voice may simply be a third-person **narrator** such as we might find in a short story or novel. While it is perhaps true that many poems (including the majority of those included here) are in fact spoken by the poet out of his or her most private feelings, it is not a good idea to leap too quickly to the assumption that the persona of a poem is identical to the poet and shares his or her views. Conclusions about the degree to which a poem is autobiographical can only be verified by research and familiarity with a poet's other works.

To return to our question: Who is speaking *to whom?* Another useful term is **auditor**, the person or persons spoken to in a poem. Some poems identify no auditor; others clearly do specify an auditor or auditors, in most cases identified by name or by the second-person pronoun "you" (or "thee/thou" in older poetry). Again, the title may give clues: Poe's "To Helen" is addressed to the famous beauty of Homeric legend; Robert Herrick's "To the Virgins, to Make Much of Time" is addressed to a group of young women; William Cullen Bryant's "To a Waterfowl" is addressed to, yes, a *duck*—or at least to some other type of migratory waterfowl. (The figure of speech **apostrophe** is used when a non-human, inanimate, or abstract thing is directly addressed). Relatively few poems are addressed directly to the reader, so when we read the opening of William Shakespeare's Sonnet 18 ("Shall I compare thee to a summer's day?") we should keep in mind that he is not addressing us but another individual, in this case a young friend who is referred to in many of the sonnets. A powerful poem like Claude McKay's "If We Must Die" begins in this manner:

> If we must die, let it not be like hogs
> Hunted and penned in an inglorious spot,

While round us bark the mad and hungry dogs,
Making their mock at our accursed lot.

Later in the poem McKay identifies his auditors as "Kinsmen." Without outside help about all we can say with certainty at first glance is that the poet seems to be addressing a group of companions who share his desperate situation; when we learn, possibly through research, that McKay was an African-American poet writing in the 1920s, the symbolic nature of his exhortation becomes clearer.

Now the final part of the question: Who is speaking to whom *under what circumstances?* First, we might ask if there is a relationship, either implied or stated, between persona and auditor. Obviously many love poems take the form of verbal transactions between two parties, and, since relationships have their ups and downs, these shifts of mood are reflected in the poetry. One famous example is Michael Drayton's sonnet "Since There's No Help," which begins with the persona threatening to end the relationship with the auditor but which ends with an apparent reconciliation. Such "courtship ritual" poems as John Donne's "The Flea" and Andrew Marvell's "To His Coy Mistress" are witty arguments in favor of the couple's engaging in sexual intercourse—no more, no less. An example from love poetry is Matthew Arnold's "Dover Beach," with ends with the plea "Ah, love, let us be true / To one another" as the only hope for stability the persona can find in a world filled with uncertainty and fear. Even an age disparity between persona and auditor can lend meaning to a poem, which is the case with the Herrick poem mentioned earlier and a dialogue poem like John Crowe Ransom's "Piazza Piece," a classic example of the debate between innocence and experience.

Other questions relating to circumstances of the dramatic situation might concern the poem's physical setting (if any), time (of day, year, historical era), even such matters as weather. Thomas Hardy's "Neutral Tones" provides a good example of a poem in which the setting, a gray winter day in a barren outdoor place, symbolically reinforces the persona's memory of the bitter end of a love affair. The shift in setting from the springtime idyll to the "cold hillside" in John Keats's "La Belle Dame sans Merci" cannot be overlooked in discussing the persona's disillusionment. Of course, many poems are explicitly occasional and may even contain an **epigraph**, a brief explanatory statement or quotation, or a **dedication** which explains the setting. Sometimes footnotes or even outside research may be necessary. John Milton's "On the Late Massacre in Piedmont" will make little sense to readers if they do not know that the poet is reacting to the massacre of a group of Protestants by Roman Catholic soldiers and that Milton, an English Puritan, uses the occasion to attack the Papacy as a "triple tyrant" and the "Babylonian woe."

To return, then, one final time to "The Star-Spangled Banner," let's apply our question to the poem. We have already determined that Key is the persona. Who is the "you" mentioned four words into the poem? It seems clear that Key is addressing an auditor standing close to him, either a single individual or a group, as he asks the auditor if he can see the flag that they both observed for the last time the previous day at sundown. Key tells us that it is now just at the moment of dawn, and that even though the flag could be glimpsed periodically in the "rockets' red glare" of the bombardment throughout the night, it cannot be clearly seen now. It is a crucial question, for if the flag is no longer flying "o'er the ramparts" it will mean that the fort has fallen to the enemy. The tension mounts and moves into the second stanza, where at last, "thro' the mists of the deep," the flag can be discerned, "dimly seen" at first, then clearly as it "catches the gleam" of the full sunlight.

The full story of how Key came to write the poem is fairly well known and supports this reading. The events which the poem describes took place on September 13 and 14, 1814, during the War of 1812. A lawyer, Key came aboard a British warship anchored off Baltimore to argue for the release of a client and friend who had been taken hostage by the British. Key won his friend's release, but the British captain, fearing that he might reveal information he had learned on board, kept Key overnight, releasing him and his client in the morning. It was during that night that Key witnessed the bombardment and, with it, the failure of the British to take Baltimore. The final half of the poem celebrates the victory and offers a hopeful prayer that God will continue to smile on America "when our cause it is just." One might well argue that Key's phrase "conquer we must" contradicts the spirit of the earlier parts of the poem, but few people have argued that "The Star-Spangled Banner" is a consistently great poem. Still, it is an effective piece of patriotic verse that has a few moments of real drama, expressed in a vivid manner that lets its readers become eyewitnesses to an incident from American history.

Lyric, Narrative, Dramatic

The starting point for all literary criticism in Western civilization is Aristotle's *Poetics*, a work dating from the fourth century B.C. While Aristotle's remarks on drama, tragedy in particular, are more complete than his analysis of other types of literature, he does mention three main types of poetry: lyric, epic, and dithyrambic. In doing so, Aristotle outlines for the first time a theory of literature based on **genres**, or separate categories delineated by distinct style, form, and content. This three-fold division remains useful today, though in two cases different terminology is employed. The first genre, **lyric poetry**, originally comprised brief poems that were meant to be sung or chanted. Today we still use the word "lyrics" in a specialized sense when referring to the words of a song, but lyric poetry has become such a large category that it includes virtually all poems that are primarily *about* a subject and contain little narrative content. The subject of a lyric poem may be the poet's emotions, an abstract idea, a satirical insight, or a description of a person or place. The persona in a lyric is usually closely identified with the poet himself or herself; since we tend to identify the essence of poetry with personal, subjective expression of feelings or ideas, lyric poetry remains the largest genre, with a number of subtypes. Among them are the **epigram**, a short, satirical lyric usually aimed at a specific person; the **elegy**, a lyric on the occasion of a death; and the **ode**, a long lyric in elevated language on a serious theme.

Aristotle's second genre, the epic, has been expanded to include all types of **narrative poetry**, that is, poetry whose main function is to tell a story. Like prose fiction, narrative poems have plots, characters, setting, and point-of-view, and may be discussed in the same terms as, say, a short story. The **epic** is a long narrative poem about the exploits of a hero. **Folk epics** like *The Iliad* or *Beowulf* were originally intended for public recitation and existed in oral form for long periods of time before they were transcribed. Little or nothing is known about the authors of folk epics. **Literary epics**, like Virgil's *Aeneid* or Henry Wadsworth Longfellow's *The Song of Hiawatha*, differ in that they are the products of known authors who wrote primarily for publication. **Ballads** are generally shorter narratives with song-like qualities which often include rhyme and repeated refrains. **Folk ballads**, like folk epics, come from the oral tradition and are usually published anonymously; "Bonny Barbara Allan" and "Sir Patrick Spens" are typical examples. **Art** or **literary ballads**, on the other hand, are conscious imitations of the ballad style by later poets and are generally somewhat more sophisticated than folk ballads in their techniques. Examples of this popular genre include Keats's "La Belle Dame sans Merci" and as recent a specimen as Marilyn Nelson's "Ballad of Aunt Geneva." There are also other types of narrative poetry that have been popular through the centuries. **Metrical romances**, verse tales of the exploits of knights, were a popular genre of the Middle Ages and Renaissance; Edmund Spenser's *The Faerie Queene* is one of the most ambitious examples of the type. At the opposite extreme are **mock-heroic narratives** like John Dryden's *MacFlecknoe* or Lord Byron's *Don Juan*, which spoof the conventions of epic poetry for comic or satirical effect. **Realistic narratives** of medium length (under 1000 lines) like Wordsworth's "Michael," a story of the dissolution of a shepherd's family, or Robert Frost's "Home Burial" have been popular since the beginning of the nineteenth century and are sometimes discussed as "poetic novels" or "short stories in verse."

There is no exact contemporary analogue for Aristotle's third category, **dithyrambic poetry**. This type of poem was composed to be chanted at religious rituals by a chorus and was the forerunner of tragedy. Today the third type is usually called **dramatic poetry**, since it has perhaps as much in common with the separate genre of drama as with lyric and narrative poetry. In general, the persona in a dramatic poem is an invented character or characters not to be identified with the poet. The poem is presented as a speech or dialogue that might be acted out like a soliloquy or scene from a play. The **dramatic monologue** is a speech for a single character, usually delivered to a silent auditor. Notable examples are Tennyson's "Ulysses" and Browning's "My Last Duchess." A dramatic monologue sometimes implies, in the words of its persona, a distinct setting and interplay between persona and auditor. At the close of "Ulysses" the aged hero urges his listening "mariners" to listen closely and to observe the ship in the harbor waiting to take them off on a final voyage. Dramatic poetry can also take the form of **dialogue poetry**, in which two personae speak alternately. Examples are Christina Rossetti's "Up-Hill" and Hardy's "The Ruined Maid." A popular type of dialogue poem in the past was the **débat**, or mock-debate, in which two characters, usually personified abstractions like the Soul and the Body, argued their respective merits.

While it is easy enough to find examples of "pure" lyrics, narratives, and dramatic monologues, sometimes the distinction between the three major types may become blurred, even in the same poem. "The Star-Spangled Banner," for example, contains elements of all three genres. The opening stanza, with its vivid re-creation of a question asked at dawn, is closest to dramatic poetry. The second and third stanzas, which tell of the outcome of the battle, are primarily narrative. The final stanza, with its patriotic effusion and religious sentiment, is lyrical. Still, the three-fold division is useful in discussing a single author's various ways of dealing with subjects or in comparing examples of one type by separate authors. To cite three poems by the same poet in this collection, we might look at William Blake's "The Tyger," "A Poison Tree," and "The Little Black Boy." The first of these is a descriptive lyric, dwelling primarily on the symbolic meaning of the tiger's appearance; the second is a narrative that relates, in the allegorical manner of a parable, the events leading up to a murder; the third is a dramatic monologue spoken by the persona identified in the title.

The Language of Poetry

One of the most persistent myths about poetry is that its language is artificial, "flowery," and essentially different from the language that people speak in going about their daily lives. While these beliefs may be true of *some* poetry, one can easily find numerous examples that reveal the opposite side of the coin. It is impossible to characterize poetic language narrowly, for poetry, which is after all the *art* of language, covers the widest possible range of linguistic possibilities. For example, here are several passages from different poets, all describing birds:

> Hail to thee, blithe Spirit!
>   Bird thou never wert—
> That from Heaven, or near it,
>   Pourest thy full heart
> In profuse strains of unpremeditated art.
>
> Higher still and higher
>   From the earth thou springest
> Like a cloud of fire;
>   The blue deep thou wingest,
> And singing still dost soar, and soaring ever singest.
>
> Percy Bysshe Shelley, "To a Skylark"

I caught this morning morning's minion, king-
dom of daylight's dauphin, dapple-dawn-drawn Falcon, in his riding
Of the rolling level underneath him steady air, and striding
High there, how he rung upon the rein of a wimpling wing
In his ecstacy!

> *Gerard Manley Hopkins, "The Windhover"*

When the lilac-scent was in the air and Fifth-month
    grass was growing,
Up this seashore in some briers,
Two feather'd guests from Alabama, two together,
And their nest, and four light-green eggs spotted with brown,
And every day the he-bird to and fro near at hand,
And every day the she-bird crouch'd on her nest,
    silent, with bright eyes,
And every day I, a curious boy, never too close, never
    disturbing them,
Cautiously peering, absorbing, translating.

> *Walt Whitman, "Out of the Cradle Endlessly Rocking"*

At once a voice arose among
    The bleak twigs overhead
In a full-hearted evensong
    Of joy illimited;
An aged thrush, frail, gaunt, and small,
    In blast-beruffled plume,
Had chosen thus to fling his soul
    Upon the growing gloom.

> *Thomas Hardy, "The Darkling Thrush"*

There is a singer everyone has heard,
Loud, a mid-summer and a mid-wood bird,
Who makes the solid tree trunks sound again.
He says that leaves are old and that for flowers
Mid-summer is to spring as one to ten.

> *Robert Frost, "The Oven Bird"*

The blue booby lives
on the bare rocks
of Galápagos
and fears nothing.
It is a simple life:
they live on fish,
and there are few predators.

> *James Tate, "The Blue Booby"*

Of these quotes only the oldest, from the early nineteenth century, pos-
sesses the stereotypical characteristics of what we mean when we use the term

"poetic" in a negative sense. Poetry, like any other art form, follows fashions that change over the years; by Shelley's day, the use of "thee" and "thou" and their related verb forms ("wert" and "wingest") had come full circle from their original use as a familiar form of the second person employed to address intimates and servants to an artificially heightened grammatical form reserved for prayers and poetry. Hopkins's language, from a poem of the 1870s, is artificial in an entirely different way; here the poet's **idiom**, the personal use of words that marks his poetry, is highly idiosyncratic; indeed, it would be hard to mistake a poem by Hopkins with one by any other poet. Whitman, on the other hand, should present few difficulties; the only oddity here is "Fifth-month" instead of "May," a linguistic inheritance, perhaps, from Whitman's Quaker mother. Of course, one might argue that Whitman's "naturalness" results from his use of his free verse, but both Hardy and Frost, who are writing rhymed, metrical verse, are hardly less natural. When we move to the contemporary period, we can find little difference between the language of many poems and conversational speech, as Tate's lines indicate.

Still, in reading a poem, particularly one from the past, we should be aware of certain problems that may impede our understanding. **Diction** refers to the individual words in a poem and may be classified in several ways. A poem's **level of diction** can range from slang at one extreme to formal usage at the other, though in an age in which most poems use a level of diction that stays in the middle of the scale, ranging between conversational and standard levels, these distinctions are useful only when a poet is being self-consciously formal (perhaps for ironic effect) or going to the opposite extreme to imitate the language of the streets. In past eras the term **poetic diction** was used to indicate a level of speech somehow refined above ordinary usage and, thus, somehow superior to it; today the same term would most likely be used as a way of condemning a poet's language. We should keep in mind that the slang of one era is the standard usage of another, o.k.?

A good dictionary is useful in many ways, particulary in dealing with **archaisms** (words that are no longer commonly in use) and other words that may not be familiar to the reader. Take, for example, the opening lines of Edgar Allan Poe's "To Helen":

> Helen, thy beauty is to me
> Like those Nicean barks of yore,
> That gently, o'er a perfumed sea,
> The weary, way-worn wanderer bore
> To his own native shore.

There are several words here that may give trouble to the average reader. First, "o'er," like "ne'er" or similar words like "falt'ring" and "glimm'ring," is simply a contraction; this dropping of a letter, called **syncope**, is done for the sake of rhythm. "Barks of yore" will probably send most of us to the dictionary, for our sense of "bark" as either the outer surface of a tree or the noise that a dog makes does not fit here; likewise, "yore" is unfamiliar, possibly archaic. Looking up the literal sense of a word in a dictionary discloses its **denotation**, or literal meaning. Thus, we find that "barks" are small sailing ships and that "yore" refers to the distant past. Of course, Poe could have said "ships of the past" or a similar phrase, but his word choice was perhaps dictated by **connotation**, the implied meaning or *feel* that some words have acquired; it may be that even in Poe's day "barks of yore" had a remote, exotic quality that somehow evoked ancient Greece. But what are we to make of "Nicean," a proper adjective that sounds geographical but does not appear in either the dictionary or gazetteer? In this case we have encountered an example of a **coinage** or **neologism**, a word made up by the poet. Speculation on the source of "Nicean" has ranged from Nice, in the South of France, to Phoenician, but it is likely that Poe simply coined the word. Similarly, we might note that the phrase "weary, way-worn wanderer" contains words that seem to have been chosen primarily for their sounds.

When we put a poem into our own words, we **paraphrase** it, a practice that is often useful when passages are hard to understand. Other than diction, **syntax**, the order of words in a sentence, may also give us problems. Syntax in poetry, particulary in poems that use rhyme, is likely to be different from that of both speech and prose; if a poet decides to rhyme in a certain pattern, he or she must modify word order to fit the formal design, and this may present difficulties to readers in understanding the grammar of a passage. Here is the opening of a familiar piece of American patriotic verse: "My country, 'tis of thee, / Sweet land of liberty, / Of thee I sing." What is the subject of this sentence? Would you be surprised to learn that the subject is *it* (contained in the contraction *'tis*)? The passage from Poe presents few difficulties of this order but does contain one example of **inversion**, words that fall out of their expected order (a related syntactical problem lies in **ellipsis**, words that are consciously omitted by the poet). If we do not allow for this, we are likely to be confused by "the weary, way-worn wanderer bore / To his own native shore." The wanderer bore *what*? A quick mental sentence diagram shows that "wanderer" is the direct object of "bore," not its subject. A good paraphrase should simplify both diction and syntax: "Helen, to me your beauty is like those Nicean (?) ships of the ancient past that carried the weary, travel-worn wanderer gently over a perfumed sea to his own native land." In paraphrasing, only the potentially troublesome words and phrases should be substituted, leaving as much of the original language intact as possible. Paraphrasing is a useful first step toward unfolding a poem's literal sense, but it obviously takes few of a poet's specific nuances of language into account.

Several other matters relevant to poetic language are worth mentioning. **Etymology**, the study of the sources of words, is a particularly rewarding topic in English since our language has such an unusually rich history—compare an unabridged French dictionary to its English counterpart. Old English (or Anglo-Saxon), the original language of the British Isles, was part of the Germanic family of languages. When the Norman French successfully invaded the British Isles in 1066 they brought with them their own language, part of the Romance language family (all originally derived from Latin). By the time of Chaucer's death in 1400 these two linguistic traditions had merged into a single language, Middle English, that can be read today, despite its differences in spelling, pronunciation, and vocabulary. We can still, however, distinguish the words that show their Germanic heritage from those of Latinate origin, and despite the fact that English is rich in synonyms, the Germanic and Latinate words often have different connotations. "Smart" is not quite the same as "intelligent," and a "mapmaker" is subtly different from a "cartographer." A poet's preference for words of a certain origin is not always immediately clear, but we can readily distinguish the wide gulf that separates a statement like "I live in a house with my folks" from "I abide in a residence with my parents."

A final tension exists in poems between their use of **concrete diction** and **abstract diction**. Concrete words denote that which can be perceived by the senses, and the vividness of a poem's language resides primarily in the way it uses **imagery**, sensory details denoting specific details of experience. Since it is the most important of the five senses, visual imagery ("a dim light"; "a dirty rag"; "a golden daffodil") predominates in poems, but we should also be wary for striking examples of the other types of imagery: auditory ("a pounding surf"), tactile ("a rough floor"), olfactory ("the scent of apple blossoms"), and gustatory ("the bitter tang of gin"). Abstract words are likewise important since they carry the burden of a poem's overall meaning or theme. William Butler Yeats's "Leda and the Swan" provides a good example of how concrete and abstract words coexist in a poem. Reading this account of the myth in which Zeus, in the form of a swan, impregnates a human woman and thus sets in action the chain of events that leads to the Trojan War (Leda was the mother of Helen of Troy), we will probably be struck at first by the way that tactile imagery ("a sudden blow"; fingers attempting to "push / The feathered glory" away; "A shudder in the loins") is used to describe an act of sexual violence. Even though some abstract words ("terrified"; "vague"; "glory"; "strange") appear in the first eight lines of the poem they are all linked closely to concrete words like "fingers," "feathered," and "heart." In the last two lines of the poem, Yeats uses three large abstractions—"knowledge," "power," and "indifferent"—to state his theme (or at least ask the crucial question about the meaning of the myth). More often than not, one can expect to encounter the largest number of abstract words near the conclusions of poems. Probably the most famous abstract statement in English poetry— John Keats's "'Beauty is truth, truth beauty,'—that is all / Ye know on earth, and all ye need to know."—appears in the last two lines of a fifty-line poem.

Two final devices aid poets in determining the best choice of words. **Onomatopoeia** refers to individual words like "splash" or "thud" whose meanings are closely related to their sounds. Auditory imagery in a poem can often be enhanced by the use of onomatopoeic words. In some cases, however, a whole line can be called onomatopoeic, even if it contains no single word that illustrates the device. Thomas Hardy uses this line to describe the pounding of distant surf: "Where hill-hid tides throb, throe on throe." Here the repetition of similar sounds helps to imitate the sound of the ocean. A second device is the **pun**, the use of one word to imply the additional meaning of a similar-sounding word (the formal term is **paranomasia**). Thus, when Anne Bradstreet is comparing her first book to an illegitimate child, she addresses the book in this manner: "If for thy Father asked, say thou had'st none; / And for thy Mother, she alas is poor, / Which caused her thus to send thee out of door." The closeness of the interjection "alas" to the article and noun "a lass" is hardly coincidental. Poets in Bradstreet's day considered the pun a staple of their repertoire, even in serious poetry, but contemporary poets are more likely to use it primarily for comic effect:

> They have a dozen children; it's their diet,
> For they have bread too often. Please don't try it.

And so on. More often than not, puns like these will elicit a groan from the audience, a response that may be exactly what the poet intends.

Figurative Language

We use figurative language in everyday speech without thinking of the poetic functions of the same devices. We can always relate experience in a purely literal fashion: "His table manners were deplorable. Mother scolded him severely, and Dad said some angry words to him. He left the table embarrassed and with his feelings hurt." But a more vivid way of saying the same thing might employ language used not in the literal but in the figurative sense. Thus, another version might run, "His table manners were swinish. Mother jumped on his back about them, and Dad scorched his ears. You should have seen him slink off like a scolded puppy." At least four comparisons are made here in an attempt to describe one character's table manners, his mother's scolding, his father's words, and the manner in which the character retreated from the table. In every case, the thing being described, what is called the **tenor** of the figure of speech, is linked with a concrete image or **vehicle**. All of the types of figurative language, what are called **figures of speech** or **tropes**, involve some kind of comparison, either explicit or implied. Thus, two of the figures in the above example specifically compare aspects of the character's behavior to animal behavior. The other two imply parental words that were delivered with strong physical force or were extremely angry. Some of the most common figures of speech are:

Metaphor: a direct comparison between two unlike things. Metaphors may take several forms.

> His words were sharp knives.
> The sharp knife of his words cut through the silence.

He spoke sharp, cutting words with his knife-edged voice.
His words knifed through the still air.
"I will speak daggers to her. . . ." (*Shakespeare*, Hamlet)

Implied metaphor: a metaphor in which either the tenor or vehicle is implied, not stated.

The running back gathered steam and chugged toward the goal. (Compares the player to a steam locomotive without naming it explicitly.)
"While smoke on its chin, that slithering gun /
Coiled back from its windowsill" (*X. J. Kennedy*).

Simile: a comparison using *like*, *as*, or *than* as a connective device.

"My love is like a red, red rose" (*Robert Burns*).
My love smells as sweet as a rose.
My love looks fresher than a newly budded rose.

Conceit: an extended or far-fetched metaphor, in most cases comparing things that apparently have almost nothing in common.

"Make me, O Lord, thy spinning wheel complete. . . ."
(*Edward Taylor*)
(The poem draws an analogy between the process of salvation and the manufacture of cloth, ending with the persona attired in "holy robes.")

The **Petrarchan conceit**, named perhaps unfairly after the first great master of the sonnet, is a clichéd comparison usually relating to a woman's beauty (see Thomas Campion's "There Is a Garden in Her Face"; Shakespeare's Sonnet 130 parodies this type of trope). The **Metaphysical conceit** refers to the extended comparisons favored by poets like John Donne, George Herbert, and Edward Taylor. The conceit in the final three stanzas of Donne's "A Valediction: Forbidding Mourning" compares the poet and his wife to a pair of drafting compasses.

Hyperbole: overstatement, a comparison using conscious exaggeration.

He threw the ball so fast it caught the catcher's mitt on fire.
"And I will love thee still, my dear, / Till a' the seas gang dry."
(*Robert Burns*)

Understatement: the opposite of hyperbole.

I had to spend a moment or two filling out my tax forms before I mailed them to the IRS.
"The space between [birth and death] is but an hour, / The frail duration of a flower" (*Philip Freneau*).

Allusion: metaphor making a direct comparison to a historical or literary event or character, a myth, a biblical reference, etc.

He is a Samson of strength but a Judas of duplicity.
"He dreamed of Thebes and Camelot, / And Priam's neighbors."
(*Edwin Arlington Robinson*)

Metonymy: use of a related object to stand for the thing actually being talked about.

It's a white-collar street in a blue-collar town.
"And O ye high-flown quills [literary critics] that soar the skies,
And ever with your prey still catch your praise." (*Anne Bradstreet*)

Synecdoche: use of a part for the whole, or vice versa.

The crowned heads of Europe were in attendance.
"Before the indifferent beak could let her drop."
(*William Butler Yeats*)

Personification: giving human characteristics to non-human things or to abstractions.

Justice weighs the evidence in her golden scales.
The ocean cursed and spat at us.
"Of all her train, the hands of Spring
First plant thee [a yellow violet] in the watery mould."
(*William Cullen Bryant*)

Apostrophe: variety of personification in which a non-human thing, abstraction, or person not physically present is directly addressed as if it could respond.

"Milton! Thou shouldst be living at this hour."
(*William Wordsworth*)

"Is it, O man, with such discordant noises,
With such accursed instruments as these,
Thou drownest Nature's sweet and kindly voices,
And jarrest the celestial harmonies?" (*Henry Wadsworth Longfellow*)

Paradox: an apparent contradiction or illogical statement.

I'll never forget old what's-his-name.
"His [God's] hand hath made this noble work [the universe] which
Stands, / His Glorious Handywork not made by hands."
(*Edward Taylor*)

Oxymoron: a short paradox, usually consisting of an adjective and noun with conflicting meanings.

The touch of her lips was sweet agony.
"Progress is a comfortable disease" (*E. E. Cummings*)

Synesthesia: a conscious mixing of two different types of sensory experience.

> A raw, red wind rushed from the north.
> "Leaves cast in casual potpourris
> Whisper their scents from pits and cellar-holes." (*Richard Wilbur*)

Allegory and Symbol

Related to the figurative devices are the various types of symbolism that may occur in poems. In many cases, a poem may seem so simple on the surface that we feel impelled to read deeper meanings into it; Robert Frost's "Stopping by Woods on a Snowy Evening" is a classic case in point. There is nothing wrong with searching for larger significance in a poem, but the reader should perhaps be wary of leaping to conclusions about symbolic meanings before fully exhausting the literal sense of a poem. Whatever the case, both allegory and symbolism share the demand that the reader supply abstract or general meanings to the specific concrete details of the poem.

The simplest form that this substitution takes occurs in **allegory.** An allegory is usually a narrative that exists on at least two levels simultaneously, a concrete literal level and a second level of abstract meaning; throughout an allegory there is a consistent sequence of parallels between the literal and the abstract. Sometimes allegories may imply third or fourth levels of meaning as well, especially in long allegorical works like Dante's *The Divine Comedy*, which has been interpreted in personal, political, ethical, and Christian terms. The characters and actions in an allegory explicitly signify the abstract level of meaning, and generally this second level of meaning is what the poet primarily intends to convey. For example, Robert Southwell's "The Burning Babe" is filled with fantastic incidents and paradoxical speech that are made clear in the poem's last line: "And straight I callèd unto mind that it was Christmas day." The literal burning babe of the title is the Christ child, who predicts his own future to the amazed watcher. Thus, in interpreting the poem the reader must substitute theological terms like "redemption" or "original sin" for the literal details it contains.

Two types of prose allegories, the fable and parable, have been universally popular. A fable is a short, non-realistic narrative that is told to illustrate a universal moral concept. A parable is similar, but generally contains realistic characters and events. Thus, Aesop's fable of the tortoise and the hare, instead of telling us something about animal behavior, illustrates the virtue of persistence against seemingly unbeatable competition. Jesus' parable of the Good Samaritan tells the story of a man who is robbed and beaten and eventually rescued by a stranger of another race in order to define the concept of "neighbor" for a questioning lawyer. Poetic allegories like George Herbert's "Redemption" or Christina Rossetti's "Up-Hill" can be read in Christian terms as symbolic accounts of the process of salvation.

Many poems contain symbolic elements that are somewhat more elusive in meaning than the simple one-for-one equivalences presented by allegory. A **symbol**, then, is any concrete thing or action in a poem that implies a meaning beyond its literal sense. Many of these things or actions are called **traditional symbols**, that is, symbols that hold roughly the same meanings for members of a given society. Certain flowers, colors, natural objects, and religious emblems possess meanings that we can generally agree upon. A white lily and a red rose suggest opposite occasions, mourning and passion. Few would associate black with gaiety or red with innocence, and dawn and rainbows are traditional natural symbols of hope and new beginnings. It would be unlikely for a poet to mention a cross without expecting readers to think of its Christian associations.

Other types of symbols can be identified in poems that are otherwise not allegorical. A **private symbol** is one that has acquired certain meanings from a single poet's repeated use of it. William Butler Yeats's use of "gyres" is explained in some of his prose writings as a symbol for the turning of historical cycles, and his use of the word in his poems obviously goes beyond the literal level. Some visionary poets like William Blake have devised complicated private symbolic systems, a sort of alternative mythology, and understanding the full import of these symbols becomes primarily the task of the specialist. Other poets may employ **incidental symbols**, things that are not usually considered symbolic but may be in a particular poem, or **symbolic acts**, a situation or response that seems of greater than literal import. As earlier noted, one of the most famous poems using these two devices is Robert Frost's "Stopping by Woods on a Snowy Evening." In this poem some readers see the "lovely, dark and deep" woods as inviting, even threatening, and want to view the persona's rejection of their allure ("But I have promises to keep / And miles to go before I sleep") as some sort of life-affirming act. Frost himself was not particularly helpful in guiding his readers, often scoffing at those who had read too much metaphysical portent into such a simple lyric, though in other of his poems he presents objects—a rock wall between neighboring farms, an abandoned woodpile—that obviously possess some larger significance. There are many modern poems that remain so enigmatic that readers have consistently returned to them looking for new interpretations. Poems like these were to a degree influenced by the Symbolists, a group of French poets of the late nineteenth century, who deliberately wrote poems filled with vague nuances subject to multiple interpretations. Such American attempts at Symbolist experiments as Wallace Stevens's "Anecdote of the Jar" or "The Emperor of Ice-Cream" continue to perplex and fascinate readers, particularly those who are versed in recent schools of interpretation which focus on the indeterminacy of a poetic text.

Tone of Voice

Even the simplest statement is subject to multiple interpretations if it is delivered in several different tones of voice. Consider the shift in emphasis between "I *gave* you the money" and "I gave *you* the money." Even a seemingly innocent compliment like "You look lovely this morning" takes on a different meaning if it is delivered by a woman to her obviously hung-over husband. Still, these variations in **tone**, the speaker's implied attitude toward the words he or she says, depend primarily on vocal inflection. Since a poet only rarely gets the opportunity to elucidate his tones in a public performance, it is possible that readers may have difficulties in grasping the tone of a poem printed on the page. Still, some poems should present few problems. The opening of Milton's sonnet "On the Late Massacre in Piedmont"—"Avenge, O Lord, thy slaughtered saints . . ."—establishes a tone of righteous anger that is consistent throughout the poem. Keats's initial apostrophe in "Ode on a Grecian Urn"—"Thou still unravished bride of quietness, / Thou foster-child of silence and slow time . . ."—strikes the reader as both passionate and reverent in the poet's response to an undamaged artifact of the ancient past. Thus, in many cases we can relate the tone of voice in poems to the emotions we employ in our own speech, and we would have to violate quite a few rules of common sense to argue that Milton is being flippant or that Keats is speaking sarcastically.

Irony is the element of tone by which a poet may imply an attitude that is in fact contrary to what his words appear to say. Of course, the simplest form of irony is **sarcasm**, the wounding tone of voice we use to imply exactly the opposite of what we say: "That's really a *great* excuse!" "What a *wonderful* performance!" One is almost tempted to add a firm "Not!" after such deliberately insincere bits of praise. **Verbal irony** is the conscious manipulation of tone by which the poet's actual attitude is the opposite of what he says. In a poem like Thomas Hardy's "The Ruined Maid" it is obvious that one speaker considers the meaning of "ruined" to be somewhat less severe than the other, and the whole poem hinges on this ironic counterpoint of definitions and the different moral and social attitudes they imply. Consider the opening lines of Oliver Wendell Holmes's "Old Ironsides," a piece of propaganda verse which succeeded in raising enough money to save the U.S.S. *Constitution* from the scrapyard: "Ay, tear her tattered ensign down! / Long has it waved on high, / And many an eye has danced to see / That banner in the sky. . . ." Since Holmes's poetic mission is to *save* the ship, it is obvious that he is speaking ironically in the opening line; he emphatically *does not* want the ship's flag stripped from her, an attitude that is made clear in the third and fourth lines. Verbal irony is also a conspicuous feature of verse **satire**, poetry that exists primarily to mock or ridicule, though often with serious intent. One famous example, in the form of a short satirical piece, or **epigram**, is Sarah N. Cleghorn's "The Golf Links," a poem written before the advent of child-labor laws:

> The golf links lie so near the mill
>   That almost every day
> The laboring children can look out
>   And see the men at play.

Here the weight of the verbal irony falls on two words, "laboring" and "play," and the way each is incongruously applied to the wrong group of people.

"The Golf Links," taken as a whole, also represents a second form of irony, **situational irony,** in which the setting of the poem (laboring children watching playing adults) contains a built-in incongruity. One master of ironic situation is Thomas Hardy, who used the title "Satires of Circumstances" in a series of short poems illustrating this sort of irony. Hardy's "Ah, Are You Digging on My Grave?" and A. E. Housman's "Is My Team Plowing?" demonstrate similar ironic situations, a ghostly persona asking questions of living speakers who end up offering little comfort to the dead. **Dramatic irony,** the third type of irony, occurs when the persona of a poem is less aware of the full import of his or her words than is the reader. William Blake's "The Chimney Sweeper" is spoken by a child who does not seem to fully realize how badly he is being exploited by his employer, who has apparently been using the promises of religion as a way of keeping his workers in line. A similar statement could be made of the persona of Walter Savage Landor's "Mother, I Cannot," a young girl who apparently has not realized (or is deliberately unwilling to admit) that she has been sexually deceived. Dramatic irony, as the term implies, is most often found in dramatic monologues, where the gap between the speaker's perception of the situation and the reader's may be wide indeed.

Repetition: Sounds and Schemes

Because poetry uses language at its most intense level, we are aware of the weight of individual words and phrases to a degree that is usually lacking when we read prose. Poets have long known that the meanings that they attempt to convey often depend as much on the sound of the words as their meaning. We have already mentioned one sound device, onomatopoeia. Consider how much richer the experience of "the murmuring of innumerable bees" is than a synonymous phrase, "the low sound of a lot of bees." It has often been said that all art aspires to the condition of music in the way that it affects an audience on some unconscious, visceral level. By carefully exploiting the repetition of sound devices, a poet may use some of the same effects that the musical composer does.

Of course, much of this sonic level of poetry is subjective; what strikes one listener as pleasant may overwhelm the ear of another. Still, it is useful to distinguish between a poet's use of **euphony,** a series of pleasant sounds, and **cacophony,** sounds that are deliberately unpleasant. Note the following passages from Alexander Pope's "An Essay on Criticism," a didactic poem which attempts to illustrate many of the devices poets use:

Soft is the strain when Zephyr gently blows,
And the smooth stream in smoother numbers flows; . . .

The repetition of the initial consonant sounds is called **alliteration,** and here Pope concentrates on the s sound. The vowel sounds are generally long: strain, blows, smooth, and so on. Here the description of the gentle west wind is assisted by the generally pleasing sense of euphony. But

Pope, to illustrate the opposite quality, follows this couplet with a second:

> But when loud surges lash the sounding shore,
> The hoarse, rough verse should like the torrent roar.

Now the wind is anything but gentle, and the repetition of the *r* sounds in surges, shore, hoarse, rough, verse, torrent, and roar force the reader into the back of the throat, making sounds that are anything but euphonious.

Repetition of sounds has no inherent meaning values (though some linguists might argue that certain sounds do stimulate particular emotions), but this repetition does call attention to itself and can be particularly effective when a poet wishes to emphasize a certain passage. We have already mentioned alliteration. Other sound patterns are **assonance**, the repetition of similar vowel sounds (*steep, even, receive, veal*), and **consonance**, the repetition of similar consonant sounds (du*ck*, tor*que*, stri*ke*, tri*ck*le). It should go without saying that spelling has little to do with any sound pattern; an initial *f* will alliterate with an initial *ph*.

Rhyme is the most important sound device, and our pleasures in deftly executed rhymes (consider the possibilities of rhyming "neighbor" with "sabre," as Richard Wilbur does in one of his translations) goes beyond mere sound to include the pleasure we take when an unexpected word is magically made to fit with another. There are several types of rhyme. **Masculine rhyme** occurs between single stressed syllables: *fleece, release, surcease, Nice*, and so on. **Feminine rhyme**, also called **double rhyme**, matches two syllables, one stressed and one usually unstressed: *stinging, upbringing, flinging*. **Triple rhyme** goes further: *slithering, withering*. **Slant rhyme** (also called **near rhyme** and **off rhyme**) contains hints of sound repetition (sometimes related to assonance and consonance): *chill, dull, sale* are possibilities, though poets often grant themselves considerable leeway in counting as rhyming words pairs that often have only the slightest similarity. When rhymes fall in a pattern in a poem and are **end rhymes**, occurring at the end of lines, then it is convenient to assign letters to the sounds and speak of a **rhyme scheme**. Thus, a stanza of four lines ending with *heaven, hell, bell, eleven* would be said to have a rhyme scheme of ABBA. Rhymes may also occasionally be found in the interior of lines, what is called **internal rhyme**.

More complicated patterns of repetition involve more than mere sounds but whole phrases and grammatical units. Ancient rhetoricians, teaching the art of public speaking, identified several of these, and they are also found in poetry. **Parallel structure** is simply the repetition of grammatically similar phrases or clauses: Tennyson's "To strive, to seek, to find, and not to yield." **Anaphora** and **epistrophe** are repeated words or phrases at, respectively, the beginnings and ends of lines. Walt Whitman uses these schemes extensively, often in the same lines. This passage from *Song of Myself* illustrates both anaphora and epistrophe:

> If they are not yours as much as mine they are nothing,
>   or next to nothing,

> If they are not the riddle and the untying of the
>   riddle they are nothing,
> If they are not just as close as they are distant they
>   are nothing.

Antithesis is the matching of parallel units which contain contrasting meanings, such as Whitman's "I am of old and young, of the foolish as much as the wise, / Regardless of others, ever regardful of others, / Maternal as well as paternal, a child as well as a man. . . ." While the rhetorical schemes are perhaps more native to the orator, the poet can still make occasional effective use of them, particularly in open form poetry like that of Whitman, where the formal devices of meter, rhyme, and stanza are lacking.

Meter and Rhythm

The subject of poetic meter and rhythm can be a difficult one, to say the least, and it is doubtless true that such phrases as *trochaic octameter* or *spondaic substitution* have an intimidating quality. Still, discussions of meter need not be limited to experts, and even beginning readers should be able to apply a few of the metrical principles that are commonly found in poetry written in English.

First, let's distinguish between two terms that are often used synonymously: **poetry** and **verse**. Poetry refers to a whole genre of literature and thus stands with fiction and drama as one of the three major types of writing. Verse, on the other hand, refers to a mode of writing in lines of a certain length; thus, many poets still retain the old practice of capitalizing the first word of each line to indicate its integrity as a unit of composition. Virtually any piece of writing can be versified (and sometimes rhymed as well). Especially useful are bits of **mnemonic verse**, in which information like the number of days in the months or simple spelling rules ("*I* before *E* / Except after *C* . . .") is cast in a form that is easy to remember. Although it is not strictly accurate to do so, many writers use *verse* to denote metrical writing that somehow does not quite measure up to the level of true poetry; phrases like **light verse** or **occasional verse** (lines written for a specific event, like a birthday or anniversary) are often used in this way.

If, on the other hand, a writer is unconcerned about the length of individual lines and is governed only by the width of the paper being used, then he or she is not writing verse but **prose**. Verse is metrical writing; prose is not. Surprisingly enough, there is a body of writing called **prose poetry**, writing that uses language in a poetic manner but avoids any type of meter; see Carolyn Forché's "The Colonel" for one example. Perhaps the simplest way to think of **meter** in verse is to think of its synonym **measure** (think of the use of *meter* in words like *odometer* or *kilometer*). Thus, meter refers to the method by which a poet determines line length. Even if a poet writes lines of varying length, what we usually call **free verse**, he or she is still making a conscious decision about how much each line may contain and may be measuring it on the basis of grammatical phrases or his or her own breath units.

However, when we talk about meter in poetry we ordinarily mean that the poet is employing some kind of consistent **prosody** or system of measurement. There are many possible prosodies, depending on what the poet decides to count as the unit of measurement in the line, but only three of these systems are common in English poetry. Perhaps the simplest is **syllabic verse**. In verse of this type the length of the line is determined by counting the total number of syllables the line contains (see Sylvia Plath's "Metaphors" for one example). Much French poetry of the past was written in twelve-syllable lines, or **Alexandrines**, and in English a word like **octosyllabic** denotes a line of eight syllables. Because English is a language of strong stresses, most of our poets have favored other prosodic systems, but syllabic poetry has been attempted by many poets, among them Marianne Moore, Richard Wilbur, and Dylan Thomas. Moore, in particular, often writes in **quantitative syllabics**, that is, stanzas with identical numbers of syllables in corresponding lines.

More natural to the English language is **accentual verse**, a prosodic system in which only accented or strongly stressed syllables are counted in a line, which can also contain a varying number of unaccented syllables. Much folk poetry, intended perhaps to be recited to the beat of a percussion instrument, retains this stress-based pattern, and the oldest English verse, Anglo-Saxon poetry like *Beowulf*, is composed in four-stress lines which were recited to musical accompaniment. Many of the verses we recall from nursery rhymes, children's chanting games ("Red rover, red rover, / Send [any name from one to up to four syllables can be substituted here— *Bill, Susan, Latisha, Elizabeth*] right over") and sports cheers ("Two bits, four bits, six bits, a dollar! / All for the [*Owls, Cowboys, Cardinals*] stand up and holler!") retain the strong sense of rhythmical pulse that characterizes much accentual verse, a fact we recognize when we clap our hands and move rhythmically to the sound of the words. Indeed, the lyrics to most current rap music are actually composed to a four-stress accentual line, and the stresses or "beats" can be heard plainly when we listen or dance. More subtle, perhaps, is the method of many contemporary poets; indeed, what often passes for free verse is revealed, on closer inspection, to be a poem written in accentual meter. Richard Wilbur's "The Writer," for example, is written in a stanza containing lines of three, five, and three strong stresses, respectively, but the stresses do not overwhelm the reader insistently.

Accentual-syllabic verse is the most important prosodic system in English, dominating our poetry for the five centuries from Chaucer's time down to the early years of our century; it has only been within the last fifty years that free verse has become the prevailing style, and accentual-syllabic verse still has many able practitioners. An accentual-syllabic prosody is somewhat more complicated than the two systems we have mentioned, because it requires that the poet count both the strongly stressed syllables *and* the total number of syllables in the line. Because stressed and unstressed syllables alternate fairly regularly in this system, four **metrical**

feet, representing the most common patterns, designate the subdivisions of rhythm that make up the line (think of a yardstick divided into three feet). These feet are the **iamb** (or **iambic foot**), one unstressed and one stressed syllable; the **trochee** (or **trochaic foot**), one stressed and one unstressed syllable; the **anapest** (or **anapestic foot**), two unstressed syllables and one stressed syllable; and the **dactyl** (or **dactylic foot**), one stressed and two unstressed syllables. The first two of these, iambic and trochaic, are called **double meters**; the second two, **triple meters.** Iambic and anapestic meters are sometimes called **rising meters** because they "rise" toward the stressed syllable; trochaic and dactylic meters are called **falling meters** for the opposite reason. Simple repetition of words or phrases can give us the sense of how these lines sound in a purely schematic sense. The **breve** (⌣) and **ictus** (ʹ) are used to denote unstressed and stressed syllables, respectively.

Iambic:

⌣ ʹ   ⌣ ʹ   ⌣ ʹ
release / release / release

⌣ ʹ   ⌣ ʹ   ⌣ ʹ
to fall / into / despair

⌣ ʹ   ⌣ ʹ   ⌣ ʹ ⌣
Marie / discov / ers candy

Trochaic:

ʹ ⌣   ʹ ⌣   ʹ ⌣   ʹ ⌣
melting / melting / melting / melting

ʹ ⌣   ʹ ⌣   ʹ ⌣   ʹ ⌣
Peter / disa / greed en / tirely

ʹ ⌣   ʹ ⌣   ʹ ⌣   ʹ
clever / writing / filled the / page

Anapestic:

⌣ ⌣ ʹ   ⌣ ⌣ ʹ
to the top / to the top

⌣ ⌣ ʹ   ⌣ ⌣ ʹ
a retriev / er appeared

⌣ ⌣ ʹ   ⌣ ⌣ ʹ ⌣
and a ter / rible thunder

Dactylic:

ʹ ⌣ ⌣   ʹ ⌣ ⌣   ʹ ⌣ ⌣   ʹ ⌣ ⌣   ʹ ⌣ ⌣
shivering / shivering / shivering / shivering / shivering

ʹ ⌣ ⌣   ʹ ⌣ ⌣   ʹ ⌣ ⌣   ʹ ⌣ ⌣   ʹ ⌣ ⌣
terribly / ill with the / symptoms of / viral pneu / monia

ʹ ⌣ ⌣   ʹ ⌣ ⌣   ʹ ⌣ ⌣   ʹ ⌣ ⌣   ʹ
note how the / minister / whispered at / Emily's / grave

Because each of these lines contains a certain number of feet, a second specialized term is used to denote how many times a pattern is repeated in a line:

one foot	monometer
two feet	dimeter
three feet	trimeter
four feet	tetrameter
five feet	pentameter
six feet	hexameter
seven feet	heptameter
eight feet	octameter

Thus, in the examples opposite, the first set of lines is iambic trimeter; the second, trochaic tetrameter; the third, anapestic dimeter; and the fourth, dactylic pentameter. The third lines in the iambic and trochaic examples are **hypermetrical**; that is, they contain an extra unstressed syllable or **feminine ending**. Conversely, the third lines in the trochaic and dactylic examples are missing one and two unstressed final syllables, respectively, a common practice called **catalexis**. Although over thirty combinations of foot type and number per line are theoretically possible, relatively few are ordinarily encountered in poetry. The iambic foot is most common in English, followed by the anapest and the trochee; the dactylic foot is relatively rare. Line lengths tend to be from three to five feet, with anything shorter or longer used only sparingly. Still, there are famous exceptions like Poe's "The Raven," which is composed in trochaic octameter or Southwell's "The Burning Babe," in iambic heptameter.

Meter denotes regularity, the "blueprint" for a line from which the poet works. Since iambic pentameter is the most common meter used in English, our subsequent discussion will focus on poems written in it. But most good poets quickly learn that a metronomic regularity, five iambic feet marching in lockstep line after line, is not a virtue and quickly becomes predictable. Thus, there are several ways by which poets can add variety to their lines. One is by varying the placement of the **caesura** (||) or pause within a line (usually indicated by a mark of punctuation). Another is by mixing **end-stopped lines**, which clearly pause at their conclusion, with **enjambed lines**, which run on into the next line with no pause. These lines from Tennyson's "Ulysses" illustrate these techniques:

This is my son, mine own Telemachus,
To whom I leave the scepter and the isle,
Well-loved of me, discerning to fulfill
This labor, by slow prudence to make mild
A rugged people, and through soft degrees
Subdue them to the useful and the good.

Lines two and six have no caesurae; the others do, after either the third, fourth, or fifth syllable. Lines one, two, and six are end-stopped; the others are enjambed.

Another technique of varying regularity is **metrical substitution**, where feet of a different type are substituted for what the meter calls for. In iambic meter, trochaic feet are often encountered at the beginnings of lines, or after a caesura. Two other feet, the **pyrrhic** (˘ ˘), consisting of two unstressed syllables, and the **spondee** (′ ′), consisting of two stressed syllables, are also commonly substituted. Here are Tennyson's lines with their **scansion** marked.

$$\text{Th\'is \'is / m\u{y} s\'on, | |/ m\'ine \u{o}wn / T\'elem / \'achus,}$$

$$\text{To wh\'om / \u{I} le\'ave / the sc\'ep / ter \u{and} / the \'isle}$$

$$\text{W\'ell-l\'oved / of m\u{e}, | |/ disc\'ern /\u{ing} t\u{o} / fulf\'ill}$$

$$\text{This l\'a / b\u{o}r, | | b\u{y} / sl\'ow pr\'u / d\'ence t\u{o} / m\'ake m\'ild}$$

$$\text{\u{A} r\'ug / g\u{e}d p\'eo / pl\u{e}, | | \u{and} / thr\'ough s\'oft / d\'egr\'ees}$$

$$\text{Subd\'ue / th\u{e}m t\u{o} / th\u{e} \'use / f\u{ul} \u{and} / th\u{e} g\'ood.}$$

Even though these are fairly regular iambic pentameter lines it should be observed that no single line is without some substitution. Still, the dominant pattern of five iambic feet per line should be apparent (out of thirty total feet, about twenty are iambs); there is even a strong tendency on the reader's part to "promote" the middle syllable of three unstressed syllables ("Subdue / them to / the use / ful and / the good") to keep the sense of the iambic rhythm.

How far can a poet depart from the pattern without losing contact with the original meter? That is a question that is impossible to answer in general terms. The following scansion will probably strike us at first as a far departure from regular iambic pentameter:

$$\text{′ | | ′ / ˘ | | ′ / ˘ ˘ | | ′ ˘ / ˘ ′}$$

Yet it is actually the opening line of one of Shakespeare's most often quoted passages, Mark Antony's funeral oration from *Julius Caesar*:

$$\text{Fr\'iends, | | R\'o / m\u{a}ns, | | c\'oun / trymen, | |/ l\'end m\u{e} / your \'ears}$$

Poets who have learned to use the resources of meter do not consider it a restraint; instead, they are able to stretch the pattern to its limits without breaking it. A good analogy might be made between poetry and dance.

Beginning dancers watch their feet and count the steps while making them; after considerable practice, the movements become second nature, and a skillful pair of partners can add dips and passes without losing the basic step of the music.

Poetic Form: Open Versus Closed

All poems have form, the arrangement of the poem on the page that differentiates it from prose. Sometimes this arrangement indicates that the poet is following a preconceived plan—a metrical pattern, a rhyme scheme, a purely visual design like that of **concrete** or **spatial poetry,** or a scheme like that of **acrostic verse,** in which the first letters of the lines spell a message. An analysis of poetic form notes how the lines are arranged, how long they are, and how they are grouped into blocks or **stanzas.** Further analysis might reveal the existence of types of repetition, rhyme or the use of a **refrain,** or a repeated line or groups of lines. A large number of the poems written in this century have been written in **open form,** which simply means that there is no strict pattern of regularity in the elements mentioned above; in other words, there is no consistent meter and no rhyme scheme. Still, even a famous poem in open form like William Carlos Williams's "The Red Wheelbarrow" can be described in formal terms:

so much depends
upon

a red wheel
barrow

glazed with rain
water

beside the white
chickens.

Here we might observe that the eight-line poem is divided into **uniform stanzas** of two lines each (or couplets). Line length varies between four and two syllables per line. The odd-numbered lines each contain three words; the even, one. There is no apparent use of rhyme or repetition.

Closed form, on the other hand, denotes the existence of some kind of regular pattern of meter, stanza, rhyme, or repetition. **Stanza forms** are consistent patterns in the individual units of the poem (*stanza* means "room" in Italian); **fixed forms** are patterns that encompass a complete poem, for example, a sonnet. **Traditional forms** are patterns that have been used for long periods of time and thus may be associated with certain subjects, themes, or types of poems. **Nonce forms** are patterns that originate in an individual poem and have not been widely used by other poets. Of course, it goes without saying that every traditional form was at first a nonce form; the first Italian poet (now lost to memory) who first wrote a lyric consisting of fourteen rhymed iambic pentameter lines could not have foreseen that poets the world over in subsequent centuries would produce literally millions of sonnets that are all variations on the original model. Some of the most common stanza and fixed forms are briefly discussed below.

Stanza Forms

Blank verse is not, strictly speaking, a stanza form since it consists of individual lines of iambic pentameter that do not rhyme. However, long poems in blank verse may be arranged into **verse paragraphs** or stanzas with a varying number of lines. Blank verse originally appeared in English with the Earl of Surrey's translation of the *Aeneid* in the fifteenth century; it has been used extensively for narrative and dramatic purposes since, particularly in epics like Milton's *Paradise Lost* and in Shakespeare's plays. Also written in stanzas of varying lengths is the **irregular ode**, a poem which employs lines of varying length (though usually of a rhythm that is iambic or matches one of the other feet) and an irregular rhyme scheme.

Paired rhyming lines (*aabbcc* . . .) are called **couplets**, though they are only rarely printed as separate stanzas. **Short couplets** have a meter of iambic tetrameter (and are sometimes called **octosyllabic couplets**). If their rhymes are predominantly feminine and seem chosen for comic effect, they may be called **Hudibrastic couplets** after Samuel Butler's satirical poem of the late 1600s. **Heroic couplets** have a meter of iambic pentameter and take their name from John Dryden's translation of the *Aeneid* (1697) and Alexander Pope's hugely successful translation of Homer's *Iliad* and *Odyssey* (1720-1726), all of these "heroic" or epic poems. Heroic couplets have also been used effectively in satirical poems like Pope's "mock epic" *The Dunciad* (1728-1743) and even in dramatic monologues like Browning's "My Last Duchess," where the rhymes are so effectively buried by enjambment that the poem approximates speech. Other couplet forms include **poulter's measure**, rhyming pairs of alternating lines of iambic hexameter and iambic heptameter, and **fourteeners**, pairs of iambic heptameter (fourteen-syllable) lines, which, since there is generally a caesura after the fourth foot, closely resemble common measure (see below).

A three-line stanza is called a **tercet**. If it rhymes in an *aaa bbb* . . . pattern it is a **triplet**; sometimes triplets appear in poems written in heroic couplets, especially at the end of sections or where special emphasis is desired. Iambic pentameter tercets rhyming *aba bcb cdc* . . . form **terza rima**, a pattern invented by Dante for *The Divine Comedy*.

A four-line stanza is known as a **quatrain**. Alternating lines of tetrameter and trimeter in any foot, rhyming *abcb* or *abab*, make up a **ballad stanza**; if the feet are strictly iambic, the quatrain is called **common measure**, the form of many popular hymns like "Amazing Grace." **Long measure**, also widely used in hymns, consists of iambic tetrameter lines rhyming *abcb* or *abab*. The **In Memoriam stanza**, named after Tennyson's long poetic sequence, is iambic tetrameter rhyming *abba*. The **Rubaiyat** stanza, an import from ancient Persia, consists of lines of either iambic tetrameter or pentameter, rhyming *aaba bbcb* . . . ; Edward FitzGerald's translation *The Rubaiyat of Omar Khayyam* employs this form. Four lines of iambic pentameter rhyming *abab* are known as an **English quatrain**, also known as the **elegiac stanza** (after Thomas Gray's "Elegy Written in a Country Churchyard"). Lines of the same meter rhyming *abba* make up an **Italian quatrain**. One other unusual quatrain stanza is an import from ancient Greece, the **Sapphic stanza**, named after the poet Sappho. The Sapphic stanza consists of three **hendecasyllabic** (eleven-syllable) lines of this pattern:

$$/\cup/\ /\cup/\ /\cup\cup/\ /\cup/\ /\cup$$

and a fourth line called an **Adonic**, which is five syllables long and consists of one dactylic foot and one trochaic foot. The Sapphic is usually unrhymed. The quatrain stanza is also used in another import, the **pantoum**, a poem in which the second and fourth lines of the first stanza become the first and third of the second, and the second and fourth of the second become the first and third of the fourth, and so on. Pantoums may be written in any meter and may or may not employ rhyme.

A five-line stanza is known as a **quintet** and is relatively rare in English poetry. The **sestet**, or six-line stanza, can be found with a number of different meters and rhyme schemes. A seven-line stanza is called a **septet**; one of Chaucer's favorite stanza patterns is **rime royal**, seven lines of iambic pentameter rhyming *ababbcc* (see "The Knight's Tale" for one example). An eight-line stanza is called an **octave**; one widely used stanza of this length is **ottava rima**, iambic pentameter lines rhyming *abababcc*. Another octave form is the **Monk's Tale stanza**, named after another of Chaucer's tales. It is iambic pentameter and rhymes *ababbcbc*. The addition of a ninth line, rhyming *c* and having a meter of iambic hexameter, makes a **Spenserian stanza**, named after Edmund Spenser, the poet who invented it for *The Faerie Queene*.

Fixed Forms

Fixed forms are combinations of meter, rhyme scheme, and repetition that make up complete poems. One familiar three-line fixed form is the **haiku**, a Japanese import consisting of lines of 5, 7, and 5 syllables, respectively. Related to the haiku is the **tanka**, which adds two additional seven-syllable lines.

Two five-line fixed forms are the **limerick** and the **cinquain**. The limerick consists of anapestic trimeter in lines one, two, and five, and anapestic dimeter in three and four. The rhymes, *aabba*, are usually feminine for a comic effect. A cinquain, the invention of American poet Adelaide Crapsey, consists of five unrhymed lines of two, four, six, eight, and two syllables, respectively.

The most important of the fixed forms is the **sonnet**, fourteen lines of rhymed iambic pentameter. The original form of the sonnet is called the **Italian sonnet** or the **Petrarchan sonnet** after the fourteenth-century poet who popularized it. An Italian sonnet is usually cast in two stanzas, an octave rhyming *abbaabba* and a sestet with a variable rhyme scheme; *cdcdcd, cdecde, cddcee* are some of the possible patterns. A **volta** or "turn," usually a conjunction or conjunctive adverb like "but" or "then," may appear at the beginning of the sestet, signifying a slight change of direction in thought. Many Italian sonnets have a strong logical connection between octave and sestet—problem/solution, cause/effect, question/answer—and the volta helps to clarify the transition. The **English sonnet**, also known as the **Shakespearean sonnet** after one of its prime exemplars, was developed in the sixteenth century after the sonnet was imported to England and employs a different rhyme scheme that takes into consideration the relative scarcity of rhymes in English (as compared to Italian). The English sonnet has a rhyme scheme of *ababcd-cdefefgg* and is usually printed as a single stanza. The pattern of three English quatrains plus a heroic couplet often forces a slightly different organizational scheme on the poet, though many of Shakespeare's sonnets still employ a strong volta at the beginning of the ninth line. Other English sonnets may withhold the turn until the beginning of the closing couplet. A third sonnet type, relatively rare, is the **Spenserian sonnet**, named after Edmund Spenser, author of *Amoretti*, one of the earliest sonnet sequences in English. The Spenserian sonnet rhymes *ababbcbccdcdee*. There are many other sonnets written over the years which have other rhyme schemes, often hybrids of the Italian and English types. These are usually termed **nonce sonnets**; Shelley's "Ozymandias," with its unusual rhyme scheme of *ababacdcedefef*, is one notable example. In "Ode to the West Wind" Shelley also employs a fourteen-line stanza rhyming *aba bcb cdc ded ff*, which has been called a **terza rima sonnet**.

Four other fixed forms, all French imports, have appeared frequently in English poetry. The **rondeau** has fifteen lines of iambic tetrameter or pentameter arranged in three stanzas: *aabba aabR aabbaR*; the R here stands for the unrhymed refrain, which repeats the first few words of the poem's first line. The **villanelle** is a nineteen-line poem, usually written in iambic pentameter, employing two refrain lines, A_1 and A_2, in a pattern of five tercets and a final quatrain: A_1bA_2 abA_1 abA_2 abA_1 abA_2 abA_1A_2. The **ballade** is twenty-eight lines of iambic tetrameter employing a refrain that appears at the end of its three octaves and final quatrain, or **envoy**: *ababbcbC ababbcbC ababbcbC bcbC*. Obviously the rhyming demands of both the villanelle and the ballade pose serious challenges to English-language poets. A final fixed form is the thirty-nine-line **sestina**, which may be either metered or in free verse and which uses a complicated sequence repeating, in different order, the six words that end the lines of the initial stanza. The sequence for the first six sestets is *123456 615243 364125 532614 451362 246531*. A final tercet uses three words in the interior of the lines and three at the ends in the pattern *(2)5(4)3(6)1*. Many sestinas hinge on the poet's choice of six end words that have multiple meanings and can serve as more than one part of speech.

There are many other less familiar types of stanza forms and fixed forms; Lewis Turco's *The New Book of Forms* and Miller Williams's *Patterns of Poetry* are two reference sources useful in identifying them. An index of the poetic forms found in this book has been included.

A Brief Note: Literary History and Poetic Conventions

What a poet attempts to do in any given poem is always governed by the tension that exists between originality and convention, in other words, between the poet's desire, in Ezra Pound's famous phrase, to "make it new" and the various stylistic devices that other poets and readers are familiar with through their understanding of the poetic tradition. If we look at some of the most obscure passages of Pound's *Cantos* we may think that the poet has departed about as far from conventional modes of expression as possible, leaving his audience far behind him. Yet it is important to keep two facts in mind. First, this style was not arrived at overnight; Pound's early poetry is relatively traditional and should present little difficulty to most readers. He arrived at the style of the *Cantos* after a twenty-year apprenticeship to the styles of writers as different as Li-Po, Robert Browning, and William Butler Yeats. Second, by the time Pound was writing his mature poetry the modernist movement was in full flower, forcing the public not only to read poems but also to look at paintings and sculpture and to listen to music in ways that would have been unimaginable only a decade or two earlier. When we talk about the stylistic conventions of any given literary period, we should keep in mind that poets are rarely willing to go much beyond what they have educated their audiences to understand. This mutual sense of agreement is the essence of poetic convention.

One should be wary of making sweeping generalizations about "schools" of poetry or the shared conventions of literary periods. In any era, there is always a significant amount of diversity among individual poets. Further, an anthology of this limited scope, which by its very nature must exclude most long poems, is likely to contribute to a misleading view of literary history and the development of poetry in English. When we read Shakespeare's sonnets or Milton's shorter poems, we should not forget that their major reputations rest on poetry of a very different sort. The Neoclassical era in English poetry, stretching from the late seventeenth century until almost the end of the eighteenth is poorly represented here because the satires of Dryden and Pope and long philosophical poems like *An Essay on Man* do not readily lend themselves to being excerpted. Edgar Allan Poe once claimed that a long poem is "simply a contradiction in terms," but the continued high reputation of *The Faerie Queene*, *Paradise Lost*, *Don Juan*, and even a modern verse-novella like Robinson Jeffers's "The Roan Stallion" demonstrate that Poe's was far from the last word on the subject.

The earliest poems in this volume, all anonymous, represent poetry's links to the oral folk tradition. The American folk songs that children learn to sing in elementary school represent our own inheritance of this rich legacy. The poets of the Tudor (1485-1558) and Elizabethan (1558-1603) eras excelled at lyrical poetry; Wyatt and Surrey had imported the sonnet form from Italy, and the form was perfected during this period. Much of the love poetry of the age is characterized by conventional imagery, so-called

Petrarchan conceits, which even a later poet like Campion employs in "There Is a Garden in Her Face" and which Shakespeare satirizes brilliantly in his Sonnet 130 ("My mistress' eyes are nothing like the sun").

The poetry of the first half of the seventeenth century has several major schools: a smooth lyricism influenced by Ben Jonson that can be traced through the work of Herrick, Waller, and Lovelace; a serious body of devotional poetry by Donne, Herbert, and Milton; and the Metaphysical style, which uses complex extended metaphors or Metaphysical conceits—Donne and Herbert are its chief exemplars, followed by early American poets Bradstreet and Taylor. Shortly after the English Restoration in 1660, a profound period of conservatism began in the arts, and the Neoclassical era, lasting through most of the eighteenth century, drew heavily on Greek and Roman models. Poetry during this period—the age of Swift, Pope, and Gray—was dominated by one form, the heroic couplet; the genres of epic and satire; and an emphasis on human reason as the poet's chief guide. Never has the private voice been so subordinated to the public as in this period when, as Pope put it, a poet's highest aspiration should be to utter "What oft was thought, but ne'er so well expressed."

The first inklings of the Romantic era coincide with the American and French Revolutions, and poets of the latter half of the eighteenth century like Freneau and Blake exhibit some of its characteristics. But it was not until the publication of *Lyrical Ballads*, a 1798 book containing the best early work of Wordsworth and Coleridge, that the Romantic era can be said to have truly flowered. Wordsworth's famous formulation of a poem as "the spontaneous overflow of powerful feeling recollected in tranquillity" remains one of Romanticism's key definitions, with its emphasis on emotion and immediacy and reflection, and Wordsworth's own poetry, with its focus on the natural world, was tremendously influential. Most of the English and American poets of the first half of the nineteenth century have ties to Romanticism in its various guises, and even a poet as late as Whitman (b. 1819) inherits many of its liberal, democratic attitudes. Poets of the Victorian era (1837–1901) continued to explore many of the same themes and genres as their Romantic forebears, but certainly much of the optimism of the early years of the century had dissipated by the time poets like Hardy, Housman, and Yeats, with their omnipresent irony and pessimism, came on the scene in the century's last decades.

The present century has been ruled by the upheavals that modernism caused in every art form. If anything characterized the first half of the century it was its tireless experimentation with the forms of poetry. There is a continuum in English-language poetry from Chaucer through Frost and Robinson, but Pound, Williams, and Cummings, to mention only three chief modernists, published poetry that would have totally mystified readers of their grandparents' day, just as Picasso and Dali produced paintings that represented radical breaks with the forms of the past. Though many of the experiments of movements like imagism and surrealism seem quaint today, they parallel the general direction that most of the other arts took during the same period.

For the sake of convenience more than anything else, it has been useful to refer to the era following the end of World War II as the postmodern era. Certainly many of the hard-won modernist gains—open form and increased candor in language and subject matter—have been taken for granted by poets writing in the contemporary period. The confessional poem, a frankly autobiographical narrative that reveals what poets in earlier ages might have striven desperately to conceal, surfaced in the late 1950s in the works of Lowell, Snodgrass, Plath, and Sexton, and remains one of the chief post-modern genres. Still, as the selections here will attest, there is considerable variety to be found in the contemporary scene, and it will perhaps be many years before critics have the necessary historical distance to assess the unique characteristics of the present period.

POETRY

Anonymous

Some of the popular ballads and lyrics of England and Scotland, composed for the most part between 1300 and 1500, were first collected in their current forms by Thomas Percy, whose *Reliques of Ancient English Poetry* (1765) helped to revive interest in folk poetry. Francis James Child (1825-1896), an American, gathered over a thousand variant versions of the three hundred-odd core of poems. The Romantic poets of the early nineteenth century showed their debt to the folk tradition by writing imitative "art ballads" (see Keats's "La Belle Dame sans Merci" or Whittier's "Skipper Ireson's Ride") which incorporate many of their stylistic devices.

Western Wind

Western wind, when will thou blow,
   The small rain down can rain?
Christ, if my love were in my arms
   And I in my bed again!

—1450?

Bonny Barbara Allan

It was in and about the Martinmas° time,
   When the green leaves were a falling,
That Sir John Græme, in the West Country,
   Fell in love with Barbara Allan.

He sent his men down through the town,   5
   To the place where she was dwelling.
"O haste and come to my master dear,
   Gin° ye be Barbara Allan."

O hooly,° hooly rose she up,
   To the place where he was lying,   10

---

1 **Martinmas** November 11 8 **Gin** if 9 **hooly** slowly

And when she drew the curtain by:
   "Young man, I think you're dying."

"O it's I'm sick, and very, very sick,
   And 'tis a'° for Barbara Allan."
"O the better for me ye s'° never be,   15
   Though your heart's blood were a-spilling.

"O dinna° ye mind, young man," said she,
   "When ye was in the tavern a drinking,
That ye made the healths gae° round and round,
   And slighted Barbara Allan?"   20

He turned his face unto the wall,
   And death was with him dealing:
"Adieu, adieu, my dear friends all,
   And be kind to Barbara Allan."

And slowly, slowly raise she up,   25
   And slowly, slowly left him,
And sighing said she could not stay,
   Since death of life had reft him.

She had not gane° a mile but twa,°
   When she heard the dead-bell ringing,   30
And every jow° that the dead-bell geid,°
   It cried, "Woe to Barbara Allan!"

"O mother, mother, make my bed!
   O make it saft° and narrow!
Since my love died for me to-day,   35
   I'll die for him to-morrow."

                                            −1500?

Sir Patrick Spens

The king sits in Dumferling town,
   Drinking the blude-reid° wine:
"O whar will I get guid sailor,
   To sail this ship of mine?"

---

14 a' all 15 s' shall 17 dinna do not 19 gae go 29 gane gone twa two 31 jow stroke
geid gave 34 saft soft
2 blude-reid blood-red

Up and spak an eldern knicht,°   5
    Sat at the king's richt° knee:
"Sir Patrick Spens is the best sailor
    That sails upon the sea."

The king has written a braid° letter,
    And signed it wi' his hand,   10
And sent it to Sir Patrick Spens,
    Was walking on the sand.

The first line that Sir Patrick read,
    A loud lauch° lauched he;
The next line that Sir Patrick read,   15
    The tear blinded his ee.°

"O wha is this has done this deed,
    This ill deed done to me,
To send me out this time o' the year,
    To sail upon the sea?   20

"Mak haste, mak haste, my mirry men all,
    Our guid ship sails the morn."
"O say na sae,° my master dear,
    For I fear a deadly storm.

"Late, late yestre'en° I saw the new moon,   25
    Wi' the auld moon in hir arm,
And I fear, I fear, my dear master,
    That we will come to harm."

O our Scots nobles wer richt laith°
    To weet° their cork-heeled shoon,°   30
But lang or a'° the play were played,
    Their hats they swam aboon.°

O lang, lang may their ladies sit,
    Wi' their fans into their hand,
Or ere they see Sir Patrick Spens   35
    Come sailing to the land.

---

5 **eldern knicht** elderly knight   6 **richt** right   9 **braid** long   14 **lauch** laugh   16 **ee** eye
23 **na sae** not so   25 **yestre'en** last evening   29 **laith** loath   30 **weet** wet   **shoon** shoes
31 **lang or a'** long before   32 **Their hats they swam aboon** their hats swam above them

O lang, lang may the ladies stand,
   Wi' their gold kems° in their hair,
Waiting for their ain dear lords,
   For they'll see them na mair.   40

Half o'er, half o'er to Aberdour
   It's fifty fadom deep,
And therĕ lies guid Sir Patrick Spens
   Wi' the Scots lords at his feet.

                                                −1500?

SIR THOMAS WYATT   1503?–1542

While serving Henry VIII as a diplomat in Italy, Wyatt read the love poetry of Petrarch (1304-1374), and is generally credited with having imported both the fashions of these lyrics—hyperbolic "conceits" or metaphorical descriptions of the woman's beauty and the lover's suffering—and their form, the sonnet, to England. "They Flee from Me," an example of one of his original lyrics, displays Wyatt's unique grasp of the rhythms of speech.

They Flee from Me

They flee from me, that sometime did me seek,
With naked foot stalking in my chamber.
I have seen them gentle, tame and meek,
That now are wild, and do not remember
That sometime they put themself in danger   5
To take bread at my hand; and now they range,
Busily seeking with a continual change.

Thanked be Fortune it hath been otherwise,
Twenty times better; but once in special,
In thin array, after a pleasant guise,°   10
When her loose gown from her shoulders did fall,
And she me caught in her arms long and small,
And therewith all sweetly did me kiss
And softly said, "Dear heart, how like you this?"

It was no dream, I lay broad waking.   15
But all is turned, thorough° my gentleness,

---

38 **kems** combs
10 **guise** appearance   16 **thorough** through

Into a strange fashion of forsaking;
And I have leave to go, of her goodness,
And she also to use newfangleness.
But since that I so kindely° am served,   20
I fain° would know what she hath deserved.

—1557

Henry Howard,
Earl of Surrey   1517?–1547

Like Wyatt, Surrey was heavily influenced by Petrarchan love poetry.
His two major innovations are formal: his translation of Virgil's
Aeneid introduced blank verse to English poetry, and he was first
to use the English sonnet form, with its relaxed rhyme scheme
(see Introduction). This type of sonnet became, in the hands of
Shakespeare and later poets, the most enduring of all traditional
poetic forms in English. In "The Soote Season" he experiments with
a sonnet turning on only two rhymes.

The Soote Season

The soote° season, that bud and bloom forth brings,
With green hath clad the hill and eke° the vale;
The nightingale with feathers new she sings;
The turtle° to her make° hath told her tale.
Summer is come, for every spray now springs;   5
The hart hath hung his old head on the pale;
The buck in brake his winter coat he flings,
The fishes float with new repairèd scale;
The adder° all her slough away she slings,
The swift swallow pursueth the flies small;   10
The busy bee her honey now she mings.°
Winter is worn, that was the flowers' bale.°
And thus I see among these pleasant things,
Each care decays, and yet my sorrow springs.

—1557

---

20 kindely in this manner   **21 fain** gladly
1 soote sweet   **2 eke** also   **4 turtle** turtledove   **make** mate   **9 adder** any snake   **11 mings**
remembers   **12 bale** threat

Queen Elizabeth I   1533–1603

Elizabeth's skills as an amateur poet drew praise from the members of her court, many of whom were also versifiers. A handful of her lyrics survives, as do translations she made from the Roman writers Seneca and Horace. Her reign (1558-1603) established England as a world power and also nurtured the talents of Edmund Spenser, William Shakespeare, Christopher Marlowe, and Ben Jonson.

When I Was Fair and Young

When I was fair and young, and favor gracèd me,
Of many was I sought, their mistress for to be;
But I did scorn them all, and answered them therefore,
    "Go, go, go seek some otherwhere!
                    Importune me no more!"   5

How many weeping eyes I made to pine with woe,
How many sighing hearts, I have no skill to show;
Yet I the prouder grew, and answered them therefore,
    "Go, go, go seek some otherwhere!
                    Importune me no more!"   10

Then spake fair Venus' son,° that proud victorious boy,
And said, "Fine dame, since that you be so coy,
I will so pluck your plumes that you shall say no more,
    'Go, go, go seek some otherwhere!
                    Importune me no more!'"   15

When he had spake these words, such change grew in my breast
That neither night nor day since that, I could take any rest.
Then lo! I did repent that I had said before,
    "Go, go, go seek some otherwhere!
                    Importune me no more!"   20

Edmund Spenser   1552–1599

Born in London, Spenser spent most of his adult life in Ireland, where he held a variety of minor government posts. *The Faerie Queene*, a long allegorical romance about Elizabethan England, was uncompleted at his death. The eighty-odd sonnets that make up the

---

11 **Venus' son** Eros or Cupid, god of love

sequence called *Amoretti* are generally thought to detail his courtship
of his second wife, Elizabeth Boyle, whom he married in 1594.

Amoretti: Sonnet 75

One day I wrote her name upon the strand,
But came the waves and washèd it away:
Agayne I wrote it with a second hand,°
But came the tyde, and made my paynes his pray.
"Vayne man," sayd she, "that doest in vaine assay,°   5
A mortall thing so to immortalize,
For I my selve shall lyke° to this decay
And eek° my name bee wypèd out lykewize."
"Not so," quod° I, "let baser things devize
To dy in dust, but you shall live by fame: 10
My verse your vertues rare shall eternize,
And in the hevens wryte your glorious name.
Where whenas death shall all the world subdew
Our love shall live, and later life renew."

                                                          —1595

SIR PHILIP SIDNEY   1554–1586

Sidney embodied many of the aspects of the ideal man of the
Renaissance; he was a courtier, scholar, patron of the arts, and soldier who died of wounds received at the battle of Zutphen. His sonnet sequence *Astrophel and Stella* appeared in 1591, several years
before Spenser's *Amoretti*, and helped to precipitate the fashion for
sonnets that lasted in England well into the next century.

from *Astrophel and Stella*

1

Loving in truth, and fain° in verse my love to show,
That she dear she might take some pleasure of my pain,
Pleasure might cause her read, reading might make her know,
Knowledge might pity win, and pity grace obtain,
I sought fit words to paint the blackest face of woe: 5
Studying inventions fine, her wits to entertain,
Oft turning others' leaves,° to see if thence would flow

---

3 second hand second time   **5 assay** attempt   **7 lyke** be similar to   **8 eek** also   **9 quod** said
1 fain glad   **7 leaves** pages

Some fresh and fruitful showers upon my sunburned brain.
But words came halting forth, wanting Invention's stay;
Invention, Nature's child, fled stepdame Study's blows;   10
And others' feet° still seemed but strangers in my way.
Thus, great with child to speak, and helpless in my throes,
Biting my truant pen, beating myself for spite:
"Fool," said my Muse to me, "look in thy heart, and write."

—1582

ROBERT SOUTHWELL   1561?–1595

Southwell, a Roman Catholic priest in Elizabeth's Protestant
England, was executed for his religious beliefs. His devotional
poems, most of them on the subject of spiritual love, were largely
written during his three years in prison. Southwell was declared a
saint in the Roman Catholic Church in 1970.

The Burning Babe

As I in hoary winter's night stood shivering in the snow,
Surprised I was with sudden heat which made my heart to glow;
And lifting up a fearful eye to view what fire was near,
A pretty babe all burning bright did in the air appear;
Who, scorchèd with excessive heat, such floods of tears did shed   5
As though his floods should quench his flames which with his tears
    were fed.
"Alas," quoth he, "but newly born in fiery heats I fry,
Yet none approach to warm their hearts or feel my fire but I!
My faultless breast the furnace is, the fuel wounding thorns,
Love is the fire, and sighs the smoke, the ashes shame and scorns;   10
The fuel justice layeth on, and mercy blows the coals,
The metal in this furnace wrought are men's defilèd souls,
For which, as now on fire I am to work them to their good,
So will I melt into a bath to wash them in my blood."
With this he vanished out of sight and swiftly shrunk away,   15
And straight I callèd unto mind that it was Christmas day.

—1602

---

11 **feet** metrical feet in poetry

Michael Drayton   1563–1631

Like his contemporary Shakespeare, Drayton excelled in several literary genres. He collaborated on plays with Thomas Dekker and
wrote long poems on English history, biography, and topography.
Drayton labored almost three decades on the sixty-three sonnets in
Idea, publishing them in their present form in 1619.

Idea: Sonnet 61

Since there's no help, come let us kiss and part;
Nay, I have done, you get no more of me,
And I am glad, yea glad with all my heart
That thus so cleanly I myself can free;
Shake hands forever, cancel all our vows,   5
And when we meet at any time again,
Be it not seen in either of our brows
That we one jot of former love retain.
Now at the last gasp of love's latest breath,
When, his pulse failing, passion speechless lies,   10
When faith is kneeling by his bed of death,
And innocence is closing up his eyes,
    Now if thou wouldst, when all have given him over,
    From death to life thou mightst him yet recover.

                                  –1619

William Shakespeare   1564–1616

Shakespeare's sonnets were first printed in 1609, during the last
years of his active career as a playwright, but they had circulated privately a dozen years before. Given the lack of concrete details about
Shakespeare's life outside the theatre, critics have found the sonnets
fertile ground for biographical speculation, and the sequence of 154
poems does contain distinct characters—a handsome youth to whom
most of the first 126 sonnets are addressed, a "Dark Lady" who figures strongly in the remaining poems, and the poet himself, whose
name is the source of many puns in the poems. There is probably no
definitive "key" to the sonnets, but there is also little doubt that their
place is secure among the monuments of English lyric verse.
Shakespeare's other non-dramatic poems include narratives, allegories, and songs, of which "When Daisies Pied," the companion
pieces from his early comedy *Love's Labour's Lost*, are perhaps the best
examples.

Sonnet 18

Shall I compare thee to a summer's day?
Thou art more lovely and more temperate:
Rough winds do shake the darling buds of May,
And summer's lease hath all too short a date:
Sometimes too hot the eye of heaven shines,   5
And often is his gold complexion dimmed;
And every fair from fair° sometimes declines,
By chance or nature's changing course untrimmed;°
But thy eternal summer shall not fade,
Nor lose possession of that fair thou ow'st;°   10
Nor shall death brag thou wander'st in his shade,
When in eternal lines to time thou grow'st:
So long as men can breathe, or eyes can see,
So long lives this, and this gives life to thee.

—1609

Sonnet 29

When, in disgrace with fortune and men's eyes,
I all alone beweep my outcast state,
And trouble deaf heaven with my bootless° cries,
And look upon myself, and curse my fate,
Wishing me like to one more rich in hope,   5
Featured like him, like him with friends possessed,
Desiring this man's art and that man's scope,
With what I most enjoy contented least;
Yet in these thoughts myself almost despising,
Haply° I think on thee—and then my state,   10
Like to the lark at break of day arising
From sullen earth, sings hymns at heaven's gate;
For thy sweet love remembered such wealth brings
That then I scorn to change my state with kings.

—1609

Sonnet 30

When to the sessions° of sweet silent thought
I summon up remembrance of things past,

---

7 **fair from fair** every fair thing from its fairness   8 **untrimmed** stripped   10 **ow'st**
ownest
3 **bootless** useless   10 **Haply** fortunately
1 **sessions** as in sessions of a court of law

I sigh the lack of many a thing I sought,
And with old woes new wail my dear time's waste:
Then can I drown an eye, unused to flow,   5
For precious friends hid in death's dateless° night,
And weep afresh love's long since canceled woe,
And moan the expense of many a vanished sight:
Then can I grieve at grievances foregone,
And heavily from woe to woe tell o'er   10
The sad account of fore-bemoanèd moan,
Which I new pay as if not paid before.
But if the while I think on thee, dear friend,
All losses are restored and sorrows end.

                                            —1609

Sonnet 73

That time of year thou mayst in me behold
When yellow leaves, or none, or few, do hang
Upon those boughs which shake against the cold,
Bare ruined choirs, where late the sweet birds sang.
In me thou see'st the twilight of such day   5
As after sunset fadeth in the west;
Which by and by black night doth take away,
Death's second self, that seals up all in rest.
In me thou see'st the glowing of such fire,
That on the ashes of his youth doth lie,   10
As the deathbed whereon it must expire,
Consumed with that which it was nourished by.
This thou perceiv'st, which makes thy love more strong,
To love that well which thou must leave ere long.

                                            —1609

Sonnet 116

Let me not to the marriage of true minds
Admit impediments. Love is not love
Which alters when it alteration finds,
Or bends with the remover to remove:
Oh, no! it is an ever-fixèd mark,   5
That looks on tempests and is never shaken:
It is the star to every wandering bark,
Whose worth's unknown, although his height be taken.°

---

6 **dateless** endless
8 **height be taken** elevation be measured

Love's not Time's fool, though rosy lips and cheeks
Within his bending sickle's compass° come;   10
Love alters not with his brief hours and weeks,
But bears it out even to the edge of doom.
If this be error and upon me proved,
I never writ, nor no man ever loved.

—1609

Sonnet 130

My mistress' eyes are nothing like the sun;
Coral is far more red than her lips' red;
If snow be white, why then her breasts are dun;
If hairs be wires, black wires grow on her head.
I have seen roses damasked,° red and white,   5
But no such roses see I in her cheeks;
And in some perfumes is there more delight
Than in the breath that from my mistress reeks.
I love to hear her speak, yet well I know
That music hath a far more pleasing sound;   10
I grant I never saw a goddess go;
My mistress, when she walks, treads on the ground.
And yet, by heaven, I think my love as rare
As any she belied° with false compare.°

—1609

When Daisies Pied°

SPRING

When daisies pied and violets blue
    And ladysmocks all silver-white
And cuckoobuds of yellow hue
    Do paint the meadows with delight,
The cuckoo then, on every tree,   5
Mocks married men;° for thus sings he,
            Cuckoo;
Cuckoo, cuckoo: Oh word of fear,
Unpleasing to a married ear!

---

10 compass range
5 damasked multi-colored   **14 belied** lied about   **compare** comparisons
Pied multi-colored   **6 Mocks married men** The pun is on the similarity between "cuckoo"
and "cuckold."

When shepherds pipe on oaten straws,   10
    And merry larks are plowmen's clocks,
When turtles tread,° and rooks, and daws,
    And maidens bleach their summer smocks,
The cuckoo then, on every tree,
Mocks married men; for thus sings he,   15
            Cuckoo:
Cuckoo, cuckoo: Oh word of fear,
Unpleasing to a married ear!

WINTER

When icicles hang by the wall
And Dick the shepherd blows his nail°   20
And Tom bears logs into the hall,
    And milk comes frozen home in pail,
When blood is nipped and ways be foul,
Then nightly sings the staring owl,
            Tu-who;   25
Tu-whit, tu-who: a merry note,
While greasy Joan doth keel° the pot.

When all aloud the wind doth blow,
    And coughing drowns the parson's saw,°
And birds sit brooding in the snow,   30
    And Marian's nose looks red and raw,
When roasted crabs° hiss in the bowl,
Then nightly sings the staring owl,
            Tu-who;
Tu-whit, tu-who: a merry note   35
While greasy Joan doth keel the pot.

                                        —1598

THOMAS CAMPION   1567–1620

A poet and physician, Campion wrote music and lyrics in a manner
that was "chiefly aimed to couple my words and notes lovingly
together." The imagery in "There Is a Garden in Her Face" represents a late flowering of the conceits of Petrarchan love poetry, so wit-
tily mocked by Shakespeare in "Sonnet 130."

---

12 turtles tread turtledoves mate   **20 nail** fingernails   **27 keel** stir   **29 saw** saying   **32 crabs**
crabapples

There Is a Garden in Her Face

There is a garden in her face,
Where roses and white lilies grow,
A heavenly paradise is that place,
Wherein all pleasant fruits do flow.
There cherries grow which none may buy   5
Till "Cherry-ripe!" themselves do cry.

Those cherries fairly do enclose
Of orient pearl a double row,
Which when her lovely laughter shows,
They look like rosebuds filled with snow.   10
Yet them nor peer nor prince can buy,
Till "Cherry-ripe!" themselves do cry.

Her eyes like angels watch them still;
Her brows like bended bows do stand,
Threatening with piercing frowns to kill   15
All that attempt with eye or hand
Those sacred cherries to come nigh,
Till "Cherry-ripe!" themselves do cry.

—1617

JOHN DONNE   1572–1631

Trained in the law for a career in government service, Donne became the greatest preacher of his day, ending his life as dean of St. Paul's Cathedral in London. Only two of Donne's poems and a handful of his sermons were printed during his life, but both circulated widely in manuscript and his literary reputation among his contemporaries was considerable. His poetry falls into two distinct periods: the witty love poetry of his youth and the sober religious meditations of his maturity. In both, however, Donne shows remarkable originality in rhythm, diction, and the use of metaphor and conceit which mark him as the chief poet of what has become commonly known as the Metaphysical style.

The Canonization

For God's sake hold your tongue, and let me love,
    Or chide my palsy, or my gout,
My five gray hairs, or ruined fortune, flout,

With wealth your state, your mind with arts improve,
    Take you a course, get you a place,   5
    Observe His Honor, or His Grace,
Or the king's real,° or his stampèd face
    Contèmplate; what you will, approve,°
    So you will let me love.

Alas, alas, who's injured by my love?   10
    What merchant's ships have my sighs drowned?
Who says my tears have overflowed his ground?
    When did my colds a forward° spring remove?
      When did the heats which my veins fill
      Add one more to the plaguy bill?°   15
Soldiers find wars, and lawyers find out still
    Litigious men, which quarrels move,
    Though she and I do love.

Call us what you will, we're made such by love;
    Call her one, me another fly,   20
We're tapers too, and at our own cost die,°
    And we in us find th' eagle and the dove.
      The phoenix° riddle hath more wit
      By us: we two being one, are it.
So, to one neutral thing both sexes fit,   25
    We die and rise the same, and prove
    Mysterious by this love.

We can die by it, if not live by love,
    And if unfit for tomb and hearse
Our legend be, it will be fit for verse;   30
    And if no piece of chronicle° we prove,
      We'll build in sonnets pretty rooms;
      As well a well-wrought urn becomes
The greatest ashes, as half-acre tombs;
      And by these hymns, all shall approve   35
      Us canonized for love:

And thus invoke us, "You whom reverend love
    Made one another's hermitage;
You, to whom love was peace, that now is rage;
    Who did the whole world's soul contract, and drove   40

---

7 **real** coinage   8 **approve** attempt   13 **forward** early   15 **plaguy bill** list of dead by plague
21 **die** i.e., to have sexual intercourse   23 **phoenix** legendary bird which is reborn from its
own ashes   31 **chronicle** history

Into the glasses of your eyes
(So made such mirrors, and such spies,°
That they did all to you epitomize)
Countries, towns, courts: Beg from above
A pattern of your love!"   45

—1633

The Flea

Mark but this flea, and mark in this,
How little that which thou deniest me is;
Me it sucked first, and now sucks thee,
And in this flea our two bloods mingled be;
Thou know'st that this cannot be said   5
A sin, or shame, or loss of maidenhead,
    Yet this enjoys before it woo,
    And pampered swells with one blood made of two,
    And this, alas, is more than we would do.

Oh stay, three lives in one flea spare,   10
Where we almost, nay more than married are.
This flea is you and I, and this
Our marriage bed and marriage temple is;
Though parents grudge, and you, we are met,
And cloistered in these living walls of jet.°   15
    Though use° make you apt to kill me
    Let not to that, self-murder added be,
    And sacrilege, three sins in killing three.

Cruel and sudden, hast thou since
Purpled thy nail° in blood of innocence?   20
Wherein could this flea guilty be,
Except in that drop which it sucked from thee?
Yet thou triumph'st, and say'st that thou
Find'st not thy self nor me the weaker now;
    'Tis true; then learn how false fears be: 25
    Just so much honor, when thou yield'st to me,
    Will waste, as this flea's death took life from thee.

—1633

---

42 **spies** telescopes
15 **jet** black   16 **use** familiarity, especially in the sexual sense   20 **Purpled thy nail** blood-
ied your fingernail

Holy Sonnet 10

Death, be not proud, though some have callèd thee
Mighty and dreadful, for thou art not so;
For those whom thou think'st thou dost overthrow
Die not, poor Death, nor yet canst thou kill me.
From rest and sleep, which but thy pictures be,   5
Much pleasure; then from thee much more must flow,
And soonest our best men with thee do go,
Rest of their bones, and soul's delivery.
Thou'art slave to fate, chance, kings, and desperate men,
And dost with poison, war, and sickness dwell,   10
And poppy° or charms can make us sleep as well
And better than thy stroke; why swell'st thou then?
One short sleep past, we wake eternally,
And death shall be no more; Death, thou shalt die.

                                                —1633

Holy Sonnet 14

Batter my heart, three-personed God; for You
As yet but knock, breathe, shine, and seek to mend;
That I may rise, and stand, o'erthrow me, and bend
Your force to break, blow, burn, and make me new.
I, like an usurped town, to another due,   5
Labor to admit You, but O, to no end;
Reason, Your viceroy in me, me should defend,
But is captived, and proves weak or untrue.
Yet dearly I love You, and would be lovèd fain,°
But am betrothed unto Your enemy.   10
Divorce me, untie or break that knot again;
Take me to You, imprison me, for I,
Except You enthrall me, never shall be free,
Nor ever chaste, except You ravish me.

                                                —1633

A Valediction:° Forbidding Mourning

As virtuous men pass mildly away,
    And whisper to their souls to go,

---

11 **poppy** opium
9 **fain** gladly
Valediction farewell speech; Donne is addressing his wife before leaving on a diplomatic mission.

Whilst some of their sad friends do say
    The breath goes now, and some say, No;

So let us melt, and make no noise,   5
    No tear-floods, nor sigh-tempests move,
'Twere profanation of our joys
    To tell the laity our love.

Moving of th' earth brings harms and fears,
    Men reckon what it did and meant;   10
But trepidation of the spheres,°
    Though greater far, is innocent.

Dull sublunary° lovers' love,
    (Whose soul is sense) cannot admit
Absence, because it doth remove   15
    Those things which elemented it.

But we by a love so much refined
    That our selves know not what it is,
Inter-assurèd of the mind,
    Care less, eyes, lips, and hands to miss.   20

Our two souls therefore, which are one,
    Though I must go, endure not yet
A breach, but an expansion,
    Like gold to airy thinness beat.

If they be two, they are two so   25
    As stiff twin compasses° are two;
Thy soul, the fixed foot, makes no show
    To move, but doth, if th' other do.

And though it in the center sit,
    Yet when the other far doth roam,   30
It leans and hearkens after it,
    And grows erect, as that comes home.

Such wilt thou be to me, who must
    Like th' other foot, obliquely run;
Thy firmness makes my circle just,°   35
    And makes me end where I begun.

                                    —1633

---

11 **trepidation of the spheres** natural trembling of the heavenly spheres, a concept of Ptolemaic astronomy   13 **sublunary** under the moon, hence, changeable (a Ptolemaic concept)   26 **stiff twin compasses** drafting compasses   35 **just** complete

BEN JONSON   1573–1637

Jonson was Shakespeare's chief rival on the stage, and their con-
tentious friendship has been the subject of much speculation.
Jonson became England's first unofficial poet laureate, receiving a
royal stipend from James I, and was a great influence of a group
of younger poets who became known as the "Tribe of Ben." His
tragedies are little regarded today, and his comedies, while still performed occasionally, have nevertheless failed to hold stage as brilliantly as Shakespeare's. Still, he was a poet of considerable talents,
particularly in short forms. His elegy on Shakespeare contains a
famous assessment: "He was not of an age, but for all time!"

On My First Son

Farewell, thou child of my right hand,° and joy;
My sin was too much hope of thee, loved boy:
Seven years thou'wert lent to me, and I thee pay,
Exacted by thy fate, on the just day.°
Oh, could I lose all father now! for why   5
Will man lament the state he should envy,
To have so soon 'scaped world's and flesh's rage,
And, if no other misery, yet age?
Rest in soft peace, and asked, say, "Here doth lie
Ben Jonson his best piece of poetry."   10
For whose sake henceforth all his vows be such
As what he loves may never like too much.

                                                     —1616

Slow, Slow, Fresh Fount°

FROM CYNTHIA'S REVELS

Slow, slow, fresh fount, keep time with my salt tears;
Yet slower, yet, O faintly, gentle springs!
List to the heavy part the music bears,
Woe weeps out her division,° when she sings.
        Droop herbs and flowers;   5
        Fall grief in showers;
Our beauties are not ours. O, I could still,
Like melting snow upon some craggy hill,
        Drop, drop, drop, drop,
Since nature's pride is now a withered daffodil.   10

                                                     —1600

---

1 **child of my right hand** Benjamin, the child's name, means this in Hebrew.   **4 the just
day** Jonson's son died on his seventh birthday.
Slow, Slow, Fresh Fount from Cynthia's Revels; spoken by the nymph Echo to the dead
Narcissus   **4 division** part of a song

ROBERT HERRICK   1591–1674

The most distinguished member of the "Tribe of Ben," Herrick is grouped with the Cavalier poets, whose graceful lyrics are marked by wit and gentle irony. Surprisingly, Herrick was a minister; his Royalist sympathies during the English Civil War caused him hardship during the Puritan era, but his position in the church was returned to him by Charles II after the Restoration.

To the Virgins, to Make Much of Time

Gather ye rosebuds while ye may,
    Old time is still a-flying;
And this same flower that smiles today
    Tomorrow will be dying.

The glorious lamp of heaven, the sun,   5
    The higher he's a-getting,
The sooner will his race be run,
    And nearer he's to setting.

That age is best which is the first,
    When youth and blood are warmer;   10
But being spent, the worse, and worst
    Times still succeed the former.

Then be not coy, but use your time,
    And, while ye may, go marry;
For, having lost but once your prime,   15
    You may forever tarry.

                       —1648

GEORGE HERBERT   1593–1633

The great master of the English devotional lyric, Herbert was born into a distinguished family which included his mother, the formidable literary patroness Lady Magdalen Herbert, and the poet and statesman Edward, Lord Herbert of Cherbury. Like John Donne, with whom he shares the Metaphysical label, Herbert early aimed at a political career but turned to the clergy, spending several happy years as rector of Bemerton before his death at age 40. *The Temple*, which contains most of his poems, was published posthumously in 1633.

Easter Wings

Lord, who createdst man in wealth and store,°
Though foolishly he lost the same,
Decaying more and more
Till he became
Most poor: 5
With Thee
O let me rise
As larks, harmoniously,
And sing this day Thy victories:
Then shall the fall further the flight in me.   10

My tender age in sorrow did begin;
And still with sicknesses and shame
Thou didst so punish sin,
That I became
Most thin.   15
With Thee
Let me combine,
And feel this day thy victory;
For, if I imp my wing on thine,°
Affliction shall advance the flight in me.   20

                                    —1633

Love (III)

Love bade me welcome: yet my soul drew back,
    Guilty of dust and sin.
But quick-eyed Love, observing me grow slack
    From my first entrance in,
Drew nearer to me, sweetly questioning   5
    If I lacked anything.

"A guest," I answered, "worthy to be here":
    Love said, "You shall be he."
"I, the unkind, ungrateful? Ah, my dear,
    I cannot look on thee."   10
Love took my hand, and smiling did reply,
    "Who made the eyes but I?"

---

1 **store** abundance   19 **imp my wing on thine** to graft feathers from a strong wing onto a
weak one, a term from falconry

"Truth, Lord, but I have marred them; let my shame
    Go where it doth deserve."
"And know you not," says Love, "who bore the blame?"   15
    "My dear, then I will serve."
"You must sit down," says Love, "and taste my meat."
    So I did sit and eat.

                                                    —1633

The Pulley

When God at first made man,
Having a glass of blessings standing by,
    "Let us," said he, "pour on him all we can.
Let the world's riches, which dispersèd lie,
    Contract into a span."°   5

So strength first made a way;
Then beauty flowed, then wisdom, honor, pleasure.
    When almost all was out, God made a stay,
Perceiving that, alone of all his treasure,
    Rest in the bottom lay.   10

"For if I should," said he,
"Bestow this jewel also on my creature,
    He would adore my gifts instead of me,
And rest in Nature, not the God of Nature;
    So both should losers be.   15

"Yet let him keep the rest,
But keep them with repining restlessness.
    Let him be rich and weary, that at least,
If goodness lead him not, yet weariness
    May toss him to my breast."   20

                                                    —1633

Redemption

Having been tenant long to a rich lord,
    Not thriving, I resolvèd to be bold,
    And make a suit° unto him, to afford°
A new small-rented lease, and cancel the old.
In heaven at his manor I him sought;   5

---

5 **span** the distance between thumb tip and the tip of the little finger
3 **make a suit** formally request   **afford** grant (me)

They told me there that he was lately gone
About some land, which he had dearly bought
Long since on earth, to take possession.

I straight returned, and knowing his great birth,
  Sought him accordingly in great resorts;   10
    In cities, theaters, gardens, parks, and courts;
At length I heard a ragged noise and mirth
  Of thieves and murderers; there I him espied,°
  Who straight, Your suit is granted, said, and died.

                                  —1633

Edmund Waller   1606–1687

Another Royalist sympathizer who suffered during Oliver
Cromwell's protectorate, Waller is noted for having pioneered the
use of the heroic couplet as a popular verse form. He has been often
praised for the smoothness of his rhythms and sound patterns.

Song

  Go, lovely rose!
Tell her that wastes her time and me
  That now she knows,
When I resemble° her to thee,
How sweet and fair she seems to be.   5

  Tell her that's young,
And shuns to have her graces spied,
  That hadst thou sprung
In deserts, where no men abide,
Thou must have uncommended died.   10

  Small is the worth
Of beauty from the light retired;
  Bid her come forth,
Suffer herself to be desired,
And not blush so to be admired.   15

  Then die! that she
The common fate of all things rare

---

13 **him espied** saw him
4 **resemble** compare

May read in thee;
How small a part of time they share
That are so wondrous sweet and fair!   20

—1645

J OHN M ILTON   1608–1674

Milton's true genius was realized in *Paradise Lost*, the greatest English
epic poem. His life included service in the Puritan government of
Cromwell, pamphleteering for liberal political causes, brief impris-
onment after the Restoration, and blindness in his later years. He
excelled in the sonnet, a form to which he returned throughout his
long literary life.

How Soon Hath Time

How soon hath Time, the subtle thief of youth,
    Stol'n on his wing my three and twentieth year!
    My hasting days fly on with full career,
    But my late spring no bud or blossom shew'th.°
Perhaps my semblance might deceive the truth,   5
    That I to manhood am arrived so near,
    And inward ripeness doth much less appear,
    That some more timely-happy spirits endu'th.°
Yet be it less or more, or soon or slow,
    It shall be still in strictest measure even°   10
    To that same lot, however mean or high,
Toward which Time leads me, and the will of Heaven;
    All is, if I have grace to use it so,
    As ever in my great Taskmaster's eye.

—1645

On the Late Massacre in Piedmont°

Avenge, O Lord, thy slaughtered saints, whose bones
    Lie scattered on the Alpine mountains cold,
    Even them who kept thy truth so pure of old
    When all our fathers worshiped stocks and stones,°
Forget not: in thy book record their groans   5
    Who were thy sheep and in their ancient fold

---

4 **shew'th** shows   8 **endu'th** endows   10 **even** equal
Massacre in Piedmont 1,700 Protestants from this North Italian state were massacred by Papal
forces on Easter Day, 1655.   4 **stocks and stones** idols

Slain by the bloody Piedmontese that rolled
Mother with infant down the rocks. Their moans
The vales redoubled to the hills, and they
    To Heaven. Their martyred blood and ashes sow   10
    O'er all th'Italian fields where still doth sway
The triple tyrant:° that from these may grow
    A hundredfold, who having learnt thy way
    Early may fly the Babylonian woe.°

                                                    —1655

When I Consider How My
Light Is Spent

When I consider how my light is spent
    Ere half my days, in this dark world and wide,
    And that one talent which is death to hide°
Lodged with me useless, though my soul more bent
To serve therewith my Maker, and present   5
    My true account, lest he returning chide;
    "Doth God exact day-labor, light denied?"
    I fondly° ask; but Patience to prevent
That murmur, soon replies, "God doth not need
    Either man's work or his own gifts; who best   10
    Bear his mild yoke, they serve him best. His state
Is kingly. Thousands at his bidding speed
    And post o'er land and ocean without rest:
    They also serve who only stand and wait."

                                                    —1673

ANNE BRADSTREET   1612–1672

Bradstreet was an American Puritan who was one of the first settlers
of the Massachusetts Bay Colony, along with her husband Simon,
later governor of the colony. *The Tenth Muse Lately Sprung Up in
America*, published abroad by a relative without her knowledge, was
the first American book of poetry published in England, and the circumstances of its appearance lie behind the witty tone of "The
Author to Her Book."

---

12 triple tyrant the Pope   **14 Babylonian woe** Early Protestants often linked ancient Babylon
to modern Rome as centers of vice.
3 talent which is death to hide See the Parable of the Talents, Matthew 25:14-30.   **8 fond-
ly** foolishly

The Author to Her Book

Thou ill-formed offspring of my feeble brain,
Who after birth didst by my side remain,
Till snatched from thence by friends, less wise than true,
Who thee abroad, exposed to public view,
Made thee in rags, halting to th' press° to trudge,   5
Where errors were not lessened (all may judge).
At thy return my blushing was not small,
My rambling brat (in print) should mother call,
I cast thee by as one unfit for light,
Thy visage was so irksome in my sight;   10
Yet being mine own, at length affection would
Thy blemishes amend, if so I could:
I washed thy face, but more defects I saw,
And rubbing off a spot still made a flaw.
I stretched thy joints to make thee even feet,°   15
Yet still thou run'st more hobbling than is meet;
In better dress to trim thee was my mind,
But nought save homespun cloth i' th' house I find.
In this array 'mongst vulgars° may'st thou roam.
In critic's hands beware thou dost not come,   20
And take thy way where yet thou art not known;
If for thy father asked, say thou hadst none;
And for thy mother, she alas is poor,
Which caused her thus to send thee out of door.

           —1678

To My Dear and Loving Husband

If ever two were one, then surely we;
If ever man were loved by wife, then thee;
If ever wife was happy in a man,
Compare with me, ye women, if you can.
I prize thy love more than whole mines of gold,   5
Or all the riches that the East° doth hold.
My love is such that rivers cannot quench,
Nor aught° but love from thee give recompense.
Thy love is such I can no way repay;
The heavens reward thee manifold, I pray.   10

---

5 **press** printing press; also a clothes closet or chest   15 **even feet** a pun on metrical feet   19
vulgars common people, i.e., average readers
6 **East** the Orient   8 **aught** anything

Then while we live in love let's so persever
That when we live no more we may live ever.

—1678

RICHARD LOVELACE   1618–1658

Another Cavalier lyricist, Lovelace composed many of his poems in
prison following the English Civil War, during which he was a staunch
supporter of Charles I, serving as a soldier in Scotland and France.

To Lucasta, Going to the Wars

Tell me not, sweet, I am unkind
That from the nunnery
Of thy chaste breast and quiet mind,
To war and arms I fly.

True, a new mistress now I chase,   5
The first foe in the field;
And with a stronger faith embrace
A sword, a horse, a shield.

Yet this inconstancy is such
As you too shall adore;   10
I could not love thee, dear, so much,
Loved I not honor more.

—1649

ANDREW MARVELL   1621–1678

Although widely known for the playful sexual wit of this most famous
example of the *carpe diem* poem in English, Marvell was a learned
Latin scholar who moved in high circles of government under both
the Puritans and Charles II, serving as a member of parliament for
two decades. Oddly, Marvell was almost completely forgotten as a lyric
poet for almost two hundred years after his death, though today he is
considered the last of the great exemplars of the Metaphysical style.

To His Coy Mistress

Had we but world enough, and time,
This coyness,° lady, were no crime.

---

2 **coyness** here, artificial sexual reluctance

We would sit down, and think which way
To walk, and pass our long love's day.
Thou by the Indian Ganges' side   5
Shouldst rubies find; I by the tide
Of Humber° would complain. I would
Love you ten years before the flood,
And you should, if you please, refuse
Till the conversion of the Jews.°   10
My vegetable° love should grow
Vaster than empires, and more slow;
An hundred years should go to praise
Thine eyes, and on thy forehead gaze;
Two hundred to adore each breast,   15
But thirty thousand to the rest;
An age at least to every part,
And the last age should show your heart.
For, lady, you deserve this state,°
Nor would I love at lower rate.   20
   But at my back I always hear
Time's wingèd chariot hurrying near;
And yonder all before us lie
Deserts of vast eternity.
Thy beauty shall no more be found;   25
Nor, in thy marble vault, shall sound
My echoing song; then worms shall try°
That long-preserved virginity,
And your quaint° honor turn to dust,
And into ashes all my lust: 30
The grave's a fine and private place,
But none, I think, do there embrace.
   Now therefore, while the youthful hue
Sits on thy skin like morning glow,
And while thy willing soul transpires   35
At every pore with instant fires,
Now let us sport us while we may,
And now, like amorous birds of prey,
Rather at once our time devour
Than languish in his slow-chapped° power.   40
Let us roll all our strength and all
Our sweetness up into one ball,
And tear our pleasures with rough strife

---

7 **Humber** an English river near Marvell's home   10 **conversion of the Jews** at the end
of time   11 **vegetable** flourishing   19 **state** estate   27 **try** test   29 **quaint** too subtle
40 **chapped** jawed

Thorough the iron gates of life:
Thus, though we cannot make our sun   45
Stand still, yet we will make him run.

—1681

JOHN DRYDEN   1631–1700

Short poems do not do justice to Dryden's talents, for he excelled
at long forms—verse dramas like *All for Love*, his version of
Shakespeare's *Antony and Cleopatra*, his translation of Virgil's *Aeneid*,
political allegories like *Absalom and Achitophel*, and *MacFlecknoe*, the
first great English literary satire. Dryden's balance and formal conservatism introduced the Neoclassical style to English poetry, a manner that prevailed for a century after his death. He became Poet
Laureate of England in 1668.

To the Memory of Mr. Oldham°

Farewell, too little, and too lately known,
Whom I began to think and call my own:
For sure our souls were near allied, and thine
Cast in the same poetic mold with mine.
One common note on either lyre did strike,   5
And knaves and fools we both abhorred alike.
To the same goal did both our studies drive;
The last set out the soonest did arrive.
Thus Nisus° fell upon the slippery place,
While his young friend performed and won the race.   10
O early ripe! to thy abundant store
What could advancing age have added more?
It might (what nature never gives the young)
Have taught the numbers° of thy native tongue.
But satire needs not those, and wit will shine   15
Through the harsh cadence of a rugged line:
A noble error, and but seldom made,
When poets are by too much force betrayed.
Thy generous fruits, though gathered ere their prime,
Still showed a quickness, and maturing time   20
But mellows what we write to the dull sweets of rhyme.
Once more, hail and farewell; farewell, thou young,
But ah too short, Marcellus° of our tongue;

John Oldham (1653-1683) was a poet and a satirist.   **9 Nisus** In Virgil's *Aeneid* he is defeat-
ed in a footrace by Euryalus, his friend.   **14 numbers** poetic meters   **23 Marcellus** Roman
military leader who died at twenty

Thy brows with ivy, and with laurels bound
But fate and gloomy night encompass thee around.   25

—1684

Epigram on Milton

Three poets, in three distant ages born,
Greece,° Italy,° and England did adorn.
The first in loftiness of thought surpassed,
The next in majesty, in both the last:
The force of Nature could no farther go;   5
To make a third, she joined the former two.

—1688

EDWARD TAYLOR   1642–1729

Taylor was a Calvinist minister in a village outside of Boston whose
eccentric religious poems (obviously influenced by Donne and
Herbert) remained in manuscript for over two centuries after his
death, when they were discovered in the Yale University Library.
Taylor was a true amateur, writing in isolation and apparently
intending his poems as meditative exercises to assist him in his cler-
ical duties. Taylor's poems were not published until the twentieth
century.

Housewifery

Make me, O Lord, thy spinning wheel complete.
    Thy holy word my distaff° make for me.
Make mine affections thy swift flyers° neat,
    And make my soul thy holy spool° to be.
My conversation make to be thy reel,°   5
And reel the yarn thereon spun of thy wheel.

Make me thy loom then, knit therein this twine;
    And make thy holy spirit, Lord, wind quills.°
Then weave the web thyself. The yarn is fine.
    Thine ordinances make my fulling mills.°   10
    Then dye the same in heavenly colors choice,
    All pinked° with varnished° flowers of paradise.

---

2 **Greece** i.e., Homer   **Italy** i.e., Virgil
2 **distaff** part of a spinning wheel that holds raw material   3 **flyers** impart twist to yarn
4 **spool** collects spun yarn   5 **reel** receives finished thread   8 **quills** spools   10 **fulling mills**
where cloth is cleaned after weaving   12 **pinked** decorated   **varnished** shiny

Then clothe therewith mine understanding, will,
  Affections, judgment, conscience, memory,
My words, and actions, that their shine may fill   15
  My ways with glory and thee glorify.
Then mine apparel shall display before ye
That I am clothed in holy robes for glory.

                                —1685?

JONATHAN SWIFT   1667–1745

> As the author of *Gulliver's Travels,* Swift stands unchallenged as the
> greatest English prose satirist, but his poetry too is remarkable in the
> unsparing realism of its best passages. Like many poets of the
> Neoclassical era, Swift adds tension to his poetry by ironically
> emphasizing parallels between the heroic past and the familiar char-
> acters and scenes of contemporary London. A native of Dublin,
> Swift returned to Ireland in his maturity as dean of St. Patrick's
> Cathedral.

A Description of a City Shower

  Careful observers may foretell the hour
(By sure prognostics)° when to dread a shower:
While rain depends,° the pensive cat gives o'er
Her frolics, and pursues her tail no more.
Returning home at night, you'll find the sink°   5
Strike your offended sense with double stink.
If you be wise, then go not far to dine;
You'll spend in coach hire more than save in wine.
A coming shower your shooting corns presage,
Old achès throb, your hollow tooth will rage.   10
Sauntering in coffeehouse is Dulman° seen;
He damns the climate and complains of spleen.°
  Meanwhile the South, rising with dabbled wings,
A sable cloud athwart the welkin° flings,
That swilled more liquor than it could contain,   15
And, like a drunkard, gives it up again.
Brisk Susan whips her linen from the rope,
While the first drizzling shower is borne aslope:
Such is that sprinkling which some careless quean°
Flirts on you from her mop, but not so clean: 20

---

2 **prognostics** forecasts   3 **depends** is imminent   5 **sink** sewer   11 **Dulman** i.e., dull man
12 **spleen** mental depression   14 **welkin** sky   19 **quean** ill-mannered woman

You fly, invoke the gods; then turning, stop
To rail; she singing, still whirls on her mop.
Not yet the dust had shunned the unequal strife,
But, aided by the wind, fought still for life,
And wafted with its foe by violent gust,   25
'Twas doubtful which was rain and which was dust.
Ah! where must needy poet seek for aid,
When dust and rain at once his coat invade?
Sole coat, where dust cemented by the rain
Erects the nap, and leaves a mingled stain.   30
    Now in contiguous drops the flood comes down,
Threatening with deluge this devoted° town.
To shops in crowds the daggled° females fly,
Pretend to cheapen° goods, but nothing buy.
The Templar° spruce, while every spout's abroach,°   35
Stays till 'tis fair, yet seems to call a coach.
The tucked-up sempstress walks with hasty strides,
While streams run down her oiled umbrella's sides.
Here various kinds, by various fortunes led,
Commence acquaintance underneath a shed.   40
Triumphant Tories and desponding Whigs°
Forget their feuds, and join to save their wigs.
Boxed in a chair° the beau impatient sits,
While spouts run clattering o'er the roof by fits,
And ever and anon with frightful din   45
The leather sounds; he trembles from within.
So when Troy chairmen bore the wooden steed,
Pregnant with Greeks impatient to be freed
(Those bully Greeks, who, as the moderns do,
Instead of paying chairmen, run them through),   50
Laocoön° struck the outside with his spear,
And each imprisoned hero quaked for fear.
    Now from all parts the swelling kennels° flow,
And bear their trophies with them as they go:
Filth of all hues and odors seem to tell   55
What street they sailed from, by their sight and smell.
They, as each torrent drives with rapid force,
From Smithfield° or St. Pulchre's shape their course,
And in huge confluence joined at Snow Hill ridge,
Fall from the conduit prone to Holborn Bridge.   60
Sweepings from butchers' stalls, dung, guts, and blood,

---

32 devoted doomed   **33 daggled** spattered   **34 cheapen** inspect prices of   **35 Templar** law
student **abroach** pouring   **41 Tories . . . Whigs** rival political factions   **43 chair** sedan chair
51 Laocoön For his attempt to warn the Trojans, he was crushed by sea serpents sent by
Poseidon.   **53 kennels** storm drains   **58 Smithfield** site of London cattle exchange

Drowned puppies, stinking sprats,° all drenched in mud,
Dead cats, and turnip tops, come tumbling down the flood.

—1710

ALEXANDER POPE   1688–1744

A tiny man who was afflicted in childhood by a crippling disease,
Pope was the dominant poet of eighteenth-century England, particularly excelling as a master of mock-epic satire in "The Rape of the
Lock" and "The Dunciad." His translations of the *Iliad* and the
Odyssey made him famous and financially independent and remained the standard versions of Homer for almost two hundred
years. "An Essay on Criticism," a long didactic poem modeled on
Horace's *Ars Poetica*, remains the most complete statement of the
neoclassical aesthetic.

from An Essay on Criticism

But most by numbers judge a poet's song,
And smooth or rough with them is right or wrong.
In the bright Muse though thousand charms conspire,
Her voice is all these tuneful fools admire,
Who haunt Parnassus° but to please their ear,   5
Not mend their minds; as some to church repair,
Not for the doctrine, but the music there.
These equal syllables alone require,
Though oft the ear the open vowels tire,
While expletives° their feeble aid do join,   10
And ten low words oft creep in one dull line:
While they ring round the same unvaried chimes,
With sure returns of still expected rhymes;
Where'er you find "the cooling western breeze,"
In the next line, it "whispers through the trees";   15
If crystal streams "with pleasing murmurs creep,"
The reader's threatened (not in vain) with "sleep";
Then, at the last and only couplet fraught
With some unmeaning thing they call a thought,
A needless Alexandrine° ends the song   20
That, like a wounded snake, drags its slow length along.
Leave such to tune their own dull rhymes, and know

---

62 **sprats** small fish
5 **Parnassus** mountain of the Muses   10 **expletives** unnecessary filler words   20 **Alexan-
drine** line of six iambic feet (as in the next line)

What's roundly smooth or languishingly slow;
And praise the easy vigor of a line
Where Denham's strength and Waller's° sweetness join.   25
True ease in writing comes from art, not chance,
As those move easiest who have learned to dance.
'Tis not enough no harshness gives offense,
The sound must seem an echo to the sense.
Soft is the strain when Zephyr° gently blows,   30
And the smooth stream in smoother numbers flows;
But when loud surges lash the sounding shore,
The hoarse, rough verse should like the torrent roar.
When Ajax° strives some rock's vast weight to throw,
The line too labors, and the words move slow;   35
Not so when swift Camilla° scours the plain,
Flies o'er the unbending corn, and skims along the main.
Hear how Timotheus'° varied lays surprise,
And bid alternate passions fall and rise!
While at each change the son of Libyan Jove°   40
Now burns with glory, and then melts with love;
Now his fierce eyes with sparkling fury glow,
Now sighs steal out, and tears begin to flow:
Persians and Greeks like turns of nature found
And the world's victor stood subdued by sound!   45
The power of music all our hearts allow,
And what Timotheus was is Dryden now.
    Avoid extremes; and shun the fault of such
Who still are pleased too little or too much.
At every trifle scorn to take offense: 50
That always shows great pride, or little sense.
Those heads, as stomachs, are not sure the best,
Which nauseate all, and nothing can digest.
Yet let not each gay turn thy rapture move;
For fools admire, but men of sense approve: 55
As things seem large which we through mists descry,
Dullness is ever apt to magnify.

                                                            —1711

Ode on Solitude

Happy the man whose wish and care
    A few paternal acres bound,

---

25 **Denham's . . . Waller's** earlier English poets praised by Pope   **30 Zephyr** the west wind
34 Ajax legendary strong man of the *Iliad*   **36 Camilla** messenger of the goddess Diana
38 Timotheus a legendary musician   **40 son of Libyan Jove** Alexander the Great

Content to breathe his native air,
    In his own ground.

Whose herds with milk, whose fields with bread,   5
    Whose flocks supply him with attire,
Whose trees in summer yield him shade,
    In winter fire.

Blest, who can unconcernedly find
    Hours, days, and years slide soft away,   10
In health of body, peace of mind,
    Quiet by day,

Sound sleep by night; study and ease,
    Together mixed; sweet recreation;
And innocence, which most does please   15
    With meditation.

Thus let me live, unseen, unknown;
    Thus unlamented let me die;
Steal from the world, and not a stone
    Tell where I lie.   20

—1736

Thomas Gray   1716–1771

Gray's contemporary reputation rests primarily on a single poem, but it remains one of the most often quoted in the whole English canon, and the quatrain stanza is often called "elegiac" in its honor. Gray lived almost all of his adult life at Cambridge University, where he was a professor of history and languages. He declined the poet laureateship of England in 1757.

Elegy Written in a Country Churchyard

The curfew tolls the knell of parting day,
    The lowing herd wind slowly o'er the lea,
The plowman homeward plods his weary way,
    And leaves the world to darkness and to me.

Now fades the glimmering landscape on the sight,   5
    And all the air a solemn stillness holds,

Save where the beetle wheels his droning flight,
   And drowsy tinklings lull the distant folds;

Save that from yonder ivy-mantled tower
   The moping owl does to the moon complain   10
Of such, as wandering near her secret bower,
   Molest her ancient solitary reign.

Beneath those rugged elms, that yew tree's shade,
   Where heaves the turf in many a moldering heap,
Each in his narrow cell forever laid,   15
   The rude° forefathers of the hamlet sleep.

The breezy call of incense-breathing morn,
   The swallow twittering from the straw-built shed,
The cock's shrill clarion, or the echoing horn,
   No more shall rouse them from their lowly bed.   20

For them no more the blazing hearth shall burn,
   Or busy housewife ply her evening care;
No children run to lisp their sire's return,
   Or climb his knees the envied kiss to share.

Oft did the harvest to their sickle yield,   25
   Their furrow oft the stubborn glebe° has broke;
How jocund did they drive their team afield!
   How bowed the woods beneath their sturdy stroke!

Let not Ambition mock their useful toil,
   Their homely joys, and destiny obscure;   30
Nor Grandeur hear with a disdainful smile
   The short and simple annals of the poor.

The boast of heraldry, the pomp of power,
   And all that beauty, all that wealth e'er gave,
Awaits alike the inevitable hour.   35
   The paths of glory lead but to the grave.

Nor you, ye proud, impute to these the fault,
   If Memory o'er their tomb no trophies raise,
Where through the long-drawn aisle and fretted° vault
   The pealing anthem swells the note of praise.   40

---

16 **rude** unlearned   26 **glebe** plot of farmland   39 **fretted** carved

Can storied urn or animated bust
    Back to its mansion call the fleeting breath?
Can Honor's voice provoke the silent dust,
    Or Flattery soothe the dull cold ear of Death?

Perhaps in this neglected spot is laid   45
    Some heart once pregnant with celestial fire;
Hands that the rod of empire might have swayed,
    Or waked to ecstasy the living lyre.

But Knowledge to their eyes her ample page
    Rich with the spoils of time did ne'er unroll;   50
Chill Penury repressed their noble rage,
    And froze the genial current of the soul.

Full many a gem of purest ray serene,
    The dark unfathomed caves of ocean bear:
Full many a flower is born to blush unseen,   55
    And waste its sweetness on the desert air.

Some village Hampden,° that with dauntless breast
    The little tyrant of his field withstood;
Some mute inglorious Milton here may rest,
    Some Cromwell° guiltless of his country's blood.   60

The applause of listening senates to command,
    The threats of pain and ruin to despise,
To scatter plenty o'er a smiling land,
    And read their history in a nation's eyes,

Their lot forbade: nor circumscribed alone   65
    Their growing virtues, but their crimes confined;
Forbade to wade through slaughter to a throne,
    And shut the gates of mercy on mankind,

The struggling pangs of conscious truth to hide,
    To quench the blushes of ingenuous shame,   70
Or heap the shrine of Luxury and Pride
    With incense kindled at the Muse's flame.

Far from the madding° crowd's ignoble strife,
    Their sober wishes never learned to stray;

---

57 Hampden hero of the English Civil War   **60 Cromwell** Lord Protector of England from 1653 to 1658   **73 madding** frenzied

Along the cool sequestered vale of life   75
    They kept the noiseless tenor of their way.

Yet even these bones from insult to protect
    Some frail memorial still erected nigh,
With uncouth rhymes and shapeless sculpture decked,
    Implores the passing tribute of a sigh.   80

Their name, their years, spelt by the unlettered Muse,
    The place of fame and elegy supply:
And many a holy text around she strews,
    That teach the rustic moralist to die.

For who to dumb Forgetfulness a prey,   85
    This pleasing anxious being e'er resigned,
Left the warm precincts of the cheerful day,
    Nor cast one longing lingering look behind?

On some fond breast the parting soul relies,
    Some pious drops the closing eye requires;   90
Even from the tomb the voice of Nature cries,
    Even in our ashes live their wonted fires.

For thee, who mindful of the unhonored dead
    Dost in these lines their artless tale relate;
If chance, by lonely contemplation led,   95
    Some kindred spirit shall inquire thy fate,

Haply some hoary°-headed swain° may say,
    "Oft have we seen him at the peep of dawn
Brushing with hasty steps the dews away
    To meet the sun upon the upland lawn.   100

"There at the foot of yonder nodding beech
    That wreathes its old fantastic roots so high,
His listless length at noontide would he stretch,
    And pore upon the brook that babbles by.

"Hard by yon wood, now smiling as in scorn,   105
    Muttering his wayward fancies he would rove,
Now drooping, woeful wan, like one forlorn,
    Or crazed with care, or crossed in hopeless love.

---

97 hoary frosty, white   **swain** peasant

"One morn I missed him on the customed hill,
    Along the heath and near his favorite tree;   110
Another came; nor yet beside the rill,
    Nor up the lawn, nor at the wood was he;

"The next with dirges due in sad array
    Slow through the churchway path we saw him borne.
Approach and read (for thou canst read) the lay,   115
    Graved on the stone beneath yon aged thorn."

                    The Epitaph

Here rests his head upon the lap of Earth
    A youth to Fortune and to Fame unknown.
Fair Science frowned not on his humble birth,   120
    And Melancholy marked him for her own.

Large was his bounty, and his soul sincere,
    Heaven did a recompense as largely send:
He gave to Misery all he had, a tear,
    He gained from Heaven ('twas all he wished) a friend.   125

No farther seek his merits to disclose,
    Or draw his frailties from their dread abode
(There they alike in trembling hope repose),
    The bosom of his Father and his God.

                                                        —1751

CHRISTOPHER SMART   1722–1771

Educated, like Thomas Gray, at Cambridge, Smart fell victim to religious mania and insanity but continued to write throughout his life. *Jubilate Agno* ("Rejoice in the Lamb") is a long meditation on the immanence of God, even in such insignificant forms as Gray's cat Jeoffry. The poem is one of the earliest examples of free verse in English.

from *Jubilate Agno*

For I will consider my Cat Jeoffry.
For he is the servant of the Living God, duly and daily serving him.
For at the first glance of the glory of God in the East he worships in his way.
For is this done by wreathing his body seven times round with elegant quickness.

For then he leaps up to catch the musk,° which is the blessing of
    God upon his prayer.   5
For he rolls upon prank to work it in.
For having done duty and received blessing he begins to consider
    himself.
For this he performs in ten degrees.
For first he looks upon his forepaws to see if they are clean.
For secondly he kicks up behind to clear away there.   10
For thirdly he works it upon stretch with the forepaws extended.
For fourthly he sharpens his paws by wood.
For fifthly he washes himself.
For sixthly he rolls upon wash.
For seventhly he fleas himself, that he may not be interrupted
    upon the beat.°   15
For eighthly he rubs himself against a post.
For ninthly he looks up for his instructions.
For tenthly he goes in quest of food.
For having considered God and himself he will consider his
    neighbor.
For if he meets another cat he will kiss her in kindness.   20
For when he takes his prey he plays with it to give it a chance.
For one mouse in seven escapes by his dallying.
For when his day's work is done his business more properly begins.
For he keeps the Lord's watch in the night against the adversary.°
For he counteracts the powers of darkness by his electrical skin and
    glaring eyes.   25
For he counteracts the Devil, who is death, by brisking about
    the life.
For in his morning orisons he loves the sun and the sun loves him.
For he is of the tribe of Tiger.
For the Cherub Cat is a term° of the Angel Tiger.
For he has the subtlety and hissing of a serpent, which in
    goodness he suppresses.   30
For he will not do destruction if he is well-fed, neither will he spit
    without provocation.
For he purrs in thankfulness when God tells him he's a good Cat.
For he is an instrument for the children to learn benevolence upon.
For every house is incomplete without him, and a blessing is
    lacking in the spirit.
For the Lord commanded Moses concerning the cats at the
    departure of the Children of Israel from Egypt.   35
For every family had one cat at least in the bag.
For the English Cats are the best in Europe.

---

5 **musk** scented object or toy   15 **beat** accustomed path   24 **adversary** i.e., Satan   29 **term**
immature version

For he is the cleanest in the use of his forepaws of any quadruped.
For the dexterity of his defense is an instance of the love of God
    to him exceedingly.
For he is the quickest to his mark of any creature.   40
For he is tenacious of his point.
For he is a mixture of gravity and waggery.
For he knows that God is his Saviour.
For there is nothing sweeter than his peace when at rest.
For there is nothing brisker than his life when in motion.   45
For he is of the Lord's poor, and so indeed is he called by
    benevolence perpetually—Poor Jeoffry! poor Jeoffry!
    the rat has bit thy throat.
For I bless the name of the Lord Jesus that Jeoffry is better.
For the divine spirit comes about his body to sustain it in
    complete cat.
For his tongue is exceeding pure so that it has in purity what it
    wants in music.
For he is docile and can learn certain things.   50
For he can sit up with gravity, which is patience upon
    approbation.
For he can fetch and carry, which is patience in employment.
For he can jump over a stick, which is patience upon proof
    positive.
For he can spraggle upon waggle at the word of command.
For he can jump from an eminence into his master's bosom.   55
For he can catch the cork and toss it again.
For he is hated by the hypocrite and miser.
For the former is afraid of detection.
For the latter refuses the charge.
For he camels his back to bear the first notion of business.   60
For he is good to think on, if a man would express himself neatly.
For he made a great figure in Egypt for his signal services.
For he killed the Icneumon° rat, very pernicious by land.
For his ears are so acute that they sting again.
For from this proceeds the passing quickness of his attention.   65
For by stroking of him I have found out electricity.
For I perceived God's light about him both wax and fire.
For the electrical fire is the spiritual substance which God sends
    from heaven to sustain the bodies both of man and beast.
For God has blessed him in the variety of his movements.
For, though he cannot fly, he is an excellent clamberer.   70
For his motions upon the face of the earth are more than any
    other quadruped.

---

63 Icneumon resembling the mongoose (Herpestes ichneumon)

For he can tread to all the measures upon the music.
For he can swim for life.
For he can creep.

—ca. 1760

PHILIP FRENEAU   1752–1832

A friend and political ally of Thomas Jefferson, Freneau was a popular journalist and writer whose patriotic verse earned him the moniker "Poet of the Revolution." This reputation has unfortunately overshadowed his considerable talents as a lyric poet whose fine eye for nature prefigures the next generation of American Romantics.

The Wild Honey Suckle

Fair flower, that dost so comely grow,
Hid in this silent, dull retreat,
Untouched thy honied blossoms blow,
Unseen thy little branches greet:
    No roving foot shall crush thee here,   5
    No busy hand provoke a tear.°

By Nature's self in white arrayed,
She bade thee shun the vulgar° eye,
And planted here the guardian shade,
And sent soft waters murmuring by;   10
    Thus quietly thy summer goes,
    Thy days declining to repose.

Smit with those charms, that must decay,
I grieve to see your future doom;
They died—nor were those flowers more gay,   15
The flowers that did in Eden bloom;
    Unpitying frosts, and Autumn's power
    Shall leave no vestige of this flower.

From morning suns and evening dews
At first thy little being came: 20
If nothing once, you nothing lose,
For when you die you are the same;
    The space between, is but an hour,
    The frail duration of a flower.

—1788

---

6 **provoke a tear** i.e., the nectar of the flower   8 **vulgar** common

William Blake   1757–1827

Poet, painter, engraver, and visionary, Blake does not fit into any easy categories, though his political sympathies link him to the later Romantic poets. His first book, *Poetical Sketches*, attracted little attention, but his mature works, starting with *Songs of Innocence* and *Songs of Experience*, combine poetry with his own remarkable illustrations and are unique in English literature. Thought mad by many in his own day, Blake anticipated many future directions of both literature and modern psychology.

The Chimney Sweeper

When my mother died I was very young,
And my father sold me while yet my tongue
Could scarcely cry "'weep! 'weep! 'weep! 'weep!"
So your chimneys I sweep & in soot I sleep.

There's little Tom Dacre, who cried when his head   5
That curl'd like a lamb's back, was shav'd, so I said,
"Hush, Tom! never mind it, for when your head's bare,
You know that the soot cannot spoil your white hair."

And so he was quiet, & that very night,
As Tom was a-sleeping, he had such a sight!   10
That thousands of sweepers, Dick, Joe, Ned, & Jack,
Were all of them lock'd up in coffins of black;

And by came an Angel who had a bright key,
And he open'd the coffins & set them all free;
Then down a green plain, leaping, laughing, they run,   15
And wash in a river and shine in the Sun.

Then naked & white, all their bags left behind,
They rise upon clouds, and sport in the wind.
And the Angel told Tom, if he'd be a good boy,
He'd have God for his father, & never want joy.   20

And so Tom awoke; and we rose in the dark,
And got with our bags & our brushes to work.
Tho' the morning was cold, Tom was happy & warm;
So if all do their duty, they need not fear harm.

—1789

The Little Black° Boy

My mother bore me in the southern wild,
And I am black, but O! my soul is white;
White as an angel is the English child:
But I am black as if bereav'd of light.

My mother taught me underneath a tree,   5
And sitting down before the heat of day,
She took me on her lap and kissèd me,
And pointing to the east, began to say:

"Look on the rising sun: there God does live,
And gives his light, and gives his heat away;   10
And flowers and trees and beasts and men receive
Comfort in morning, joy in the noon day.

"And we are put on earth a little space,
That we may learn to bear the beams of love,
And these black bodies and this sun-burnt face   15
Is but a cloud, and like a shady grove.

"For when our souls have learn'd the heat to bear,
The cloud will vanish; we shall hear his voice,
Saying: 'Come out from the grove, my love & care,
And round my golden tent like lambs rejoice.'"   20

Thus did my mother say, and kissèd me;
And thus I say to little English boy:
When I from black and he from white cloud free,
And round the tent of God like lambs we joy,

I'll shade him from the heat till he can bear   25
To lean in joy upon our father's knee:
And then I'll stand and stroke his silver hair,
And be like him, and he will then love me.

—1789

A Poison Tree

I was angry with my friend:
I told my wrath, my wrath did end.

Black probably Indian rather than African

I was angry with my foe:
I told it not, my wrath did grow.

And I water'd it in fears,   5
Night & morning with my tears;
And I sunnèd it with smiles,
And with soft deceitful wiles.

And it grew both day and night,
Till it bore an apple bright;   10
And my foe beheld it shine,
And he knew that it was mine,

And into my garden stole
When the night had veil'd the pole;
In the morning glad I see   15
My foe outstretch'd beneath the tree.

                                              —1794

The Tyger

Tyger! Tyger! burning bright
In the forests of the night,
What immortal hand or eye
Could frame thy fearful symmetry?

In what distant deeps or skies   5
Burnt the fire of thine eyes?
On what wings dare he aspire?
What the hand, dare seize the fire?

And what shoulder, & what art,
Could twist the sinews of thy heart?   10
And when thy heart began to beat,
What dread hand? & what dread feet?

What the hammer? what the chain?
In what furnace was thy brain?
What the anvil? what dread grasp   15
Dare its deadly terrors clasp?

When the stars threw down their spears,
And water'd heaven with their tears,
Did he smile his work to see?
Did he who made the Lamb make thee?   20

Tyger! Tyger! burning bright
In the forests of the night,
What immortal hand or eye,
Dare frame thy fearful symmetry?

—1794

Robert Burns　　　　　　　　1759–1796

Burns, a Scot known in his day as the "Ploughman Poet," was one of the first English poets to put dialect to serious literary purpose. Chiefly known for his realistic depictions of peasant life, he was also an important lyric poet who prefigured many of the later concerns of the Romantic era.

A Red, Red Rose

O my luve's like a red, red rose,
　　That's newly sprung in June;
O my luve's like the melodie
　　That's sweetly played in tune.

As fair art thou, my bonnie lass,　　　　　　　　5
　　So deep in luve am I;
And I will luve thee still, my dear,
　　Till a' the seas gang° dry.

Till a' the seas gang dry, my dear,
　　And the rocks melt wi' the sun;　　　　　　　　10
O I will luve thee still, my dear,
　　While the sands o' life shall run.

And fare thee weel, my only luve,
　　And fare thee weel awhile!
And I will come again, my luve　　　　　　　　15
　　Though it were ten thousand mile.

—1796

William Wordsworth　　　　　　　　1770–1850

Wordsworth is generally considered the first of the English Romantics, and *Lyrical Ballads*, the 1798 volume that introduced both his poetry and Samuel Taylor Coleridge's to a wide readership,

---

8 gang go

remains one of the most influential collections of poetry ever published. Wordsworth's preface to the revised edition of 1800 contains the famous Romantic formulation of poetry as the "spontaneous overflow of powerful feelings," a theory exemplified in short lyrics like "I Wandered Lonely as a Cloud" and in longer meditative pieces like "Tintern Abbey." Wordsworth served as poet laureate from 1843 to his death.

I Wandered Lonely as a Cloud

I wandered lonely as a cloud
That floats on high o'er vales and hills,
When all at once I saw a crowd,
A host, of golden daffodils;
Beside the lake, beneath the trees,   5
Fluttering and dancing in the breeze.

Continuous as the stars that shine
And twinkle on the milky way,
They stretched in never-ending line
Along the margin of a bay: 10
Ten thousand saw I at a glance,
Tossing their heads in sprightly dance.

The waves beside them danced, but they
Outdid the sparkling waves in glee;
A poet could not but be gay,   15
In such a jocund company;
I gazed—and gazed—but little thought
What wealth the show to me had brought:

For oft, when on my couch I lie
In vacant or in pensive mood,   20
They flash upon that inward eye
Which is the bliss of solitude;
And then my heart with pleasure fills,
And dances with the daffodils.

                                        —1807

It Is a Beauteous Evening

It is a beauteous evening, calm and free,
The holy time is quiet as a Nun
Breathless with adoration; the broad sun

Is sinking down in its tranquillity;
The gentleness of heaven broods o'er the Sea: 5
Listen! the mighty Being is awake,
And doth with his eternal motion make
A sound like thunder—everlastingly.
Dear Child! dear Girl!° that walkest with me here,
If thou appear untouched by solemn thought,   10
Thy nature is not therefore less divine:
Thou liest in Abraham's bosom° all the year,
And worship'st at the Temple's inner shrine,
God being with thee when we know it not.

                                                          —1807

Lines

*Composed a Few Miles Above Tintern Abbey on Revisiting the Banks of the Wye
During a Tour. July 13, 1798*

Five years have passed; five summers, with the length
Of five long winters! and again I hear
These waters, rolling from their mountain-springs
With a sweet inland murmur.—Once again
Do I behold these steep and lofty cliffs,   5
That on a wild secluded scene impress
Thoughts of more deep seclusion; and connect
The landscape with the quiet of the sky.
The day is come when I again repose
Here, under this dark sycamore, and view   10
These plots of cottage ground, these orchard tufts,
Which at this season, with their unripe fruits,
Are clad in one green hue, and lose themselves
'Mid groves and copses. Once again I see
These hedgerows, hardly hedgerows, little lines   15
Of sportive wood run wild; these pastoral farms,
Green to the very door; and wreaths of smoke
Sent up, in silence, from among the trees!
With some uncertain notice, as might seem
Of vagrant dwellers in the houseless woods,   20
Or of some Hermit's cave, where by his fire
The Hermit sits alone.

---

9 Dear Child! dear Girl! the poet's daughter   **12 Abraham's bosom** where souls rest in
Heaven

                            These beauteous forms,
Through a long absence, have not been to me
As is a landscape to a blind man's eye;
But oft, in lonely rooms, and 'mid the din   25
Of towns and cities, I have owed to them,
In hours of weariness, sensations sweet,
Felt in the blood, and felt along the heart;
And passing even into my purer mind,
With tranquil restoration:—feelings too   30
Of unremembered pleasure; such, perhaps,
As have no slight or trivial influence
On that best portion of a good man's life,
His little, nameless, unremembered, acts
Of kindness and of love. Nor less, I trust,   35
To them I may have owed another gift,
Of aspect more sublime; that blessed mood,
In which the burthen° of the mystery,
In which the heavy and the weary weight
Of all this unintelligible world,   40
Is lightened—that serene and blessed mood,
In which the affections gently lead us on—
Until, the breath of this corporeal frame
And even the motion of our human blood
Almost suspended, we are laid asleep   45
In body, and become a living soul;
While with an eye made quiet by the power
Of harmony, and the deep power of joy,
We see into the life of things.

                            If this
Be but a vain belief, yet, oh! how oft—   50
In darkness and amid the many shapes
Of joyless daylight; when the fretful stir
Unprofitable, and the fever of the world,
Have hung upon the beatings of my heart—
How oft, in spirit, have I turned to thee,   55
O sylvan Wye! Thou wanderer through the woods,
How often has my spirit turned to thee!

      And now, with gleams of half-extinguished thought,
With many recognitions dim and faint,
And somewhat of a sad perplexity,   60
The picture of the mind revives again:

----

38 burthen burden

While here I stand, not only with the sense
Of present pleasure, but with pleasing thoughts
That in this moment there is life and food
For future years. And so I dare to hope,   65
Though changed, no doubt, from what I was when first
I came among these hills; when like a roe
I bounded o'er the mountains, by the sides
Of the deep rivers, and the lonely streams,
Wherever nature led—more like a man   70
Flying from something that he dreads than one
Who sought the thing he loved. For nature then
(The coarser pleasures of my boyish days,
And their glad animal movements all gone by)
To me was all in all.—I cannot paint   75
What then I was. The sounding cataract
Haunted me like a passion: the tall rock,
The mountain, and the deep and gloomy wood,
Their colours and their forms, were then to me
An appetite: a feeling and a love,   80
That had no need of a remoter charm,
By thought supplied, or any interest
Unborrowed from the eye.—That time is past,
And all its aching joys are now no more,
And all its dizzy raptures. Not for this   85
Faint I, nor mourn nor murmur: other gifts
Have followed; for such loss, I would believe,
Abundant recompense. For I have learned
To look on nature, not as in the hour
Of thoughtless youth; but hearing oftentimes   90
The still, sad music of humanity,
Nor harsh nor grating, though of ample power
To chasten and subdue. And I have felt
A presence that disturbs me with the joy
Of elevated thoughts; a sense sublime   95
Of something far more deeply interfused,
Whose dwelling is the light of setting suns,
And the round ocean and the living air,
And the blue sky, and in the mind of man:
A motion and a spirit, that impels   100
All thinking things, all objects of all thought,
And rolls through all things. Therefore am I still
A lover of the meadows and the woods,
And mountains; and of all that we behold
From this green earth; of all the mighty world   105
Of eye, and ear—both what they half create,

And what perceive; well pleased to recognize
In nature and the language of the sense
The anchor of my purest thoughts, the nurse,
The guide, the guardian of my heart, and soul   110
Of all my moral being.

                    Nor, perchance,
If I were not thus taught, should I the more
Suffer my genial spirits° to decay:
For thou art with me, here, upon the banks
Of this fair river; thou, my dearest Friend,°   115
My dear, dear Friend; and in thy voice I catch
The language of my former heart, and read
My former pleasures in the shooting lights
Of thy wild eyes. Oh! yet a little while
May I behold in thee what I was once,   120
My dear, dear Sister! And this prayer I make,
Knowing that Nature never did betray
The heart that loved her; 'tis her privilege,
Through all the years of this our life, to lead
From joy to joy: for she can so inform   125
The mind that is within us, so impress
With quietness and beauty, and so feed
With lofty thoughts, that neither evil tongues,
Rash judgments, nor the sneers of selfish men,
Nor greetings where no kindness is, nor all   130
The dreary intercourse of daily life,
Shall e'er prevail against us, or disturb
Our cheerful faith, that all which we behold
Is full of blessings. Therefore let the moon
Shine on thee in thy solitary walk;   135
And let the misty mountain winds be free
To blow against thee: and, in after years,
When these wild ecstasies shall be matured
Into a sober pleasure; when thy mind
Shall be a mansion for all lovely forms,   140
Thy memory be as a dwelling place
For all sweet sounds and harmonies; oh! then,
If solitude, or fear, or pain, or grief,
Should be thy portion, with what healing thoughts
Of tender joy wilt thou remember me,   145
And these my exhortations! Nor, perchance—
If I should be, where I no more can hear

---

113 **genial spirits** natural abilities   115 **Friend** the poet's sister Dorothy (1771-1855)

Thy voice, nor catch from thy wild eyes these gleams
Of past existence—wilt thou then forget
That on the banks of this delightful stream   150
We stood together; and that I, so long
A worshipper of Nature, hither came,
Unwearied in that service: rather say
With warmer love,—oh! with far deeper zeal
Of holier love. Nor wilt thou then forget,   155
That after many wanderings, many years
Of absence, these steep woods and lofty cliffs,
And this green pastoral landscape, were to me
More dear, both for themselves and for thy sake!

                                                    —1798

Nuns Fret Not at Their Convent's Narrow Room

Nuns fret not at their convent's narrow room;
And hermits are contented with their cells;
And students with their pensive citadels;
Maids at the wheel, the weaver at his loom,
Sit blithe and happy; bees that soar for bloom,   5
High as the highest Peak of Furness-fells,°
Will murmur by the hour in foxglove bells:
In truth the prison, into which we doom
Ourselves, no prison is: and hence for me,
In sundry moods, 'twas pastime to be bound   10
Within the Sonnet's scanty plot of ground;
Pleased if some Souls (for such there needs must be)
Who have felt the weight of too much liberty,
Should find brief solace there, as I have found.

                                                    —1807

Ode

Intimations of Immortality
from Recollections of Early Childhood

    The Child is Father of the Man;
    And I could wish my days to be
    Bound each to each by natural piety.°

---

6 **Furness-fells** mountains located in the English Lake District
The Child . . . natural piety last three lines of the poet's "My Heart Leaps Up"

1

There was a time when meadow, grove, and stream,
The earth, and every common sight,
    To me did seem
    Appareled in celestial light,
The glory and the freshness of a dream.   5
It is not now as it hath been of yore;—
    Turn wheresoe'er I may,
    By night or day,
The things which I have seen I now can see no more.

2

    The Rainbow comes and goes,   10
    And lovely is the Rose,
    The Moon doth with delight
Look round her when the heavens are bare,
    Waters on a starry night
    Are beautiful and fair;   15
    The sunshine is a glorious birth;
    But yet I know, where'er I go,
That there hath past away a glory from the earth.

3

Now, while the birds thus sing a joyous song,
    And while the young lambs bound   20
    As to the tabor's° sound,
To me alone there came a thought of grief:
A timely utterance gave that thought relief,
    And I again am strong:
The cataracts blow their trumpets from the steep;   25
No more shall grief of mine the season wrong;
I hear the Echoes through the mountains throng,
The Winds come to me from the fields of sleep,
    And all the earth is gay;
    Land and sea   30
    Give themselves up to jollity,
    And with the heart of May
    Doth every Beast keep holiday;—
    Thou Child of Joy,
Shout round me, let me hear thy shouts, thou happy
    Shepherd-boy!   35

4

Ye blessèd Creatures, I have heard the call
    Ye to each other make; I see

---

21 **tabor's** small drum's

The heavens laugh with you in your jubilee;
   My heart is at your festival,   40
   My head hath its coronal,°
The fulness of your bliss, I feel—I feel it all.
      Oh evil day! if I were sullen
      While Earth herself is adorning,
         This sweet May-morning,   45
      And the Children are culling
         On every side,
      In a thousand valleys far and wide,
      Fresh flowers; while the sun shines warm,
And the Babe leaps up on his Mother's arm:—   50
   I hear, I hear, with joy I hear!
   —But there's a Tree, of many, one,
A single Field which I have looked upon,
Both of them speak of something that is gone:
      The Pansy at my feet   55
      Doth the same tale repeat:
Whither is fled the visionary gleam?
Where is it now, the glory and the dream?

5

Our birth is but a sleep and a forgetting:
The Soul that rises with us, our life's Star,   60
      Hath had elsewhere its setting,
        And cometh from afar:
      Not in entire forgetfulness,
      And not in utter nakedness,
But trailing clouds of glory do we come   65
      From God, who is our home:
Heaven lies about us in our infancy!
Shades of the prison-house begin to close
      Upon the growing Boy,
But he beholds the light, and whence it flows,   70
      He sees it in his joy;
The Youth, who daily farther from the east
      Must travel, still is Nature's Priest,
      And by the vision splendid
      Is on his way attended;   75
At length the Man perceives it die away,
And fade into the light of common day.

---

41 **coronal** floral crown

6

Earth fills her lap with pleasures of her own;
Yearnings she hath in her own natural kind,
And, even with something of a Mother's mind,   80
    And no unworthy aim,
    The homely Nurse doth all she can
To make her Foster-child, her Inmate Man,
    Forget the glories he hath known,
And that imperial palace whence he came.   85

7

Behold the Child among his new-born blisses,
A six years' Darling of a pigmy size!
See where 'mid work of his own hand he lies,
Fretted° by sallies of his mother's kisses,
With light upon him from his father's eyes!   90
See, at his feet, some little plan or chart,
Some fragment from his dream of human life,
Shaped by himself with newly-learnèd art;
    A wedding or a festival,
    A mourning or a funeral;   95
      And this hath now his heart,
      And unto this he frames his song:
      Then will he fit his tongue
To dialogues of business, love, or strife;
    But it will not be long   100
    Ere this be thrown aside,
    And with new joy and pride
The little Actor cons another part;
Filling from time to time his "humorous stage"°
With all the Persons, down to palsied Age,   105
That Life brings with her in her equipage;
    As if his whole vocation
    Were endless imitation.

8

Thou whose exterior semblance doth belie
    Thy Soul's immensity;   110
Thou best Philosopher, who yet dost keep
Thy heritage, thou Eye among the blind,
That, deaf and silent, read'st the eternal deep,
Haunted for ever by the eternal mind,—

---

89 fretted annoyed or marked   **104 "humorous stage"** phrase from poet Samuel Daniel
(1563-1619)

Mighty Prophet! Seer blest!   115
　　On whom those truths do rest,
Which we are toiling all our lives to find,
In darkness lost, the darkness of the grave;
Thou, over whom thy Immortality
Broods like the Day, a Master o'er a Slave,   120
A Presence which is not to be put by;
Thou little Child, yet glorious in the might
Of heaven-born freedom on thy being's height,
Why with such earnest pains dost thou provoke
The years to bring the inevitable yoke,   125
Thus blindly with thy blessedness at strife?
Full soon thy Soul shall have her earthly freight,
And custom lie upon thee with a weight,
Heavy as frost, and deep almost as life!

9

O joy! that in our embers   130
Is something that doth live,
That nature yet remembers
What was so fugitive!
The thought of our past years in me doth breed
Perpetual benediction: not indeed   135
For that which is most worthy to be blest;
Delight and liberty, the simple creed
Of Childhood, whether busy or at rest,
With new-fledged hope still fluttering in his breast:—
Not for these I raise   140
The song of thanks and praise;
But for those obstinate questionings
Of sense and outward things,
Fallings from us, vanishings;
Blank misgivings of a Creature   145
Moving about in worlds not realized,
High instincts before which our mortal Nature
Did tremble like a guilty Thing surprised:
But for those first affections,
Those shadowy recollections,   150
Which, be they what they may,
Are yet the fountain light of all our day,
Are yet a master light of all our seeing;
Uphold us, cherish, and have power to make
Our noisy years seem moments in the being   155
Of the eternal Silence: truths that wake,
To perish never;

Which neither listlessness, nor mad endeavour,
    Nor Man nor Boy,
Nor all that is at enmity with joy,   160
Can utterly abolish or destroy!
   Hence in a season of calm weather
     Though inland far we be,
Our Souls have sight of that immortal sea
    Which brought us hither,   165
   Can in a moment travel thither,
And see the Children sport upon the shore,
And hear the mighty waters rolling evermore.

10

Then sing, ye Birds, sing, sing a joyous song!
     And let the young Lambs bound   170
     As to the tabor's sound!
We in thought will join your throng,
    Ye that pipe and ye that play,
    Ye that through your hearts to-day
    Feel the gladness of the May!   175
What though the radiance which was once so bright
Be now for ever taken from my sight,
    Though nothing can bring back the hour
Of splendour in the grass, of glory in the flower;
    We will grieve not, rather find   180
    Strength in what remains behind;
    In the primal sympathy
    Which having been must ever be;
    In the soothing thoughts that spring
    Out of human suffering;   185
    In the faith that looks through death,
In years that bring the philosophic mind.

11

And O, ye Fountains, Meadows, Hills, and Groves,
Forbode not any severing of our loves!
Yet in my heart of hearts I feel your might;   190
I only have relinquished one delight
To live beneath your more habitual sway.
I love the Brooks which down their channels fret,
Even more than when I tripped lightly as they;
The innocent brightness of a new-born Day   195
    Is lovely yet;
The Clouds that gather round the setting sun
Do take a sober colouring from an eye

That hath kept watch o'er man's mortality;
Another race hath been, and other palms are won.   200
Thanks to the human heart by which we live,
Thanks to its tenderness, its joys, and fears,
To me the meanest° flower that blows can give
Thoughts that do often lie too deep for tears.

                                                    —1807

SAMUEL TAYLOR COLERIDGE   1772–1834

The inspired but erratic Coleridge did his best work, like
Wordsworth, during the great first decade of their friendship, the
period that produced *Lyrical Ballads*. Coleridge's later life is a tragic
tale of financial and marital problems, unfinished projects, and a
ruinous addiction to opium. A brilliant critic, Coleridge lectured on
Shakespeare and other writers and wrote the *Biographia Literaria*, perhaps the greatest literary autobiography ever written.

Frost at Midnight

The Frost performs its secret ministry,
Unhelped by any wind. The owlet's cry
Came loud—and hark, again! loud as before.
The inmates of my cottage, all at rest,
Have left me to that solitude, which suits   5
Abstruser musings: save that at my side
My cradled infant° slumbers peacefully.
'Tis calm indeed! so calm, that it disturbs
And vexes meditation, with its strange
And extreme silentness. Sea, hill, and wood,   10
This populous village! Sea, and hill, and wood,
With all the numberless goings-on of life,
Inaudible as dreams! the thin blue flame
Lies on my low-burnt fire, and quivers not;
Only that film,° which fluttered on the grate,   15
Still flutters there, the sole unquiet thing.
Methinks its motion in this hush of nature
Gives it dim sympathies with me who live,
Making it a companionable form,
Whose puny flaps and freaks the idling Spirit   20
By its own moods interprets, everywhere

---

203 **meanest** least significant
7 **My cradled infant** the poet's son Hartley (1796-1849)   15 **film** a piece of ash

Echo or mirror seeking of itself,
And makes a toy of Thought.

                            But O! how oft,
How oft, at school, with most believing mind,
Presageful,° have I gazed upon the bars,   25
To watch that fluttering *stranger!* and as oft
With unclosed lids, already had I dreamt
Of my sweet birthplace, and the old church tower,
Whose bells, the poor man's only music, rang
From morn to evening, all the hot Fair-day,   30
So sweetly, that they stirred and haunted me
With a wild pleasure, falling on mine ear
Most like articulate sounds of things to come!
So gazed I, till the soothing things, I dreamt,
Lulled me to sleep, and sleep prolonged my dreams!   35
And so I brooded all the following morn,
Awed by the stern preceptor's° face, mine eye
Fixed with mock study on my swimming book:
Save if the door half opened, and I snatched
A hasty glance, and still my heart leaped up,   40
For still I hoped to see the *stranger's* face,
Townsman, or aunt, or sister more beloved,
My playmate when we both were clothed alike!

        Dear Babe, that sleepest cradled by my side,
Whose gentle breathings, heard in this deep calm,   45
Fill up the interspersèd vacancies
And momentary pauses of the thought!
My babe so beautiful! it thrills my heart
With tender gladness, thus to look at thee,
And think that thou shalt learn far other lore,   50
And in far other scenes! For I was reared
In the great city, pent 'mid cloisters dim,
And saw nought lovely but the sky and stars.
But *thou*, my babe! shalt wander like a breeze
By lakes and sandy shores, beneath the crags   55
Of ancient mountain, and beneath the clouds,
Which image in their bulk both lakes and shores
And mountain crags: so shalt thou see and hear
The lovely shapes and sounds intelligible
Of that eternal language, which thy God   60
Utters, who from eternity doth teach

---

25 Presageful with hints of the future   **37 preceptor** teacher

Himself in all, and all things in himself.
Great universal Teacher! he shall mold
Thy spirit, and by giving make it ask.

Therefore all seasons shall be sweet to thee,   65
Whether the summer clothe the general earth
With greenness, or the redbreast sit and sing
Betwixt the tufts of snow on the bare branch
Of mossy apple tree, while the nigh thatch
Smokes in the sun-thaw; whether the eave-drops fall   70
Heard only in the trances of the blast,
Or if the secret ministry of frost
Shall hang them up in silent icicles,
Quietly shining to the quiet Moon.

                                            —February 1798

Kubla Khan°

<small>OR A VISION IN A DREAM,° A FRAGMENT</small>

In Xanadu did Kubla Khan
A stately pleasure-dome decree:
Where Alph, the sacred river, ran
Through caverns measureless to man
    Down to a sunless sea.   5
So twice five miles of fertile ground
With walls and towers were girdled round:
And there were gardens bright with sinuous rills,
Where blossomed many an incense-bearing tree;
And here were forests ancient as the hills,   10
Enfolding sunny spots of greenery.

But oh! that deep romantic chasm which slanted
Down the green hill athwart a cedarn cover!

Kubla Khan ruler of China (1216-1294)   **vision in a dream** Coleridge's own account tells
how he took opium for an illness and slept for three hours, during which time he envisioned
a complete poem of some 300 lines. When he awoke, he began to write down the details of
his dream. "At this moment he was unfortunately called out by a person on business from
Porlock, and detained by him above an hour, and on his return to the room found, to his no
small surprise and mortification, that though he still retained some vague and dim recollec-
tion of the general purport of the vision, yet, with the exception of some eight or ten scattered lines and images on the surface of a stream into which a stone has been cast . . ."
[Coleridge's note]

A savage place! as holy and enchanted
As e'er beneath a waning moon was haunted 15
By woman wailing for her demon lover!
And from this chasm, with ceaseless turmoil seething,
As if this earth in fast thick pants were breathing,
A mighty fountain momently was forced:
Amid whose swift half-intermitted burst 20
Huge fragments vaulted like rebounding hail,
Or chaffy grain beneath the thresher's flail:
And 'mid these dancing rocks at once and ever
It flung up momently the sacred river.
Five miles meandering with a mazy motion 25
Through wood and dale the sacred river ran,
Then reached the caverns measureless to man,
And sank in tumult to a lifeless ocean:
And 'mid this tumult Kubla heard from far
Ancestral voices prophesying war! 30

    The shadow of the dome of pleasure
    Floated midway on the waves;
    Where was heard the mingled measure
    From the fountain and the caves.
It was a miracle of rare device, 35
A sunny pleasure-dome with caves of ice!

    A damsel with a dulcimer
    In a vision once I saw:
    It was an Abyssinian maid,
    And on her dulcimer she played, 40
    Singing of Mount Abora.
    Could I revive within me
    Her symphony and song,
    To such a deep delight 'twould win me,
That with music loud and long, 45
I would build that dome in air,
That sunny dome! those caves of ice!
And all who heard should see them there,
And all should cry, Beware! Beware!
His flashing eyes, his floating hair! 50
Weave a circle round him thrice,
And close your eyes with holy dread,
For he on honey-dew hath fed,
And drunk the milk of Paradise.

                                   −1797-98

Work Without Hope

Lines Composed 21st February 1825

All Nature seems at work. Slugs leave their lair—
The bees are stirring—birds are on the wing—
And Winter slumbering in the open air
Wears on his smiling face a dream of Spring!
And I the while, the sole unbusy thing,   5
Nor honey make, nor pair, nor build, nor sing.

     Yet well I ken° the banks where amaranths° blow,
Have traced the fount whence streams of nectar flow.
Bloom, O ye amaranths! bloom for whom ye may,
For me ye bloom not! Glide, rich streams, away!   10
With lips unbrightened, wreathless brow, I stroll:
And would you learn the spells that drowse my soul?
Work without Hope draws° nectar in a sieve,
And Hope without an object cannot live.

                               —1828

WALTER SAVAGE LANDOR   1775–1864

Landor attained considerable celebrity in his final decades as the last living Romantic poet. An author of epic poems and verse dramas, he is best known today for his brilliant epigrams and other short poems, which often employ *dramatis personae*.

Dying Speech of an Old Philosopher

I strove with none, for none was worth my strife:
     Nature I loved, and, next to Nature, Art:
I warmed both hands before the fire of Life;
     It sinks; and I am ready to depart.

                               —1849

Mother, I Cannot

Mother, I cannot mind my wheel;°
     My fingers ache, my lips are dry:

---

7 **ken** know   **amaranths** legendary flowers that never fade   13 **draws** dips
1 **wheel** spinning wheel

Oh! if you felt the pain I feel!
    But oh, who ever felt as I?

No longer could I doubt him true;   5
    All other men may use deceit:
He always said my eyes were blue,
    And often swore my lips were sweet.

                                        —1806

GEORGE GORDON, LORD BYRON 1788–1824

The flamboyant Byron, whose celebrity status and unconventional lifestyle contributed to his notoriety, was the most widely read of all the English Romantic poets, but his verse romances and mock-epic poems like *Don Juan* have not proven as popular in this century. An English aristocrat who was committed to revolutionary ideals, Byron died while lending military assistance to the cause of Greek freedom.

Stanzas

When A Man Hath No Freedom To Fight For At Home

When a man hath no freedom to fight for at home,
    Let him combat for that of his neighbors;
Let him think of the glories of Greece and of Rome,
    And get knocked on his head for his labors.

To do good to mankind is the chivalrous plan,   5
    And is always as nobly requited:
Then battle for freedom wherever you can,
    And, if not shot or hanged, you'll get knighted.

                                        —1824

When We Two Parted

When we two parted
    In silence and tears,
Half broken-hearted
    To sever for years,
Pale grew thy cheek and cold,   5
    Colder thy kiss;
Truly that hour foretold
    Sorrow to this.

The dew of the morning
  Sunk chill on my brow—   10
It felt like the warning
  Of what I feel now.
Thy vows are all broken,
  And light is thy fame;
I hear thy name spoken,   15
  And share in its shame.

They name thee before me,
  A knell to mine ear;
A shudder comes o'er me—
  Why wert thou so dear?   20
They know not I knew thee,
  Who knew thee too well:—
Long, long shall I rue thee,
  Too deeply to tell.

In secret we met—   25
  In silence I grieve
That thy heart could forget,
  Thy spirit deceive.
If I should meet thee
  After long years,   30
How should I greet thee?—
  With silence and tears.

                                —1813

PERCY BYSSHE SHELLEY   1792–1822

Like his friend Byron, Shelley has not found as much favor in this century as the other English Romantics, though his political liberalism anticipates many currents of our own day. Perhaps his unbridled emotionalism sometimes is too intense for modern readers. His wife, Mary Wollstonecraft Shelley, will be remembered as the author of the classic horror novel *Frankenstein*.

Ode to the West Wind

1

O wild West Wind, thou breath of Autumn's being,
Thou, from whose unseen presence the leaves dead
Are driven, like ghosts from an enchanter fleeing,

Yellow, and black, and pale, and hectic red,
Pestilence-stricken multitudes: O thou,   5
Who chariotest to their dark wintry bed

The wingèd seeds, where they lie cold and low,
Each like a corpse within its grave, until
Thine azure sister of the Spring° shall blow

Her clarion o'er the dreaming earth, and fill   10
(Driving sweet buds like flocks to feed in air)
With living hues and odors plain and hill:

Wild Spirit, which art moving everywhere;
Destroyer and preserver; hear, oh, hear!

2

Thou on whose stream, mid the steep sky's commotion,   15
Loose clouds like earth's decaying leaves are shed,
Shook from the tangled boughs of Heaven and Ocean,

Angels of rain and lightning: there are spread
On the blue surface of thine aëry surge,
Like the bright hair uplifted from the head   20

Of some fierce Mænad,° even from the dim verge
Of the horizon to the zenith's height,
The locks of the approaching storm. Thou dirge

Of the dying year, to which this closing night
Will be the dome of a vast sepulcher,   25
Vaulted with all thy congregated might

Of vapors, from whose solid atmosphere
Black rain, and fire, and hail will burst: oh, hear!

3

Thou who didst waken from his summer dreams
The blue Mediterranean, where he lay,   30
Lulled by the coil of his crystàlline streams,

---

9 azure sister of the Spring i.e., the South Wind   **21 Mænad** female worshipper of Bacchus,
god of wine

Beside a pumice isle in Baiae's bay,°
And saw in sleep old palaces and towers
Quivering within the wave's intenser day,

All overgrown with azure moss and flowers   35
So sweet, the sense faints picturing them! Thou
For whose path the Atlantic's level powers

Cleave themselves into chasms, while far below
The sea-blooms and the oozy woods which wear
The sapless foliage of the ocean, know   40

Thy voice, and suddenly grow gray with fear,
And tremble and despoil themselves: oh, hear!

4

If I were a dead leaf thou mightest bear;
If I were a swift cloud to fly with thee;
A wave to pant beneath thy power, and share   45

The impulse of thy strength, only less free
Than thou, O uncontrollable! If even
I were as in my boyhood, and could be

The comrade of thy wanderings over Heaven,
As then, when to outstrip thy skyey speed   50
Scarce seemed a vision; I would ne'er have striven

As thus with thee in prayer in my sore need.
Oh, lift me as a wave, a leaf, a cloud!
I fall upon the thorns of life! I bleed!

A heavy weight of hours has chained and bowed   55
One too like thee: tameless, and swift, and proud.

5

Make me thy lyre, even as the forest is:
What if my leaves are falling like its own!
The tumult of thy mighty harmonies

Will take from both a deep, autumnal tone,   60
Sweet though in sadness. Be thou, Spirit fierce,
My spirit! Be thou me, impetuous one!

---

32 **Baiae's bay** near Naples

Drive my dead thoughts over the universe
Like withered leaves to quicken a new birth!
And, by the incantation of this verse,   65

Scatter, as from an unextinguished hearth
Ashes and sparks, my words among mankind!
Be through my lips to unawakened earth

The trumpet of a prophecy! O Wind,
If Winter comes, can Spring be far behind?   70

                                                            —1820

Ozymandias°

I met a traveler from an antique land
Who said: Two vast and trunkless legs of stone
Stand in the desert. . . . Near them, on the sand,
Half sunk, a shattered visage lies, whose frown,
And wrinkled lip, and sneer of cold command,   5
Tell that its sculptor well those passions read
Which yet survive, stamped on these lifeless things,
The hand that mocked them, and the heart that fed:
And on the pedestal these words appear:
"My name is Ozymandias, king of kings: 10
Look on my works, ye Mighty, and despair!"
Nothing beside remains. Round the decay
Of that colossal wreck, boundless and bare
The lone and level sands stretch far away.

                                                            —1818

WILLIAM CULLEN BRYANT   1794–1878

Bryant was often called "the American Wordsworth" for his adaptation of the techniques of English Romanticism to the American landscape. Bryant's observations of nature have rarely been equaled.

To the Fringed Gentian

Thou blossom bright with autumn dew,
And colored with the heaven's own blue,
That openest when the quiet light
Succeeds the keen and frosty night—

Ozymandias Ramses II of Egypt (c. 1250 B.C.)

Thou comest not when violets lean   5
O'er wandering brooks and springs unseen,
Or columbines, in purple dressed,
Nod o'er the ground-bird's hidden nest.

Thou waitest late and com'st alone,
When woods are bare and birds are flown,   10
And frosts and shortening days portend
The aged year is near his end.

Then doth thy sweet and quiet eye
Look through its fringes to the sky,
Blue—blue—as if that sky let fall   15
A flower from its cerulean wall.

I would that thus, when I shall see
The hour of death draw near to me,
Hope, blossoming within my heart,
May look to heaven as I depart.   20

                                                        —1829

J OHN K EATS   1795–1821

Among his fellow poets, Keats is perhaps the most admired of all the
major Romantics. Certainly his tragic death from tuberculosis in his
twenties gives poignancy to thoughts of the doomed young poet writing feverishly in a futile race against time; "Here lies one whose name
was writ in water" are the words he chose for his own epitaph. Many
of Keats's poems are concerned with glimpses of the eternal, whether
a translation of an ancient epic poem or a pristine artifact of a vanished civilization.

La Belle Dame sans Merci°

O what can ail thee, Knight at arms,
    Alone and palely loitering?
The sedge has withered from the Lake
    And no birds sing!

O what can ail thee, Knight at arms,   5
    So haggard, and so woebegone?
The squirrel's granary is full
    And the harvest's done.

La Belle Dame sans Merci "the beautiful lady without pity"

I see a lily on thy brow
    With anguish moist and fever dew,   10
And on thy cheeks a fading rose
    Fast withereth too.

"I met a Lady in the Meads,
    Full beautiful, a faery's child,
Her hair was long, her foot was light,   15
    And her eyes were wild.

"I made a Garland for her head,
    And bracelets too, and fragrant Zone;°
She looked at me as she did love
    And made sweet moan.   20

"I set her on my pacing steed
    And nothing else saw all day long,
For sidelong would she bend and sing
    A faery's song.

"She found me roots of relish sweet,   25
    And honey wild, and manna dew,
And sure in language strange she said
    'I love thee true.'

"She took me to her elfin grot°
    And there she wept and sighed full sore,   30
And there I shut her wild wild eyes
    With kisses four.

"And there she lullèd me asleep,
    And there I dreamed, Ah Woe betide!
The latest dream I ever dreamt   35
    On the cold hill side.

"I saw pale Kings, and Princes too,
    Pale warriors, death-pale were they all;
They cried, 'La belle Dame sans merci
    Hath thee in thrall!'   40

"I saw their starved lips in the gloam
    With horrid warning gapèd wide,
And I awoke, and found me here
    On the cold hill's side.

---

18 Zone belt   **29 grot** cave

"And this is why I sojourn here   45
    Alone and palely loitering;
Though the sedge is withered from the Lake,
    And no birds sing."

                                                −1819

Ode on a Grecian Urn

1
Thou still unravished bride of quietness,
    Thou foster-child of silence and slow time,
Sylvan historian, who canst thus express
    A flowery tale more sweetly than our rhyme:
What leaf-fringed legend haunts about thy shape   5
    Of deities or mortals, or of both,
        In Tempe or the dales of Arcady?°
    What men or gods are these? What maidens loath?°
What mad pursuit? What struggle to escape?
        What pipes and timbrels?° What wild ecstasy?   10

2
Heard melodies are sweet, but those unheard
    Are sweeter; therefore, ye soft pipes, play on;
Not to the sensual ear, but, more endeared,
    Pipe to the spirit ditties of no tone:
Fair youth, beneath the trees, thou canst not leave   15
    Thy song, nor ever can those trees be bare;
        Bold Lover, never, never canst thou kiss,
Though winning near the goal—yet, do not grieve;
        She cannot fade, though thou hast not thy bliss,
    Forever wilt thou love, and she be fair!   20

3
Ah, happy, happy boughs! that cannot shed
    Your leaves, nor ever bid the Spring adieu;
And, happy melodist, unwearièd,
    Forever piping songs forever new;
More happy love! more happy, happy love!   25
    Forever warm and still to be enjoyed,
        Forever panting, and forever young;
All breathing human passion far above,

---

7 **Tempe or the dales of Arcady** idealized Greek settings   8 **loath** reluctant   10 **timbrels** tambourines

That leaves a heart high-sorrowful and cloyed,
    A burning forehead, and a parching tongue.   30

4

Who are these coming to the sacrifice?
    To what green altar, O mysterious priest,
Lead'st thou that heifer lowing at the skies,
    And all her silken flanks with garlands dressed?
What little town by river or sea shore,   35
    Or mountain-built with peaceful citadel,
        Is emptied of this folk, this pious morn?
And, little town, thy streets forevermore
    Will silent be; and not a soul to tell
        Why thou art desolate, can e'er return.   40

5

O Attic° shape! Fair attitude! with brede°
    Of marble men and maidens overwrought,
With forest branches and the trodden weed;
    Thou, silent form, dost tease us out of thought
As doth eternity: Cold Pastoral!   45
    When old age shall this generation waste,
        Thou shalt remain, in midst of other woe
Than ours, a friend to man, to whom thou say'st,
    "Beauty is truth, truth beauty,"—that is all
        Ye know on earth, and all ye need to know.   50

                                                —1819

Ode to a Nightingale

1

My heart aches, and a drowsy numbness pains
    My sense, as though of hemlock° I had drunk,
Or emptied some dull opiate to the drains
    One minute past, and Lethe-wards° had sunk.
'Tis not through envy of thy happy lot,   5
    But being too happy in thine happiness—
        That thou, light-wingèd Dryad° of the trees,
           In some melodious plot
    Of beechen green, and shadows numberless,
        Singest of summer in full-throated ease.   10

---

41 Attic Greek   **brede** ornamental pattern
2 hemlock a deadly poison   **4 Lethe-wards** toward the waters of forgetfulness   **7 Dryad** tree nymph

2

O, for a draught of vintage! that hath been
    Cooled a long age in the deep-delvèd earth,
Tasting of Flora° and the country green,
    Dance, and Provençal° song, and sunburnt mirth!
O for a beaker full of the warm South,   15
    Full of the true, the blushful Hippocrene,°
       With beaded bubbles winking at the brim,
        And purple-stainèd mouth;
    That I might drink, and leave the world unseen,
      And with thee fade away into the forest dim: 20

3

Fade far away, dissolve, and quite forget
    What thou among the leaves hast never known,
The weariness, the fever, and the fret
    Here, where men sit and hear each other groan;
Where palsy shakes a few, sad, last gray hairs,   25
    Where youth grows pale, and specter-thin, and dies;
       Where but to think is to be full of sorrow
        And leaden-eyed despairs,
    Where Beauty cannot keep her lustrous eyes,
      Or new Love pine at them beyond tomorrow.   30

4

Away! away! for I will fly to thee,
    Not charioted by Bacchus° and his pards,°
But on the viewless wings of Poesy,
    Though the dull brain perplexes and retards:
Already with thee! tender is the night,   35
    And haply the Queen-Moon is on her throne,
       Clustered around by all her starry Fays;°
        But here there is no light,
    Save what from heaven is with the breezes blown
      Through verdurous glooms and winding mossy ways.   40

5

I cannot see what flowers are at my feet,
    Nor what soft incense hangs upon the boughs,
But, in embalmèd darkness, guess each sweet
    Wherewith the seasonable month endows
The grass, the thicket, and the fruit-tree wild;   45

---

13 Flora Roman goddess of spring   **14 Provençal** of Provence, in the South of France
16 Hippocrene fountain of the Muses   **32 Bacchus** Roman god of wine   **pards** leopards
37 Fays fairies

White hawthorn, and the pastoral eglantine;
   Fast fading violets covered up in leaves;
     And mid-May's eldest child,
  The coming musk-rose, full of dewy wine,
   The murmurous haunt of flies on summer eves.   50

6

Darkling° I listen; and for many a time
   I have been half in love with easeful Death,
Called him soft names in many a musèd rhyme,
   To take into the air my quiet breath;
Now more than ever seems it rich to die,   55
   To cease upon the midnight with no pain,
     While thou art pouring forth thy soul abroad
      In such an ecstasy!
  Still wouldst thou sing, and I have ears in vain—
   To thy high requiem become a sod.   60

7

Thou wast not born for death, immortal Bird!
   No hungry generations tread thee down;
The voice I hear this passing night was heard
   In ancient days by emperor and clown;
Perhaps the selfsame song that found a path   65
   Through the sad heart of Ruth, when, sick for home,
     She stood in tears amid the alien corn;°
      The same that ofttimes hath
  Charmed magic casements, opening on the foam
   Of perilous seas, in faery lands forlorn.   70

8

Forlorn! the very word is like a bell
   To toll me back from thee to my sole self!
Adieu! the fancy cannot cheat so well
   As she is famed to do, deceiving elf.
Adieu! adieu! thy plaintive anthem fades   75
   Past the near meadows, over the still stream,
     Up the hill side; and now 'tis buried deep
      In the next valley-glades:
  Was it a vision, or a waking dream?
   Fled is that music:—Do I wake or sleep?   80

                        —1819

---

51 **Darkling** in the dark   66-67 **Ruth . . . alien corn** in the Old Testament she is a
stranger working in the grain fields of Judah

On First Looking into Chapman's Homer°

Much have I traveled in the realms of gold,
    And many goodly states and kingdoms seen;
    Round many western islands have I been
Which bards in fealty to Apollo° hold.
Oft of one wide expanse had I been told   5
    That deep-browed Homer ruled as his demesne;
    Yet did I never breathe its pure serene
Till I heard Chapman speak out loud and bold:
Then felt I like some watcher of the skies
    When a new planet swims into his ken;   10
Or like stout Cortez° when with eagle eyes
    He stared at the Pacific—and all his men
Looked at each other with a wild surmise—
    Silent, upon a peak in Darien.°

                            —1816

When I Have Fears

When I have fears that I may cease to be
    Before my pen has gleaned my teeming brain,
Before high-pilèd books, in charact'ry,°
    Hold like rich garners the full-ripened grain;
When I behold, upon the night's starred face,   5
    Huge cloudy symbols of a high romance,
And think that I may never live to trace
    Their shadows, with the magic hand of chance;
And when I feel, fair creature of an hour,
    That I shall never look upon thee more,   10
Never have relish in the faery power
    Of unreflecting love!—then on the shore
Of the wide world I stand alone, and think
Till Love and Fame to nothingness do sink.

                            —1818

Chapman's Homer translation of the *Iliad* and *Odyssey* by George Chapman (1559-1634)
4 Apollo here, the god of poetry.   **11 Cortez** Balboa was actually the first European to see the Pacific.   **14 Darien** in modern-day Panama
3 charact'ry writing

Ralph Waldo Emerson   1803–1882

Emerson was more widely known in his own day as an essayist and lecturer than as a poet, and in brilliant addresses like "The American Scholar" or "The Poet" he called for a truly American literature freed from its intellectual dependence on European models. Many of his lyrics explore the mystical aspects of his Transcendentalist philosophy.

Days

Daughters of Time, the hypocritic Days,
Muffled and dumb like barefoot dervishes,°
And marching single in an endless file,
Bring diadems and fagots in their hands.
To each they offer gifts after his will,   5
Bread, kingdom, stars, and sky that holds them all.

I, in my pleachèd° garden, watched the pomp,
Forgot my morning wishes, hastily
Took a few herbs and apples, and the Day
Turned and departed silent. I, too late,   10
Under her solemn fillet° saw the scorn.

—1857, 1867

Elizabeth Barrett Browning   1806–1861

Elizabeth Barrett was already a famous poet when she met her husband-to-be, Robert Browning, who had been corresponding with her on literary matters. She originally published her famous sonnet sequence, written in the first years of her marriage, in the guise of a translation of Portuguese poems, perhaps to mask their personal revelations.

Sonnets from the Portuguese, 43

How do I love thee? Let me count the ways.
I love thee to the depth and breadth and height
My soul can reach, when feeling out of sight
For the ends of Being and ideal Grace.
I love thee to the level of everyday's   5

---

2 dervishes members of an Islamic religious order   **7 pleachèd** woven or entwined   **11 fillet** ribbon

Most quiet need, by sun and candle-light.
I love thee freely, as men strive for Right;
I love thee purely, as they turn from Praise.
I love thee with the passion put to use
In my old griefs, and with my childhood's faith.   10
I love thee with a love I seemed to lose
With my lost saints—I love thee with the breath,
Smiles, tears, of all my life!—and, if God choose,
I shall but love thee better after death.

—1845-46

Henry Wadsworth Longfellow   1807–1882

Longfellow was by far the most prominent nineteenth-century
American poet, and his international fame led to his bust being
placed in Westminster Abbey after his death. The long epic poems
like *Evangeline* and *Hiawatha* that were immensely popular among
contemporary readers are seldom read today, but his shorter poems
reveal a level of craftsmanship that few poets have equaled.

The Arsenal at Springfield

This is the Arsenal. From floor to ceiling,
    Like a huge organ, rise the burnished arms;
But from their silent pipes no anthem pealing
    Startles the villages with strange alarms.

Ah! what a sound will rise, how wild and dreary,   5
    When the death-angel touches those swift keys!
What loud lament and dismal Miserere°
    Will mingle with their awful symphonies!

I hear even now the infinite fierce chorus,
    The cries of agony, the endless groan,   10
Which, through the ages that have gone before us,
    In long reverberations reach our own.

On helm and harness rings the Saxon hammer,
    Through Cimbric° forest roars the Norseman's song,

---

7 **Miserere** Latin hymn from Psalm 1: "Have mercy on me, Lord."   14 **Cimbric** in Denmark

And loud, amid the universal clamor,   15
    O'er distant deserts sounds the Tartar gong.

I hear the Florentine, who from his palace
    Wheels out his battle-bell with dreadful din,
And Aztec priests upon their teocallis°
    Beat the wild war-drums made of serpent's skin;   20

The tumult of each sacked and burning village;
    The shout that every prayer for mercy drowns;
The soldiers' revels in the midst of pillage;
    The wail of famine in beleaguered towns;

The bursting shell, the gateway wrenched asunder,   25
    The rattling musketry, the clashing blade;
And ever and anon, in tones of thunder
    The diapason° of the cannonade.

Is it, O man, with such discordant noises,
    With such accursed instruments as these,   30
Thou drownest Nature's sweet and kindly voices,
    And jarrest the celestial harmonies?

Were half the power, that fills the world with terror,
    Were half the wealth bestowed on camps and courts,
Given to redeem the human mind from error,   35
    There were no need of arsenals or forts:

The warrior's name would be a name abhorred!
    And every nation, that should lift again
Its hand against a brother, on its forehead
    Would wear forevermore the curse of Cain!   40

Down the dark future, through long generations,
    The echoing sounds grow fainter and then cease;
And like a bell, with solemn, sweet vibrations,
    I hear once more the voice of Christ say, "Peace!"

Peace! and no longer from its brazen portals   45
    The blast of War's great organ shakes the skies!
But beautiful as songs of the immortals,
    The holy melodies of love arise.

                                                                      —1846

---

19 **teocallis** temples atop pyramids   28 **diapason** full range of pipe organ

The Cross of Snow

In the long, sleepless watches of the night,
    A gentle face—the face of one long dead—
    Looks at me from the wall, where round its head
    The night-lamp casts a halo of pale light.
Here in this room she died; and soul more white   5
    Never through martyrdom of fire° was led
    To its repose; nor can in books be read
    The legend of a life more benedight.°
There is a mountain in the distant West
    That, sun-defying, in its deep ravines   10
    Displays a cross of snow upon its side.
Such is the cross I wear upon my breast
    These eighteen years, through all the changing scenes
    And seasons, changeless since the day she died.

                               —1886

The Ropewalk°

In that building, long and low,
With its windows all a-row,
    Like the port-holes of a hulk,
Human spiders spin and spin,
Backward down their threads so thin   5
    Dropping, each a hempen bulk.

At the end, an open door;
Squares of sunshine on the floor
    Light the long and dusky lane;
And the whirring of a wheel,
Dull and drowsy, makes me feel   10
    All its spokes are in my brain.

As the spinners to the end
Downward go and reascend,
    Gleam the long threads in the sun;   15
While within this brain of mine
Cobwebs brighter and more fine
    By the busy wheel are spun.

---

6 **martyrdom of fire** Longfellow's second wife, Frances, died as the result of a household fire in 1861.   8 **benedight** blessed
Ropewalk building where rope was handmade by spinners who walked backward

Two fair maidens in a swing,
Like white doves upon the wing,   20
    First before my vision pass;
Laughing, as their gentle hands
Closely clasp the twisted strands,
    At their shadow on the grass.

Then a booth of mountebanks,   25
With its smell of tan and planks,
    And a girl poised high in air
On a cord, in spangled dress,
With a faded loveliness,
    And a weary look of care.   30

Then a homestead among farms,
And a woman with bare arms
    Drawing water from a well;
As the bucket mounts apace,
With it mounts her own fair face,   35
    As at some magician's spell.

Then an old man in a tower,
Ringing loud the noontide hour,
    While the rope coils round and round
Like a serpent at his feet,   40
And again, in swift retreat,
    Nearly lifts him from the ground.

Then within a prison-yard,
Faces fixed, and stern, and hard,
    Laughter and indecent mirth;   45
Ah! it is the gallows-tree!
Breath of Christian charity,
    Blow, and sweep it from the earth!

Then a school-boy, with his kite
Gleaming in a sky of light,   50
    And an eager, upward look;
Steeds pursued through lane and field;
Fowlers with their snares concealed;
    And an angler by a brook.

Ships rejoicing in the breeze,   55
Wrecks that float o'er unknown seas,
    Anchors dragged through faithless sand;

Sea-fog drifting overhead,
And, with lessening line and lead,
  Sailors feeling for the land.   60

All these scenes do I behold,
These, and many left untold,
  In that building long and low;
While the wheel goes round and round,
With a drowsy, dreamy sound,   65
  And the spinners backward go.

JOHN GREENLEAF WHITTIER   1807–1892

Whittier came from a Quaker background and remained close to his
rural origins in his vigorous poetry. An abolitionist and political
activist, he retained strong convictions about poetry's moral content,
and many of his once-popular poems seem stridently propagandistic
today. He is at his best in his vigorous re-creations of events from
New England's history.

Skipper Ireson's Ride

Of all the rides since the birth of time,
Told in story or sung in rhyme,—
On Apuleius's Golden Ass,°
Or one-eyed Calender's horse of brass,°
Witch astride of a human back,   5
Islam's prophet on Al-Borák;—°
The strangest ride that ever was sped
Was Ireson's, out from Marblehead!°
    Old Floyd Ireson, for his hard heart,
    Tarred and feathered and carried in a cart   10
      By the women of Marblehead!

Body of turkey, head of owl,
Wings a-droop like a rained-on fowl,
Feathered and ruffled in every part,
Skipper Ireson stood in the cart.   15
Scores of women, old and young.

---

3 **Apuleius's Golden Ass** story from Ovid's *Metamorphoses* (c. 50 B.C.)   4 **one-eyed
Calender's horse of brass** story told in the Arabian Nights 6 **Islam's prophet on Al-Borák**
Mohammed, in one legend, rode on the back of Al-Borák, a winged creature.   8 **Marblehead**
coastal town in Massachusetts, site of Whittier's poem

Strong of muscle, and glib of tongue,
Pushed and pulled up the rocky lane,
Shouting and singing the shrill refrain:
   "Here's Flud Oirson, fur his horrd horrt,   20
   Torr'd an' futherr'd an' corr'd in a corrt
     By the women o' Morble'ead!"

Wrinkled scolds with hands on hips.
Girls in bloom of cheek and lips,
Wild-eyed, free-limbed, such as chase   25
Bacchus round some antique vase,
Brief of skirt, with ankles bare,
Loose of kerchief and loose of hair,
With conch-shells blowing and fish-horns' twang,
Over and over the Mænads° sang: 30
   "Here's Flud Oirson, fur his horrd horrt,
   Torr'd an' futherr'd an' corr'd in a corrt
     By the women o' Morble'ead!"

Small pity for him!—He sailed away
From a leaking ship in Chaleur Bay,—   35
Sailed away from a sinking wreck,
With his own town's-people on her deck!
"Lay by! lay by!" they called to him.
Back he answered, "Sink or swim!
Brag of your catch of fish again!"   40
And off he sailed through the fog and rain!
   Old Floyd Ireson, for his hard heart,
   Tarred and feathered and carried in a cart
     By the women of Marblehead!

Fathoms deep in dark Chaleur   45
That wreck shall lie forevermore.
Mother and sister, wife and maid,
Looked from the rocks of Marblehead
Over the moaning and rainy sea,—
Looked for the coming that might not be!   50
What did the winds and the sea-birds say
Of the cruel captain who sailed away?—
   Old Floyd Ireson, for his hard heart,
   Tarred and feathered and carried in a cart
     By the women of Marblehead!   55

---

30 Mænads female worshippers of Bacchus

Through the street, on either side,
Up flew windows, doors swung wide;
Sharp-tongued spinsters, old wives gray,
Treble lent the fish-horn's bray.
Sea-worn grandsires, cripple-bound,   60
Hulks of old sailors run aground,
Shook head, and fist, and hat, and cane,
And cracked with curses the hoarse refrain:
   "Here's Flud Oirson, fur his horrd horrt,
   Torr'd an' futherr'd an' corr'd in a corrt   65
     By the women o' Morble'ead!"

Sweetly along the Salem road
Bloom of orchard and lilac showed.
Little the wicked skipper knew
Of the fields so green and the sky so blue.   70
Riding there in his sorry trim,
Like an Indian idol glum and grim,
Scarcely he seemed the sound to hear
Of voices shouting, far and near:
   "Here's Flud Oirson, fur his horrd horrt,   75
   Torr'd an' futherr'd an' corr'd in a corrt
     By the women o' Morble'ead!"

"Hear me, neighbors!" at last he cried,—
"What to me is this noisy ride?
What is the shame that clothes the skin   80
To the nameless horror that lives within?
Waking or sleeping, I see a wreck,
And hear a cry from a reeling deck!
Hate me and curse me,—I only dread
The hand of God and the face of the dead!"   85
   Said old Floyd Ireson, for his hard heart,
   Tarred and feathered and carried in a cart
     By the women of Marblehead!

Then the wife of the skipper lost at sea
Said, "God has touched him! why should we!"   90
Said an old wife mourning her only son,
"Cut the rogue's tether and let him run!"
So with soft relentings and rude excuse,
Half scorn, half pity, they cut him loose,
And gave him a cloak to hide him in,   95
And left him alone with his shame and sin.
   Poor Floyd Ireson, for his hard heart,

Tarred and feathered and carried in a cart
By the women of Marblehead!

—1860

Edgar Allan Poe   1809–1849

The myth of Poe as a deranged, drug-crazed genius still lingers,
despite the wealth of evidence to the contrary that can be gleaned
from his brilliant, though erratic, career as a poet, short-story writer,
critic, and editor. Poe's brand of Romanticism seems at odds with
that of other American poets of his day and is perhaps more in keeping with the spirit of Coleridge than that of Wordsworth. "The
Raven" has been parodied perhaps more than any other American
poem, yet it still retains a powerful hold on its audience.

The Raven

Once upon a midnight dreary, while I pondered, weak and weary,
Over many a quaint and curious volume of forgotten lore—
While I nodded, nearly napping, suddenly there came a tapping,
As of some one gently rapping, rapping at my chamber door.
"'Tis some visitor," I muttered, "tapping at my chamber door—   5
                    Only this and nothing more."

Ah, distinctly I remember it was in the bleak December;
And each separate dying ember wrought its ghost upon the floor.
Eagerly I wished the morrow;—vainly I had sought to borrow
From my books surcease of sorrow—sorrow for the lost Lenore—   10
For the rare and radiant maiden whom the angels name Lenore—
                    Nameless *here* for evermore.

And the silken, sad, uncertain rustling of each purple curtain
Thrilled me—filled me with fantastic terrors never felt before;
So that now, to still the beating of my heart, I stood repeating   15
"'Tis some visitor entreating entrance at my chamber door;—
Some late visitor entreating entrance at my chamber door;—
                    This it is and nothing more."

Presently my soul grew stronger; hesitating then no longer,
"Sir," said I, "or Madam, truly your forgiveness I implore;   20
But the fact is I was napping, and so gently you came rapping,
And so faintly you came tapping, tapping at my chamber door,
That I scarce was sure I heard you"—here I opened wide the door;—
                    Darkness there and nothing more.

Deep into that darkness peering, long I stood there wondering,
    fearing,   25
Doubting, dreaming dreams no mortal ever dared to dream before;
But the silence was unbroken, and the stillness gave no token,
And the only word there spoken was the whispered word, "Lenore?"
This I whispered, and an echo murmured back the word, "Lenore!"
                  Merely this and nothing more. 30

Back into the chamber turning, all my soul within me burning,
Soon again I heard a tapping somewhat louder than before.
"Surely," said I, "surely that is something at my window lattice;
Let me see, then, what thereat is, and this mystery explore—
Let my heart be still a moment and this mystery explore;—   35
              'Tis the wind and nothing more!"

Open here I flung the shutter, when, with many a flirt and flutter,
In there stepped a stately Raven of the saintly days of yore;
Not the least obeisance made he; not a minute stopped or
    stayed he;
But, with mien of lord or lady, perched above my chamber door— 40
Perched upon a bust of Pallas° just above my chamber door—
            Perched, and sat, and nothing more.

Then this ebony bird beguiling my sad fancy into smiling,
By the grave and stern decorum of the countenance it wore,
"Though thy crest be shorn and shaven, thou," I said, "art sure no
    craven,   45
Ghastly grim and ancient Raven wandering from the Nightly shore—
Tell me what thy lordly name is on the Night's Plutonian° shore!"
          Quoth the Raven, "Nevermore."

Much I marvelled this ungainly fowl to hear discourse so plainly,
Though its answer little meaning—little relevancy bore;   50
For we cannot help agreeing that no living human being
Ever yet was blessed with seeing bird above his chamber door—
Bird or beast upon the sculptured bust above his chamber door,
         With such name as "Nevermore."

But the Raven, sitting lonely on the placid bust, spoke only   55
That one word, as if his soul in that one word he did outpour.
Nothing farther then he uttered—not a feather then he fluttered—
Till I scarcely more than muttered, "Other friends have flown
    before—

---

41 **Pallas** Athena, goddess of wisdom   47 **Plutonian** after Pluto, Roman god of the underworld

On the morrow *he* will leave me, as my Hopes have flown before."
                Then the bird said, "Nevermore." 60

Startled at the stillness broken by reply so aptly spoken,
"Doubtless," said I, "what it utters is its only stock and store
Caught from some unhappy master whom unmerciful Disaster
Followed fast and followed faster till his songs one burden bore—
Till the dirges of his Hope that melancholy burden bore   65
                Of 'Never—nevermore.'"

But the Raven still beguiling all my sad fancy into smiling,
Straight I wheeled a cushioned seat in front of bird and bust and
    door;
Then, upon the velvet sinking, I betook myself to linking
Fancy unto fancy, thinking what this ominous bird of yore—   70
What this grim, ungainly, ghastly, gaunt, and ominous bird of
    yore
                Meant in croaking "Nevermore."

This I sat engaged in guessing, but no syllable expressing
To the fowl whose fiery eyes now burned into my bosom's core;
This and more I sat divining, with my head at ease reclining   75
On the cushion's velvet lining that the lamp-light gloated o'er,
But whose velvet-violet lining with the lamp-light gloating o'er,
                She shall press, ah, nevermore!

Then, methought, the air grew denser, perfumed from an unseen
    censer
Swung by seraphim whose foot-falls tinkled on the tufted floor.   80
"Wretch," I cried, "thy God hath lent thee—by these angels he
    hath sent thee.
Respite—respite and nepenthe° from thy memories of Lenore;
Quaff, oh quaff this kind nepenthe and forget this lost Lenore!"
                Quoth the Raven, "Nevermore."

"Prophet!" said I, "thing of evil!—prophet still, if bird or devil!— 85
Whether Tempter sent, or whether tempest tossed thee here
    ashore,
Desolate yet all undaunted, on this desert land enchanted—
On this home by Horror haunted—tell me truly, I implore—
Is there—*is* there balm in Gilead?—tell me—tell me, I implore!"
                Quoth the Raven, "Nevermore." 90

---

82 nepenthe drug causing forgetfulness

"Prophet!" said I, "thing of evil!—prophet still, if bird or devil!
By that Heaven that bends above us—by that God we both adore—
Tell this soul with sorrow laden if, within the distant Aidenn,°
It shall clasp a sainted maiden whom the angels name Lenore—
Clasp a rare and radiant maiden whom the angels name Lenore."   95
                         Quoth the Raven, "Nevermore."

"Be that word our sign of parting, bird or fiend!" I shrieked,
        upstarting—
"Get thee back into the tempest and the Night's Plutonian shore!
Leave no black plume as a token of that lie thy soul hath spoken!
Leave my loneliness unbroken!—quit the bust above my door!   100
Take thy beak from out my heart, and take thy form from off
        my door!"
                         Quoth the Raven, "Nevermore."

And the Raven, never flitting, still is sitting, *still* is sitting
On the pallid bust of Pallas just above my chamber door;
And his eyes have all the seeming of a demon's that is dreaming,   105
And the lamp-light o'er him streaming throws his shadow on the
        floor;
And my soul from out that shadow that lies floating on the floor
                         Shall be lifted—nevermore!
                                              —1845

Sonnet—To Science

Science! true daughter of Old Time thou art!
    Who alterest all things with thy peering eyes.
Why preyest thou thus upon the poet's heart,
    Vulture, whose wings are dull realities?
How should he love thee? or how deem thee wise?   5
    Who wouldst not leave him in his wandering
To seek for treasure in the jeweled skies,
    Albeit he soared with an undaunted wing?
Hast thou not dragged Diana° from her car?
    And driven the Hamadryad° from the wood   10
To seek a shelter in some happier star?
    Hast thou not torn the Naiad° from her flood,
The Elfin from the green grass, and from me
The summer dream beneath the tamarind° tree?
                                              —1829

---

93 **Aidenn** Eden
9 **Diana** Roman goddess of the moon   10 **Hamadryad** wood nymph   12 **Naiad** water
nymph   14 **tamarind** exotic Oriental tree

To Helen

Helen, thy beauty is to me
   Like those Nicean° barks of yore,
That gently, o'er a perfumed sea
   The weary, way-worn wanderer bore
   To his own native shore.   5

On desperate seas long wont to roam,
   Thy hyacinth° hair, thy classic face
Thy Naiad° airs have brought me home
   To the glory that was Greece
And the grandeur that was Rome.   10

Lo! in yon brilliant window-niche
   How statue-like I see thee stand!
   The agate lamp within thy hand,
Ah! Psyche,° from the regions which
   Are Holy Land!   15

                    —1831

ALFRED, LORD TENNYSON   1809–1892

Tennyson became the most famous English poet with the 1850 publication of *In Memoriam*, a sequence of poems on the death of his friend A. H. Hallam, the same year he became Poet Laureate. Modern critical opinion has focused more favorably on Tennyson's lyrical gifts than on his talents for narrative or drama. T. S. Eliot and W. H. Auden, among other critics, praised Tennyson's rhythms and sound patterns but had reservations about his depth of intellect, especially when he took on the role of official apologist for Victorian England.

The Eagle

FRAGMENT

He clasps the crag with crooked hands;
Close to the sun in lonely lands,
Ringed with the azure world, he stands.

The wrinkled sea beneath him crawls;
He watches from his mountain walls,   5
And like a thunderbolt he falls.

                    —1851

---

2 **Nicean** possibly of Nice (in the South of France); or Phoenician 7 **hyacinth** reddish, like the flower of Greek myth 8 **Naiad** water nymph 14 **Psyche** the soul

In Memoriam A. H. H.,° 54

O, yet we trust that somehow good
   Will be the final goal of ill,
   To pangs of nature, sins of will,
Defects of doubt, and taints of blood;

That nothing walks with aimless feet;   5
   That not one life shall be destroyed,
   Or cast as rubbish to the void,
When God hath made the pile complete;

That not a worm is cloven in vain;
   That not a moth with vain desire   10
   Is shriveled in a fruitless fire,
Or but subserves another's gain.

Behold, we know not anything;
   I can but trust that good shall fall
   At last—far off—at last, to all,   15
And every winter change to spring.

So runs my dreams; but what am I?
   An infant crying in the night;
   An infant crying for the light,
And with no language but a cry.   20

                                          —1833

Tears, Idle Tears

FROM *THE PRINCESS*

   Tears, idle tears, I know not what they mean,
Tears from the depth of some divine despair
Rise in the heart, and gather to the eyes,
In looking on the happy autumn-fields,
And thinking of the days that are no more.   5

   Fresh as the first beam glittering on a sail,
That brings our friends up from the underworld,
Sad as the last which reddens over one
That sinks with all we love below the verge;
So sad, so fresh, the days that are no more.   10

A. H. H. the poet's college friend Arthur Henry Hallam (1811-1833)

Ah, sad and strange as in dark summer dawns
The earliest pipe of half-awakened birds
To dying ears, when unto dying eyes
The casement slowly grows a glimmering square;
So sad, so strange, the days that are no more.   15

Dear as remembered kisses after death,
And sweet as those by hopeless fancy feigned
On lips that are for others; deep as love,
Deep as first love, and wild with all regret;
O Death in Life, the days that are no more!   20

—1847

Ulysses°

It little profits that an idle king,
By this still hearth, among these barren crags,
Matched with an aged wife, I mete and dole
Unequal laws unto a savage race,
That hoard, and sleep, and feed, and know not me.   5
I cannot rest from travel; I will drink
Life to the lees. All times I have enjoyed
Greatly, have suffered greatly, both with those
That loved me, and alone; on shore, and when
Through scudding drifts the rainy Hyades°   10
Vexed the dim sea. I am become a name;
For always roaming with a hungry heart
Much have I seen and known—cities of men
And manners, climates, councils, governments,
Myself not least, but honored of them all—   15
And drunk delight of battle with my peers,
Far on the ringing plains of windy Troy.
I am a part of all that I have met;
Yet all experience is an arch wherethrough
Gleams that untraveled world whose margin fades   20
For ever and for ever when I move.
How dull it is to pause, to make an end,
To rust unburnished, not to shine in use!
As though to breathe were life! Life piled on life
Were all too little, and of one to me   25
Little remains; but every hour is saved
From that eternal silence, something more,

Ulysses Homer's *Odyssey* ends with the return of Odysseus (Ulysses) to his island kingdom, Ithaca. Tennyson's poem takes place some years later. **10 Hyades** a constellation thought to predict rain

A bringer of new things; and vile it were
For some three suns to store and hoard myself,
And this gray spirit yearning in desire   30
To follow knowledge like a sinking star,
Beyond the utmost bound of human thought.
　　　This is my son, mine own Telemachus,
To whom I leave the scepter and the isle,
Well-loved of me, discerning to fulfill   35
This labor, by slow prudence to make mild
A rugged people, and through soft degrees
Subdue them to the useful and the good.
Most blameless is he, centered in the sphere
Of common duties, decent not to fail   40
In offices of tenderness, and pay
Meet adoration to my household gods,
When I am gone. He works his work, I mine.
　　　There lies the port; the vessel puffs her sail;
There gloom the dark, broad seas. My mariners,   45
Souls that have toiled, and wrought, and thought with me,
That ever with a frolic welcome took
The thunder and the sunshine, and opposed
Free hearts, free foreheads—you and I are old;
Old age hath yet his honor and his toil.   50
Death closes all; but something ere the end,
Some work of noble note, may yet be done,
Not unbecoming men that strove with gods.
The lights begin to twinkle from the rocks;
The long day wanes; the low moon climbs; the deep   55
Moans round with many voices. Come, my friends,
'Tis not too late to seek a newer world.
Push off, and sitting well in order smite
The sounding furrows; for my purpose holds
To sail beyond the sunset, and the baths   60
Of all the western stars, until I die.
It may be that the gulfs will wash us down;
It may be we shall touch the Happy Isles,°
And see the great Achilles, whom we knew.
Though much is taken, much abides; and though   65
We are not now that strength which in old days
Moved earth and heaven, that which we are, we are,
One equal temper of heroic hearts,
Made weak by time and fate, but strong in will
To strive, to seek, to find, and not to yield.   70

                                              —1833

----

63 **Happy Isles** Elysium, the resting place of dead heroes

R OBERT B ROWNING   1812–1889

Browning's many successful dramatic monologues are his lasting legacy, for he brings the genre to a level of achievement rarely equaled. Less regarded during his lifetime than his contemporary Tennyson, he has consistently risen in the esteem of modern readers. Often overlooked in his gallery of often grotesque characters are his considerable metrical skills and ability to simulate speech while working in demanding poetic forms.

My Last Duchess

FERRARA°

That's my last duchess painted on the wall,
Looking as if she were alive. I call
That piece a wonder, now: Frà Pandolf's° hands
Worked busily a day, and there she stands.
Will't please you sit and look at her? I said   5
"Frà Pandolf" by design, for never read
Strangers like you that pictured countenance,
The depth and passion of its earnest glance,
But to myself they turned (since none puts by
The curtain I have drawn for you, but I)   10
And seemed as they would ask me, if they durst,
How such a glance came there; so, not the first
Are you to turn and ask thus. Sir, 'twas not
Her husband's presence only, called that spot
Of joy into the Duchess' cheek: perhaps   15
Frà Pandolf chanced to say "Her mantle laps
Over my lady's wrist too much," or "Paint
Must never hope to reproduce the faint
Half-flush that dies along her throat": such stuff
Was courtesy, she thought, and cause enough   20
For calling up that spot of joy. She had
A heart—how shall I say?—too soon made glad,
Too easily impressed; she liked whate'er
She looked on, and her looks went everywhere.
Sir, 'twas all one! My favor at her breast,   25
The dropping of the daylight in the West,
The bough of cherries some officious fool
Broke in the orchard for her, the white mule
She rode with round the terrace—all and each

Ferrara The speaker is probably Alfonso II d'Este, Duke of Ferrara (1533-158?).   **3 Frà Pandolf** an imaginary painter

Would draw from her alike the approving speech,   30
Or blush, at least. She thanked men—good! but thanked
Somehow—I know not how—as if she ranked
My gift of a nine-hundred-years-old name
With anybody's gift. Who'd stoop to blame
This sort of trifling? Even had you skill   35
In speech—which I have not—to make your will
Quite clear to such an one, and say, "Just this
Or that in you disgusts me; here you miss,
Or there exceed the mark"—and if she let
Herself be lessoned so, nor plainly set   40
Her wits to yours, forsooth, and made excuse,
—E'en then would be some stooping; and I choose
Never to stoop. Oh sir, she smiled, no doubt,
Whene'er I passed her; but who passed without
Much the same smile? This grew; I gave commands;   45
Then all smiles stopped together. There she stands
As if alive. Will't please you rise? We'll meet
The company below, then. I repeat,
The Count your master's° known munificence
Is ample warrant that no just pretense   50
Of mine for dowry will be disallowed;
Though his fair daughter's self, as I avowed
At starting, is my object. Nay, we'll go
Together down, sir. Notice Neptune, though,
Taming a sea horse, thought a rarity,   55
Which Claus of Innsbruck cast in bronze for me!

                                                   —1842

Porphyria's° Lover

The rain set early in tonight,
          The sullen wind was soon awake,
It tore the elm-tops down for spite,
          And did its worst to vex the lake:
          I listened with heart fit to break.   5
When glided in Porphyria; straight
          She shut the cold out and the storm,
And kneeled and made the cheerless grate
          Blaze up, and all the cottage warm;
          Which done, she rose, and from her form   10

---

49 Count your master's The auditor is apparently an envoy sent to arrange a marriage
between the Duke of Ferrara and a count's daughter.
Porphyria name suggesting purple, the color of nobility and royalty

Withdrew the dripping cloak and shawl,
    And laid her soiled gloves by, untied
Her hat and let the damp hair fall,
    And, last, she sat down by my side
    And called me. When no voice replied,   15
She put my arm about her waist,
    And made her smooth white shoulder bare,
And all her yellow hair displaced,
    And, stooping, made my cheek lie there,
    And spread, o'er all, her yellow hair,   20
Murmuring how she loved me—she
    Too weak, for all her heart's endeavor,
To set its struggling passion free
    From pride, and vainer ties dissever,
    And give herself to me forever.   25
But passion sometimes would prevail,
    Nor could tonight's gay feast restrain
A sudden thought of one so pale
    For love of her, and all in vain:
    So, she was come through wind and rain.   30
Be sure I looked up at her eyes
    Happy and proud; at last I knew
Porphyria worshipped me; surprise
    Made my heart swell, and still it grew
    While I debated what to do.   35
That moment she was mine, mine, fair,
    Perfectly pure and good: I found
A thing to do, and all her hair
    In one long yellow string I wound
    Three times her little throat around,   40
And strangled her. No pain felt she;
    I am quite sure she felt no pain.
As a shut bud that holds a bee,
    I warily oped her lids: again
    Laughed the blue eyes without a stain.   45
And I untightened next the tress
    About her neck; her cheek once more
Blushed bright beneath my burning kiss:
    I propped her head up as before,
    Only, this time my shoulder bore   50
Her head, which droops upon it still:
    The smiling rosy little head
So glad it has its utmost will,
    That all it scorned at once is fled,
    And I, its love, am gained instead!   55

Porphyria's love: she guessed not how
    Her darling one wish would be heard.
And thus we sit together now,
    And all night long we have not stirred,
    And yet God has not said a word!   60

                                        —1842

WALT WHITMAN   1819–1892

Whitman's pioneering use of free verse has established him as one
of the forebears of modern poetry, but his subject matter, often dealing with sexual topics, and his unsparing realism were equally controversial in his day. An admirer of Emerson, he adapted many of the
ideas of Transcendentalism in *Song of Myself*, his first major sequence,
and also incorporated many of Emerson's calls for poets to use
American subjects and patterns of speech. *Leaves of Grass*, which he
revised from 1855 until his death, expanded to include virtually all
of his poems, including the graphic poems he wrote while serving as
a volunteer in Civil War army hospitals.

A Sight in Camp in the Daybreak Gray and Dim

A sight in camp in the daybreak gray and dim,
As from my tent I emerge so early sleepless,
As slow I walk in the cool fresh air the path near by the
    hospital tent,
Three forms I see on stretchers lying, brought out there
    untended lying,
Over each the blanket spread, ample brownish woolen blanket,   5
Gray and heavy blanket, folding, covering all.

Curious I halt and silent stand,
Then with light fingers I from the face of the nearest the first
    just lift the blanket;
Who are you elderly man so gaunt and grim, with well-gray'd
    hair, and flesh all sunken about the eyes?
Who are you my dear comrade?   10
Then to the second I step—and who are you my child and
    darling?
Who are you sweet boy with cheeks yet blooming?

Then to the third—a face nor child nor old, very calm, as of
    beautiful yellow-white ivory;

Young man I think I know you—I think this face is the face of
    the Christ himself,
Dead and divine and brother of all, and here again he lies.   15

                                       —1867

Crossing Brooklyn Ferry

1

Flood-tide below me! I see you face to face!
Clouds of the west—sun there half an hour high—I see you also
    face to face.

Crowds of men and women attired in the usual costumes, how
    curious you are to me!
On the ferry-boats the hundreds and hundreds that cross,
    returning home, are more curious to me than you suppose,
And you that shall cross from shore to shore years hence are more
    to me, and more in my meditations, than you might suppose.   5

2

The impalpable sustenance of me from all things at all hours of
    the day,
The simple, compact, well-join'd scheme, myself disintegrated,
    every one disintegrated yet part of the scheme,
The similitudes of the past and those of the future,
The glories strung like beads on my smallest sights and hearings,
    on the walk in the street and the passage over the river,
The current rushing so swiftly and swimming with me far away,   10
The others that are to follow me, the ties between me and them,
The certainty of others, the life, love, sight, hearing of others.

Others will enter the gates of the ferry and cross from shore to
    shore,
Others will watch the run of the flood-tide,
Others will see the shipping of Manhattan north and west, and
    the heights of Brooklyn to the south and east,   15
Others will see the islands large and small;
Fifty years hence, others will see them as they cross, the sun half
    an hour high,
A hundred years hence, or ever so many hundred years hence,
    others will see them,
Will enjoy the sunset, the pouring-in of the flood-tide, the falling-
    back to the sea of the ebb-tide.

3

It avails not, time nor place—distance avails not,   20
I am with you, you men and women of a generation, or ever so
    many generations hence,
Just as you feel when you look on the river and sky, so I felt,
Just as any of you is one of a living crowd, I was one of a crowd,
Just as you are refresh'd by the gladness of the river and the
    bright flow, I was refresh'd,
Just as you stand and lean on the rail, yet hurry with the swift
    current, I stood yet was hurried,   25
Just as you look on the numberless masts of ships and the
    thick-stemm'd pipes of steamboats, I look'd.

I too many and many a time cross'd the river of old,
Watched the Twelfth-month° sea-gulls, saw them high in the air
    floating with motionless wings, oscillating their bodies,
Saw how the glistening yellow lit up parts of their bodies and left
    the rest in strong shadow,
Saw the slow-wheeling circles and the gradual edging toward the
    south,   30
Saw the reflection of the summer sky in the water,
Had my eyes dazzled by the shimmering track of beams,
Look'd at the fine centrifugal spokes of light round the shape
    of my head in the sunlit water,
Look'd on the haze on the hills southward and south-westward,
Look'd on the vapor as it flew in fleeces tinged with violet,   35
Look'd toward the lower bay to notice the vessels arriving,
Saw their approach, saw aboard those that were near me,
Saw the white sails of schooners and sloops, saw the ships at
    anchor,
The sailors at work in the rigging or out astride the spars,
The round masts, the swinging motion of the hulls, the slender
    serpentine pennants,   40
The large and small steamers in motion, the pilots in their
    pilothouses,
The white wake left by the passage, the quick tremulous whirl
    of the wheels,
The flags of all nations, the falling of them at sunset,
The scallop-edged waves in the twilight, the ladled cups, the
    frolicsome crests and glistening,
The stretch afar growing dimmer and dimmer, the gray walls of
    the granite storehouses by the docks,   45
On the river the shadowy group, the big steam-tug closely flank'd

---

28 **Twelfth-month** Whitman's mother was a Quaker, hence this phrase for December.

on each side by the barges, the hay-boat, the belated lighter,
On the neighboring shore the fires from the foundry chimneys
    burning high and glaringly into the night,
Casting their flicker of black contrasted with wild red and yellow
    light over the tops of houses, and down into the clefts of streets.

4

These and all else were to me the same as they are to you,
I loved well those cities, loved well the stately and rapid river,   50
The men and women I saw were all near to me,
Others the same—others who look back on me because I look'd
    forward to them,
(The time will come, though I stop here to-day and to-night.)

5

What is it then between us?
What is the count of the scores or hundreds of years between us?   55

Whatever it is, it avails not—distance avails not, and place avails
    not,
I too lived, Brooklyn of ample hills was mine,
I too walk'd the streets of Manhattan island, and bathed in the
    waters around it,
I too felt the curious abrupt questionings stir within me,
In the day among crowds of people sometimes they came upon
    me,   60
In my walks home late at night or as I lay in my bed they came
    upon me,
I too had been struck from the float forever held in solution,
I too had receiv'd identity by my body,
That I was I knew was of my body, and what I should be I knew
    I should be of my body.

6

It is not upon you alone the dark patches fall,   65
The dark threw its patches down upon me also,
The best I had done seem'd to me blank and suspicious,
My great thoughts as I supposed them, were they not in reality
    meagre?
Nor is it you alone who know what it is to be evil,
I am he who knew what it was to be evil,   70
I too knitted the old knot of contrariety,
Blabb'd, blush'd, resented, lied, stole, grudg'd,
Had guile, anger, lust, hot wishes I dared not speak,
Was wayward, vain, greedy, shallow, sly, cowardly, malignant,
The wolf, the snake, the hog, not wanting in me,   75

The cheating look, the frivolous word, the adulterous wish, not
  wanting,
Refusals, hates, postponements, meanness, laziness, none of these
  wanting,
Was one with the rest, the days and haps of the rest,
Was call'd by my nighest name by clear loud voices of young
  men as they saw me approaching or passing,
Felt their arms on my neck as I stood, or the negligent leaning
  of their flesh against me as I sat,   80
Saw many I loved in the street or ferry-boat or public assembly,
  yet never told them a word,
Lived the same life with the rest, the same old laughing, gnawing,
  sleeping,
Play'd the part that still looks back on the actor or actress,
The same old role, the role that is what we make it, as great as
  we like,
Or as small as we like, or both great and small.   85

7

Closer yet I approach you,
What thought you have of me now, I had as much of you—I laid
  in my stores in advance,
I consider'd long and seriously of you before you were born.

Who was to know what should come home to me?
Who knows but I am enjoying this?   90
Who knows, for all the distance, but I am as good as looking
  at you now, for all you cannot see me?

8

Ah, what can ever be more stately and admirable to me than mast-
  hemm'd Manhattan?
River and sunset and scallop-edg'd waves of flood-tide?
The sea-gulls oscillating their bodies, the hay-boat in the twilight,
  and the belated lighter?
What gods can exceed these that clasp me by the hand, and with
  voices I love call me promptly and loudly by my nighest name
  as I approach?   95
What is more subtle than this which ties me to the woman or
  man that looks in my face?
Which fuses me into you now, and pours my meaning into you?

We understand then do we not?
What I promis'd without mentioning it, have you not accepted?
What the study could not teach—what the preaching could not
  accomplish is accomplish'd, is it not?   100

9

Flow on, river! flow with the flood-tide, and ebb with the ebbtide!
Frolic on, crested and scallop-edg'd waves!
Gorgeous clouds of the sunset! drench with your splendor me,
    or the men and women generations after me!
Cross from shore to shore, countless crowds of passengers!
Stand up, tall masts of Mannahatta! stand up, beautiful hills of
    Brooklyn!   105
Throb, baffled and curious brain! throw out questions and answers!
Suspend here and everywhere, eternal float of solution!
Gaze, loving and thirsting eyes, in the house or street or public
    assembly!
Sound out, voices of young men! loudly and musically call me
    by my nighest name!
Live, old life! play the part that looks back on the actor or
    actress!   110
Play the old role, the role that is great or small according as one
    makes it!
Consider, you who peruse me, whether I may not in unknown
    ways be looking upon you;
Be firm, rail over the river, to support those who lean idly, yet
    haste with the hasting current;
Fly on, sea-birds! fly sideways, or wheel in large circles high
    in the air;
Receive the summer sky, you water, and faithfully hold it till all
    downcast eyes have time to take it from you!   115
Diverge, fine spokes of light, from the shape of my head, or any
    one's head, in the sunlit water!
Come on, ships from the lower bay! pass up or down, white-sail'd
    schooners, sloops, lighters!
Flaunt away, flags of all nations! be duly lower'd at sunset!
Burn high your fires, foundry chimneys! cast black shadows at
    nightfall! cast red and yellow light over the tops of the houses!
Appearances, now or henceforth, indicate what you are,   120
You necessary film, continue to envelop the soul,
About my body for me, and your body for you, be hung our
    divinest aromas,
Thrive, cities—bring your freight, bring your shows, ample and
    sufficient rivers,
Expand, being than which none else is perhaps more spiritual,
Keep your places, objects than which none else is more lasting.   125

You have waited, you always wait, you dumb, beautiful ministers,
We receive you with free sense at last, and are insatiate
    henceforward,

Not you any more shall be able to foil us, or withhold yourselves
    from us,
We use you, and do not cast you aside—we plant you permanently
    within us,
We fathom you not—we love you—there is perfection in you
    also,   130
You furnish your parts toward eternity,
Great or small, you furnish your parts toward the soul.

                                                          —1881–1882

A Noiseless Patient Spider

A noiseless patient spider,
I mark'd where on a little promontory it stood isolated,
Mark'd how to explore the vacant vast surrounding,
It launch'd forth filament, filament, filament, out of itself,
Ever unreeling them, ever tirelessly speeding them.   5

And you O my soul where you stand,
Surrounded, detached, in measureless oceans of space,
Ceaselessly musing, venturing, throwing, seeking the spheres to
    connect them,
Till the bridge you will need be form'd, till the ductile anchor
    hold,
Till the gossamer thread you fling catch somewhere, O my soul.   10

                                                              —1876

Out of the Cradle Endlessly Rocking

Out of the cradle endlessly rocking,
Out of the mocking-bird's throat, the musical shuttle,
Out of the Ninth-month° midnight,
Over the sterile sands and the fields beyond, where the child
    leaving his bed wander'd alone, bareheaded, barefoot,
Down from the shower'd halo,   5
Up from the mystic play of shadows twining and twisting as if
    they were alive,
Out from the patches of briers and blackberries,
From the memories of the bird that chanted to me,
From your memories sad brother, from the fitful risings and
    fallings I heard,
From under that yellow half-moon late-risen and swollen as if
    with tears,   10

---

3 Ninth-month Quaker term for September

From those beginning notes of yearning and love there in the mist,
From the thousand responses of my heart never to cease,
From the myriad thence-arous'd words,
From the word stronger and more delicious than any,
From such as now they start the scene revisiting,   15
As a flock, twittering, rising, or overhead passing,
Borne hither, ere all eludes me, hurriedly,
A man, yet by these tears a little boy again,
Throwing myself on the sand, confronting the waves,
I, chanter of pains and joys, uniter of here and hereafter,   20
Taking all hints to use them, but swiftly leaping beyond them,
A reminiscence sing.

Once Paumanok,°
When the lilac-scent was in the air and Fifth-month° grass was
    growing,
Up this seashore in some briers,   25
Two feather'd guests from Alabama, two together,
And their nest, and four light-green eggs spotted with brown,
And every day the he-bird to and fro near at hand,
And every day the she-bird crouch'd on her nest, silent, with
    bright eyes,
And every day I, a curious boy, never too close, never disturbing
    them,   30
Cautiously peering, absorbing, translating.

Shine! shine! shine!
Pour down your warmth, great sun!
While we bask, we two together.

Two together!   35
Winds blow south, or winds blow north,
Day come white, or night come black,
Home, or rivers and mountains from home,
Singing all time, minding no time,
While we two keep together.   40

Till of a sudden,
May-be kill'd, unknown to her mate,
One forenoon the she-bird crouch'd not on the nest,
Nor return'd that afternoon, nor the next,
Nor ever appear'd again.   45

---

23 **Paumanok** Indian name for Long Island   24 **Fifth-month** May (Quaker)

And thenceforward all summer in the sound of the sea,
And at night under the full of the moon in calmer weather,
Over the hoarse surging of the sea,
Or flitting from brier to brier by day,
I saw, I heard at intervals the remaining one, the he-bird,   50
The solitary guest from Alabama.

Blow! blow! blow!
Blow up sea-winds along Paumanok's shore;
I wait and I wait till you blow my mate to me.

Yes, when the stars glisten'd,   55
All night long on the prong of a moss-scallop'd stake,
Down almost amid the slapping waves,
Sat the lone singer wonderful causing tears.

He call'd on his mate,
He pour'd forth the meaning which I of all men know.   60
Yes my brother I know,
The rest might not, but I have treasur'd every note,
For more than once dimly down to the beach gliding,
Silent, avoiding the moonbeams, blending myself with the
    shadows,
Recalling now the obscure shapes, the echoes, the sounds and
    sights after their sorts,   65
The white arms out in the breakers tirelessly tossing,
I, with bare feet, a child, the wind wafting my hair,
Listen'd long and long.

Listen'd to keep, to sing, now translating the notes,
Following you my brother.   70

Soothe! soothe! soothe!
Close on its wave soothes the wave behind,
And again another behind embracing and lapping, every one close,
But my love soothes not me, not me.

Low hangs the moon, it rose late,   75
It is lagging—O I think it is heavy with love, with love.

O madly the sea pushes upon the land,
With love, with love.

O night! do I not see my love fluttering out among the breakers?
What is that little black thing I see there in the white?   80

Loud! loud! loud!
Loud I call to you, my love!

High and clear I shoot my voice over the waves,
Surely you must know who is here, is here,
You must know who I am, my love.   85

Low-hanging moon!
What is that dusky spot in your brown yellow?
O it is the shape, the shape of my mate!
O moon do not keep her from me any longer.
Land! land! O land!   90
Whichever way I turn, O I think you could give me my mate back
      again if you only would,
For I am almost sure I see her dimly whichever way I look.

O rising stars!
Perhaps the one I want so much will rise, will rise with some of you.

O throat! O trembling throat!   95
Sound clearer through the atmosphere!
Pierce the woods, the earth,
Somewhere listening to catch you must be the one I want.

Shake out carols!
Solitary here, the night's carols!   100
Carols of lonesome love! death's carols!
Carols under that lagging, yellow, waning moon!
O under that moon where she droops almost down into the sea!
O reckless despairing carols.

But soft! sink low!   105
Soft! let me just murmur,
And do you wait a moment you husky-nois'd sea,
For somewhere I believe I heard my mate responding to me,
So faint, I must be still, be still to listen,
But not altogether still, for then she might not come immediately to me.   110

Hither my love!
Here I am! here!
With this just-sustain'd note I announce myself to you,
This gentle call is for you my love, for you.

Do not be decoy'd elsewhere,   115
That is the whistle of the wind, it is not my voice,

That is the fluttering, the fluttering of the spray,
Those are the shadows of leaves.

O darkness! O in vain!
O I am very sick and sorrowful.   120
O brown halo in the sky near the moon, drooping upon the sea!
O troubled reflection in the sea!
O throat! O throbbing heart!
And I singing uselessly, uselessly all the night.

O past! O happy life! O songs of joy!   125
In the air, in the woods, over fields,
Loved! loved! loved! loved! loved!
But my mate no more, no more with me!
We two together no more.

The aria sinking,   130
All else continuing, the stars shining,
The winds blowing, the notes of the bird continuous echoing,
With angry moans the fierce old mother incessantly moaning,
On the sands of Paumanok's shore gray and rustling,
The yellow half-moon enlarged, sagging down, drooping, the face
    of the sea almost touching,   135
The boy ecstatic, with his bare feet the waves, with his hair the
    atmosphere dallying,
The love in the heart long pent, now loose, now at last
    tumultuously bursting,
The aria's meaning, the ears, the soul, swiftly depositing,
The strange tears down the cheeks coursing,
The colloquy there, the trio, each uttering,   140
The undertone, the savage old mother incessantly crying,
To the boy's soul's questions sullenly timing, some drown'd secret
    hissing,
To the outsetting bard.

Demon or bird! (said the boy's soul,)
Is it indeed toward your mate you sing? or is it really to me?   145
For I, that was a child, my tongue's use sleeping, now I have
    heard you,
Now in a moment I know what I am for, I awake,
And already a thousand singers, a thousand songs, clearer, louder
    and more sorrowful than yours,
A thousand warbling echoes have started to life within me, never
    to die.

O you singer solitary, singing by yourself, projecting me,   150
O solitary me listening, never more shall I cease perpetuating you,
Never more shall I escape, never more the reverberations,
Never more the cries of unsatisfied love be absent from me,
Never again leave me to be the peaceful child I was before what
     there in the night,
By the sea under the yellow and sagging moon,   155
The messenger there arous'd, the fire, the sweet hell within,
The unknown want, the destiny of me.

O give me the clew!° (it lurks in the night here somewhere,)
O if I am to have so much, let me have more!

A word then, (for I will conquer it,)   160
The word final, superior to all,
Subtle, sent up—what is it?—I listen;
Are you whispering it, and have been all the time, you sea waves?
Is that it from your liquid rims and wet sands?

Whereto answering, the sea,   165
Delaying not, hurrying not,
Whisper'd me through the night, and very plainly before daybreak,
Lisp'd to me the low and delicious word death,
And again death, death, death, death,
Hissing melodious, neither like the bird nor like my arous'd
     child's heart,   170
But edging near as privately for me rustling at my feet,
Creeping thence steadily up to my ears and laving me softly all
     over,
Death, death, death, death, death.

Which I do not forget,
But fuse the song of my dusky demon and brother,   175
That he sang to me in the moonlight on Paumanok's gray beach,
With the thousand responsive songs at random,
My own songs awaked from that hour,
And with them the key, the word up from the waves,
The word of the sweetest song and all songs,   180
That strong and delicious word which, creeping to my feet,
(Or like some old crone rocking the cradle, swathed in sweet
     garments, bending aside,)
The sea whisper'd me.

                                        —1881–1882

_____

158 clew clue

Song of Myself, 6

A child said *What is the grass?* fetching it to me with full hands;
How could I answer the child? I do not know what it is any more
    than he.

I guess it must be the flag of my disposition, out of hopeful green
    stuff woven.

Or I guess it is the handkerchief of the Lord,
A scented gift and remembrancer designedly dropped,   5
Bearing the owner's name someway in the corners, that we may
    see and remark, and say *Whose?*

Or I guess the grass is itself a child, the produced babe of the
    vegetation.

Or I guess it is a uniform hieroglyphic,
And it means, Sprouting alike in broad zones and narrow zones,
Growing among black folks as among white,   10
Kanuck,° Tuckahoe,° Congressman, Cuff,° I give them the same,
    I receive them the same.

And now it seems to me the beautiful uncut hair of graves.

Tenderly will I use you curling grass,
It may be you transpire from the breasts of young men,
It may be if I had known them I would have loved them,   15
It may be you are from old people, or from offspring taken soon
    out of their mothers' laps,
And here you are the mothers' laps.

This grass is very dark to be from the white heads of old mothers.
Darker than the colorless beards of old men.
Dark to come from under the faint red roofs of mouths.   20

O I perceive after all so many uttering tongues,
And I perceive they do not come from the roofs of mouths for
    nothing.

I wish I could translate the hints about the dead young men and
    women,
And the hints about old men and mothers, and the offspring
    taken soon out of their laps.

---

11 **Kanuck** French-Canadian   **Tuckahoe** coastal Virginian   **Cuff** a black slave

What do you think has become of the young and old men?   25
And what do you think has become of the women and children?

They are alive and well somewhere,
The smallest sprout shows there is really no death,
And if ever there was it led forward life, and does not wait at the end
    to arrest it.
And ceased the moment life appeared.   30

All goes onward and outward, nothing collapses.
And to die is different from what anyone supposed, and luckier.

                                             —1855

When I Heard the Learn'd Astronomer

When I heard the learn'd astronomer,
When the proofs, the figures, were ranged in columns before me,
When I was shown the charts and diagrams, to add, divide, and
    measure them,
When I sitting heard the astronomer where he lectured with much
    applause in the lecture-room,
How soon unaccountable I became tired and sick,   5
Till rising and gliding out I wander'd off by myself,
In the mystical moist night-air, and from time to time,
Look'd up in perfect silence at the stars.

                                             —1865

Matthew Arnold   1822–1888

Arnold, son of the headmaster of Rugby School, served as an inspector of schools during much of his adult life. An influential essayist as well as a poet, Arnold was unsparing in his criticism of middle-class "Philistinism." At least part of "Dover Beach" is thought to date from his honeymoon in 1851.

Dover Beach

The sea is calm tonight.
The tide is full, the moon lies fair
Upon the straits; on the French coast the light
Gleams and is gone; the cliffs of England stand,

Glimmering and vast, out in the tranquil bay.   5
Come to the window, sweet is the night-air!
Only, from the long line of spray
Where the sea meets the moon-blanched land,
Listen! you hear the grating roar
Of pebbles which the waves draw back, and fling,   10
At their return, up the high strand,
Begin, and cease, and then again begin,
With tremulous cadence slow, and bring
The eternal note of sadness in.

Sophocles° long ago   15
Heard it on the Aegean, and it brought
Into his mind the turbid ebb and flow
Of human misery; we
Find also in the sound a thought,
Hearing it by this distant northern sea.   20

The Sea of Faith
Was once, too, at the full, and round earth's shore
Lay like the folds of a bright girdle° furled.
But now I only hear
Its melancholy, long, withdrawing roar,   25
Retreating, to the breath
Of the night-wind, down the vast edges drear
And naked shingles° of the world.

Ah, love, let us be true
To one another! for the world, which seems   30
To lie before us like a land of dreams,
So various, so beautiful, so new,
Hath really neither joy, nor love, nor light,
Nor certitude, nor peace, nor help for pain;
And we are here as on a darkling plain   35
Swept with confused alarms of struggle and flight,
Where ignorant armies clash by night.

—1867

Emily Dickinson   1830–1886

Each generation tries to reinvent Dickinson, and readers' views of
her have ranged between two extremes—one perceiving her as the
abnormally shy "Belle of Amherst" making poetry out of her own

---

15 **Sophocles** Athenian tragic poet (496-406 B.C.)   23 **girdle** sash   28 **shingles** beach-pebbles

neuroses and another seeing her as a proto-feminist carving out a world of her own in self-willed isolation. What remains is her brilliant poetry—unique, original, and marked with the stamp of individual talent. Dickinson published only seven poems during her lifetime, but left behind hundreds of poems in manuscript at her death. Published by her relatives, they were immediately popular, but it was not until the edition of Thomas Johnson in 1955 that they were read with Dickinson's eccentric punctuation and capitalization intact.

Because I Could Not Stop for Death

Because I could not stop for Death—
He kindly stopped for me—
The Carriage held but just Ourselves—
And Immortality.

We slowly drove—He knew no haste   5
And I had put away
My labor and my leisure too,
For His Civility—

We passed the School, where Children strove
At Recess—in the Ring—   10
We passed the Fields of Gazing Grain—
We passed the Setting Sun—

Or rather—He passed Us—
The Dews drew quivering and chill—
For only Gossamer, my Gown—   15
My Tippet°—only Tulle°—

We paused before a House that seemed
A Swelling of the Ground—
The Roof was scarcely visible—
The Cornice—in the Ground—   20

Since then—'tis Centuries—and yet
Feels shorter than the Day
I first surmised the Horses' Heads
Were toward Eternity—

                                        —1890

---

16 **Tippet** shawl **Tulle** net-like fabric

I Died for Beauty—But Was Scarce

I died for Beauty—but was scarce
Adjusted in the Tomb
When One who died for Truth, was lain
In an adjoining Room—

He questioned softly "Why I failed?"   5
"For Beauty," I replied—
"And I—for Truth—Themself are One—
We Brethren, are", He said—

And so, as Kinsmen, met a Night—
We talked between the Rooms—   10
Until the Moss had reached our lips—
And covered up—our names—

                       —1890

I Heard a Fly Buzz—When I Died—

I heard a Fly buzz—when I died—
The Stillness in the Room
Was like the Stillness in the Air—
Between the Heaves of Storm—

The Eyes around—had wrung them dry—   5
And Breaths were gathering firm
For that last Onset—when the King
Be witnessed—in the Room—

I willed my Keepsakes—Signed away
What portion of me be   10
Assignable—and then it was
There interposed a Fly—

With Blue—uncertain stumbling Buzz—
Between the light—and me—
And then the Windows failed—and then   15
I could not see to see—

                       —1896

My Life Closed Twice Before Its Close

My life closed twice before its close;
It yet remains to see

If Immortality unveil
A third event to me

So huge, so hopeless to conceive   5
As these that twice befell.
Parting is all we know of heaven,
And all we need of hell.

                                        —1896

A Narrow Fellow in the Grass

A narrow Fellow in the Grass
Occasionally rides—
You may have met Him—did you not
His notice sudden is—

The Grass divides as with a Comb—   5
A spotted shaft is seen—
And then it closes at your feet
And opens further on—

He likes a Boggy Acre
A Floor to cool for Corn—   10
Yet when a Boy, and Barefoot—
I more than once at Noon
Have passed, I thought, a Whip lash
Unbraiding in the Sun
When stooping to secure it   15
It wrinkled, and was gone—

Several of Nature's People
I know, and they know me—
I feel for them a transport
Of cordiality—   20

But never met this Fellow
Attended, or alone
Without a tighter breathing
And Zero at the Bone—

                                        —1866

The Soul Selects Her Own Society—

The Soul selects her own Society—
Then—shuts the Door—

To her divine Majority—
Present no more—

Unmoved—she notes the Chariots—pausing—   5
At her low Gate—
Unmoved—an Emperor be kneeling
Upon her Mat—

I've known her—from an ample nation—
Choose One—   10
Then—close the Valves° of her attention—
Like Stone—

                                              —1890

CHRISTINA ROSSETTI   1830–1894

> The younger sister of Dante Gabriel and William, also distinguished
> writers, Rossetti was the author of numerous devotional poems and
> prose works. Her collected poems, edited by her brother William,
> appeared posthumously in 1904.

Up-Hill

Does the road wind up-hill all the way?
    Yes, to the very end.
Will the day's journey take the whole long day?
    From morn to night, my friend.

But is there for the night a resting-place?   5
    A roof for when the slow dark hours begin.
May not the darkness hide it from my face?
    You cannot miss that inn.

Shall I meet other wayfarers at night?
    Those who have gone before.   10
Then must I knock, or call when just in sight?
    They will not keep you waiting at that door.

Shall I find comfort, travel-sore and weak?
    Of labor you shall find the sum.
Will there be beds for me and all who seek?   15
    Yea, beds for all who come.

                                              —1858

___

11 **Valves** sliding doors

Thomas Hardy 1840–1928

After the disappointing response to his novel *Jude the Obscure* in 1895, Hardy returned to his first love, writing poetry for the last thirty years of his long life. The language and life of Hardy's native Wessex inform both his novels and poems. His subject matter is very much of the nineteenth century, but his ironic, disillusioned point of view marks him as one of the chief predecessors of modernism.

Ah, Are You Digging on My Grave?

"Ah, are you digging on my grave
    My loved one?—planting rue?"°
—"No: yesterday he went to wed
One of the brightest wealth has bred.
'It cannot hurt her now,' he said,   5
    'That I should not be true.'"

"Then who is digging on my grave?
    My nearest dearest kin?"
—"Ah, no; they sit and think, 'What use!
What good will planting flowers produce?   10
No tendance of her mound can loose
    Her spirit from Death's gin.'"

"But some one digs upon my grave?
    My enemy?—prodding sly?"
—"Nay: when she heard you had passed the Gate   15
That shuts on all flesh soon or late.
She thought you no more worth her hate,
    And cares not where you lie."

"Then who is digging on my grave?
Say—since I have not guessed!"   20
—"O it is I, my mistress dear,
Your little dog, who still lives near,
And much I hope my movements here
    Have not disturbed your rest?"

"Ah, yes! *You* dig upon my grave . . .   25
    Why flashed it not on me
That one true heart was left behind!
What feeling do we ever find

---

2 rue yellow flower traditionally associated with sadness

To equal among human kind
    A dog's fidelity!"   30

"Mistress, I dug upon your grave
    To bury a bone, in case
I should be hungry near this spot
When passing on my daily trot.
I am sorry, but I quite forgot   35
    It was your resting-place."

                                         −1914

Neutral Tones

We stood by a pond that winter day,
And the sun was white, as though chidden of God,
And a few leaves lay on the starving sod;
    —They had fallen from an ash, and were gray.

Your eyes on me were as eyes that rove   5
Over tedious riddles of years ago;
And some words played between us to and fro
    On which lost the more by our love.

The smile on your mouth was the deadest thing
Alive enough to have strength to die;   10
And a grin of bitterness swept thereby
    Like an ominous bird a-wing . . .

Since then, keen lessons that love deceives,
And wrings with wrong, have shaped to me
Your face, and the God-curst sun, and a tree,   15
    And a pond edged with grayish leaves.

                                         −1898

The Oxen

Christmas Eve, and twelve of the clock.
    "Now they are all on their knees,"°
An elder said as we sat in a flock
    By the embers in hearthside ease.

We pictured the meek and mild creatures where   5
    They dwelt in their strawy pen,

---

2 **Now they are all on their knees** folk belief that the oxen pray at the moment of Christ's
birth

Nor did it occur to one of us there
   To doubt they were kneeling then.

So fair a fancy few would weave
   In these years! Yet, I feel,   10
If someone said on Christmas Eve,
   "Come; see the oxen kneel,

"In the lonely barton° by yonder coomb°
   Our childhood used to know,"
I should go with him in the gloom,   15
   Hoping it might be so.

                             −1917

The Ruined Maid

"O 'Melia, my dear, this does everything crown!
Who could have supposed I should meet you in Town?
And whence such fair garments, such prosperi-ty?"
"O didn't you know I'd been ruined?" said she.

"You left us in tatters, without shoes or socks,   5
Tired of digging potatoes, and spudding up docks;°
And now you've gay bracelets and bright feathers three!"
"Yes: that's how we dress when we we're ruined," said she.

"At home in the barton° you said 'thee' and 'thou,'
And 'thik oon,' and 'theäs oon,'° and 't'other'; but now   10
Your talking quite fits 'ee for high compa-ny!"
"Some polish is gained with one's ruin," said she.

"Your hands were like paws then, your face blue and bleak
But now I'm bewitched by your delicate cheek,
And your little gloves fit as on any la-dy!"   15
"We never do work when we're ruined," said she.

"You used to call home-life a hag-ridden dream,
And you'd sigh, and you'd sock; but at present you seem
To know not of megrims° or melancho-ly!"
"True. One's pretty lively when ruined," said she.   20

---

13 **barton** barnyard   **coomb** valley
6 **docks** weeds   9 **barton** barnyard   10 **thik oon and theäs oon** dialect: "that one and this
one"   19 **megrims** migraines

"I wish I had feathers, a fine sweeping gown,
And a delicate face, and could strut about Town!"
"My dear—a raw country girl, such as you be,
Cannot quite expect that. You ain't ruined," said she.

—1866

Gerard Manley Hopkins   1844–1889

Hopkins was an English Jesuit priest who developed elaborate theories of poetic meter (what he called "sprung rhythm") and language to express his own spiritual ardor. Most of his work was posthumously printed through the efforts of his Oxford friend and later correspondent Robert Bridges, who was Poet Laureate.

God's Grandeur

The world is charged with the grandeur of God.
   It will flame out, like shining from shook foil;°
   It gathers to a greatness, like the ooze of oil
Crushed.° Why do men then now not reck his rod?
Generations have trod, have trod, have trod;   5
   And all is seared with trade; bleared, smeared with toil;
   And wears man's smudge and shares man's smell: the soil
Is bare now, nor can foot feel, being shod.

And for all this, nature is never spent;
   There lives the dearest freshness deep down things;   10
And though the last lights off the black West went
   Oh, morning, at the brown brink eastward, springs—
Because the Holy Ghost over the bent
   World broods with warm breast and with ah! bright wings.

—1877

Pied Beauty

Glory be to God for dappled things—
   For skies of couple-color as a brinded° cow;
      For rose-moles all in stipple upon trout that swim;
Fresh-firecoal chestnut-falls;° finches' wings;

---

2 **foil** gold leaf   **4 Crushed** Hopkins is referring to olive oil
2 **brinded** streaked   **4 Fresh-firecoal chestnut-falls** according to the poet, chestnuts have a
red color

Landscape plotted and pieced—fold, fallow, and plough;   5
    And all trades, their gear and tackle and trim.
All things counter, original, spare, strange;
    Whatever is fickle, freckled (who knows how?)
      With swift, slow; sweet, sour; adazzle, dim;
He fathers-forth whose beauty is past change: 10
    Praise him.

                    —1877

A. E. HOUSMAN   1859–1936

Educated in the classics at Oxford, Housman was almost forty before
he began to write verse seriously. His ballad-like poems of Shropshire
(an area in which he never actually lived) have proven some of the
most popular lyrics in English, despite their pervasive mood of bit-
tersweet pessimism.

Eight O'Clock

He stood, and heard the steeple
    Sprinkle the quarters° on the morning town.
One, two, three, four, to market-place and people
    It tossed them down.

Strapped, noosed, nighing his hour,   5
    He stood and counted them and cursed his luck;
And then the clock collected in the tower
    Its strength, and struck.

                    —1922

Is My Team Plowing

"Is my team plowing,
    That I was used to drive
And hear the harness jingle
    When I was man alive?"

Ay, the horses trample,   5
    The harness jingles now;
No change though you lie under
    The land you used to plow.

---

2 quarters quarter hours

"Is football playing
    Along the river shore,   10
With lads to chase the leather,
    Now I stand up no more?"

Ay, the ball is flying,
    The lads play heart and soul;
The goal stands up, the keeper   15
    Stands up to keep the goal.

"Is my girl happy,
    That I thought hard to leave,
And has she tired of weeping
    As she lies down at eve?"   20

Ay, she lies down lightly,
    She lies not down to weep:
Your girl is well contented
    Be still, my lad, and sleep.

"Is my friend hearty,   25
    Now I am thin and pine,
And has he found to sleep in
    A better bed than mine?"

Yes, lad, I lie easy,
    I lie as lads would choose;   30
I cheer a dead man's sweetheart,
    Never ask me whose.

                                        —1896

Loveliest of Trees, the Cherry Now

Loveliest of trees, the cherry now
Is hung with bloom along the bough,
And stands about the woodland ride
Wearing white for Eastertide.

Now, of my threescore years and ten,   5
Twenty will not come again,
And take from seventy springs a score,
It only leaves me fifty more.

And since to look at things in bloom
Fifty springs are little room,   10

About the woodlands I will go
To see the cherry hung with snow.

—1896

Stars, I Have Seen Them Fall

Stars, I have seen them fall,
    But when they drop and die
No star is lost at all
    From all the star-sown sky.
The toil of all that be   5
    Helps not the primal fault;
It rains into the sea
    And still the sea is salt.

—1936

"Terence, This Is Stupid Stuff . . ."

"Terence, this is stupid stuff:
You eat your victuals fast enough;
There can't be much amiss, 'tis clear,
To see the rate you drink your beer.
But oh, good Lord, the verse you make,   5
It gives a chap the belly-ache.
The cow, the old cow, she is dead;
It sleeps well, the hornèd head:
We poor lads, 'tis our turn now
To hear such tunes as killed the cow.   10
Pretty friendship 'tis to rhyme
Your friends to death before their time
Moping melancholy mad:
Come, pipe a tune to dance to, lad."

Why, if 'tis dancing you would be,   15
There's brisker pipes than poetry.
Say, for what were hop-yards meant,
Or why was Burton built on Trent?°
Oh many a peer of England brews
Livelier liquor than the Muse,   20
And malt does more than Milton can
To justify God's ways to man.
Ale, man, ale's the stuff to drink
For fellows whom it hurts to think:

---

18 Burton built on Trent site of breweries

Look into the pewter pot   25
To see the world as the world's not.
And faith, 'tis pleasant till 'tis past:
The mischief is that 'twill not last.
Oh I have been to Ludlow fair
And left my necktie God knows where,   30
And carried halfway home, or near,
Pints and quarts of Ludlow beer:
Then the world seemed none so bad,
And I myself a sterling lad;
And down in lovely muck I've lain,   35
Happy till I woke again.
Then I saw the morning sky:
Heigho, the tale was all a lie;
The world, it was the old world yet,
I was I, my things were wet,   40
And nothing now remained to do
But begin the game anew.

Therefore, since the world has still
Much good, but much less good than ill,
And while the sun and moon endure   45
Luck's a chance, but trouble's sure,
I'd face it as a wise man would,
And train for ill and not for good.
'Tis true, the stuff I bring for sale
Is not so brisk a brew as ale: 50
Out of a stem that scored the hand
I wrung it in a weary land.
But take it: if the smack is sour,
The better for the embittered hour;
It should do good to heart and head   50
When your soul is in my soul's stead;
And I will friend you, if I may,
In the dark and cloudy day.

There was a king reigned in the East:
There, when kings will sit to feast,   60
They get their fill before they think
With poisoned meat and poisoned drink.
He gathered all that springs to birth
From the many-venomed earth;
First a little, thence to more,   65
He sampled all her killing store;
And easy, smiling, seasoned sound,

Sate the king when healths went round.
They put arsenic in his meat
And stared aghast to watch him eat;   70
They poured strychnine in his cup
And shook to see him drink it up:
They shook, they stared as white's their shirt:
Them it was their poison hurt.
—I tell the tale that I heard told.   75
Mithridates,° he died old.

—1896

Rudyard Kipling   1865–1936

To pigeonhole Kipling as a simple-minded advocate of British impe-
rialism is to disregard the considerable talents as poet and fiction
writer that won him one of the first Nobel Prizes for literature. Best
known for his dialect ballads of English military life in far-flung colonial posts, he was also an excellent writer of lyrics.

When Earth's Last Picture Is Painted

L'ENVOI° TO "THE SEVEN SEAS"

When Earth's last picture is painted and the tubes are twisted
      and dried,
When the oldest colors have faded, and the youngest critic has
      died,
We shall rest, and, faith, we shall need it—lie down for an æon
      or two,
Till the Master of All Good Workmen shall put us to work anew.

And those that were good shall be happy: they shall sit in a
      golden chair;   5
They shall splash at a ten-league canvas with brushes of comets'
      hair.
They shall find real saints to draw from—Magdalene, Peter,
      and Paul;
They shall work for an age at a sitting and never be tired at all!

---

76 **Mithridates** legendary King of Pontus, he protected himself from poisons by taking small
doses regularly
L'Envoi closing summary

And only The Master shall praise us, and only The Master shall
   blame;
And no one shall work for money, and no one shall work for
   fame,   10
But each for the joy of the working, and each, in his separate star,
Shall draw the Thing as he sees It for the God of Things as
   They are!

                                                        —1892

William Butler Yeats   1865–1939

Yeats is the greatest Irish poet and provides an important link
between the late Romantic era and early modernism. His early
poetry, focusing on Irish legend and landscape, is regional in the
best sense of the term, but his later work, with its prophetic tone and
symbolist texture, moves on a larger stage. Yeats lived in London for
many years and was at the center of British literary life. He was
awarded the Nobel Prize in 1923.

The Lake Isle of Innisfree

I will arise and go now, and go to Innisfree,
And a small cabin build there, of clay and wattles° made:
Nine bean-rows will I have there, a hive for the honey-bee,
And live alone in the bee-loud glade.

And I shall have some peace there, for peace comes dropping slow, 5
Dropping from the veils of the morning to where the cricket sings;
There midnight's all a glimmer, and noon a purple glow,
And evening full of the linnet's wings.

I will arise and go now, for always night and day
I hear lake water lapping with low sounds by the shore;   10
While I stand on the roadway, or on the pavements gray,
I hear it in the deep heart's core.

                                                        —1892

Leda° and the Swan

A sudden blow: the great wings beating still
Above the staggering girl, her thighs caressed

---

2 **wattles** woven poles and reeds
Leda mortal mother of Helen of Troy and Clytemnestra, wife and assassin of Agamemnon

By the dark webs, her nape caught in his bill,
He holds her helpless breast upon his breast.

How can those terrified vague fingers push   5
The feathered glory from her loosening thighs?
And how can body, laid in that white rush,
But feel the strange heart beating where it lies?

A shudder in the loins engenders there
The broken wall, the burning roof and tower   10
And Agamemnon dead.°
                    Being so caught up,
So mastered by the brute blood of the air,
Did she put on his knowledge with his power
Before the indifferent beak could let her drop?

                                        −1923

Sailing to Byzantium°

1

That is no country for old men. The young
In one another's arms, birds in the trees
—Those dying generations—at their song,
The salmon-falls, the mackerel-crowded seas,
Fish, flesh, or fowl, commend all summer long   5
Whatever is begotten, born, and dies.
Caught in that sensual music all neglect
Monuments of unaging intellect.

2

An aged man is but a paltry thing,
A tattered coat upon a stick, unless   10
Soul clap its hands and sing, and louder sing
For every tatter in its mortal dress,
Nor is there singing school but studying
Monuments of its own magnificence;
And therefore I have sailed the seas and come   15
To the holy city of Byzantium.

3

O sages standing in God's holy fire
As in the gold mosaic of a wall,

10-11 The broken wall . . . Agamemnon dead events during and after the Trojan War
Byzantium Constantinople or Istanbul, capital of the Eastern Roman Empire

Come from the holy fire, perne in a gyre,°
And be the singing-masters of my soul.   20
Consume my heart away; sick with desire
And fastened to a dying animal
It knows not what it is; and gather me
Into the artifice of eternity.

4

Once out of nature I shall never take   25
My bodily form from any natural thing,
But such a form as Grecian goldsmiths make
Of hammered gold and gold enameling
To keep a drowsy Emperor awake;
Or set upon a golden bough to sing   30
To lords and ladies of Byzantium
Of what is past, or passing, or to come.

                                              —1927

The Second Coming

Turning and turning in the widening gyre°
The falcon cannot hear the falconer;
Things fall apart; the center cannot hold;
Mere anarchy is loosed upon the world,
The blood-dimmed tide is loosed, and everywhere   5
The ceremony of innocence is drowned;
The best lack all conviction, while the worst
Are full of passionate intensity.

Surely some revelation is at hand;
Surely the Second Coming is at hand.   10
The Second Coming! Hardly are those words out
When a vast image out of *Spiritus Mundi*°
Troubles my sight: somewhere in the sands of the desert
A shape with lion body and the head of a man,
A gaze blank and pitiless as the sun,   15
Is moving its slow thighs, while all about it
Reel shadows of the indignant desert birds.
The darkness drops again; but now I know
That twenty centuries of stony sleep
Were vexed to nightmare by a rocking cradle,   20

---

19 **perne in a gyre** descend in a spiral; the gyre for Yeats was a private symbol of historical cycles
1 **gyre** see note to "Sailing to Byzantium"   12 **Spiritus Mundi** World-Spirit

And what rough beast, its hour come round at last,
Slouches towards Bethlehem to be born?

—1921

The Song of Wandering Aengus°

I went out to the hazel wood,
Because a fire was in my head,
And cut and peeled a hazel wand,
And hooked a berry to a thread;
And when white moths were on the wing,   5
And moth-like stars were flickering out,
I dropped the berry in a stream
And caught a little silver trout.

When I had laid it on the floor
I went to blow the fire aflame,   10
But something rustled on the floor,
And some one called me by my name:
It had become a glimmering girl
With apple blossom in her hair
Who called me by my name and ran   15
And faded through the brightening air.

Though I am old with wandering
Through hollow lands and hilly lands,
I will find out where she has gone,
And kiss her lips and take her hands;   20
And walk among long dappled grass,
And pluck till time and times are done
The silver apples of the moon,
The golden apples of the sun.

—1899

EDWIN ARLINGTON ROBINSON   1869–1935

Robinson's poems set in "Tilbury," a re-creation of his hometown of
Gardiner, Maine, continue to present readers with a memorable cast
of eccentric characters who somehow manifest universal human
desires. Robinson languished in poverty and obscurity for many

---

Aengus Among the Sidhe (Native Irish Deities), the god of youth, love, beauty, and poetry.
Yeats once also called him the "Master of Love." Here, however, he seems a mortal.

years before his reputation began to flourish as a result of the interest taken in his work by President Theodore Roosevelt, who obtained a government job for Robinson and wrote a favorable review of one of his books.

Firelight

Ten years together without yet a cloud,
They seek each other's eyes at intervals
Of gratefulness to firelight and four walls
For love's obliteration of the crowd.
Serenely and perennially endowed   5
And bowered as few may be, their joy recalls
No snake, no sword, and over them there falls
The blessing of what neither says aloud.

Wiser for silence, they were not so glad
Were she to read the graven° tale of lines   10
On the wan face of one somewhere alone;
Nor were they more content could he have had
Her thoughts a moment since of one who shines
Apart, and would be hers if he had known.

                                        —1920

Eros Turannos°

She fears him, and will always ask
    What fated her to choose him;
She meets in his engaging mask
    All reasons to refuse him
But what she meets and what she fears   5
Are less than are the downward years,
Drawn slowly to the foamless weirs
    Of age, were she to lose him.

Between a blurred sagacity
    That once had power to sound him,   10
And Love, that will not let him be
    The Judas that she found him,
Her pride assuages her almost,
As if it were alone the cost.—
He sees that he will not be lost,   15
    And waits and looks around him.

---

10 graven engraved
Eros Turannos "Love, the Tyrant"

A sense of ocean and old trees
    Envelops and allures him;
Tradition, touching all he sees,
    Beguiles and reassures him;   20
And all her doubts of what he says
Are dimmed with what she knows of days—
Till even prejudice delays
    And fades, and she secures him.

The falling leaf inaugurates   25
    The reign of her confusion;
The pounding wave reverberates
    The dirge of her illusion;
And home, where passion lived and died
Becomes a place where she can hide,   30
While all the town and harbor side
    Vibrate with her seclusion.

We tell you, tapping on our brows,
    The story as it should be,—
As if the story of a house   35
    Were told, or ever could be;
We'll have no kindly veil between
Her visions and those we have seen,—
As if we guessed what hers have been,
    Or what they are or would be.   40

Meanwhile we do no harm; for they
    That with a god have striven,
Not hearing much of what we say
    Take what the god has given;
Though like waves breaking it may be   45
Or like a changed familiar tree,
Or like a stairway to the sea
    Where down the blind are driven.

        —1916

The Mill

The miller's wife had waited long,
    The tea was cold, the fire was dead;
And there might yet be nothing wrong
    In how he went and what he said:
"There are no millers any more,"   5
    Was all that she had heard him say;

And he had lingered at the door
   So long that it seemed yesterday.

Sick with a fear that had no form
   She knew that she was there at last;   10
And in the mill there was a warm
   And mealy fragrance of the past.
What else there was would only seem
   To say again what he had meant;
And what was hanging from a beam   15
   Would not have heeded where she went.

And if she thought it followed her,
   She may have reasoned in the dark
That one way of the few there were
   Would hide her and would leave no mark: 20
Black water, smooth above the weir
   Like starry velvet in the night,
Though ruffled once, would soon appear
   The same as ever to the sight.

                                           —1920

Richard Cory

Whenever Richard Cory went down town,
We people on the pavement looked at him:
He was a gentleman from sole to crown,
Clean favored, and imperially slim.

And he was always quietly arrayed,   5
And he was always human when he talked;
But still he fluttered pulses when he said,
"Good-morning," and he glittered when he walked.

And he was rich—yes, richer than a king—
And admirably schooled in every grace: 10
In fine, we thought that he was everything
To make us wish that we were in his place.

So on we worked, and waited for the light,
And went without the meat, and cursed the bread;
And Richard Cory, one calm summer night,   15
Went home and put a bullet through his head.

                                           —1896

Stephen Crane   1871–1900

The brilliant young journalist who wrote *The Red Badge of Courage*
was also an unconventional poet whose skeptical epigrams and fables
today seem far ahead of their time. In many ways he mirrors the cos-
mic pessimism of contemporaries like Hardy, Housman, and
Robinson, all of whom were influenced by the currents of
Determinism that ran so strongly at the end of the nineteenth
century.

The Black Riders

VI

God fashioned the ship of the world carefully.
With the infinite skill of an All-Master
Made He the hull and the sails,
Held He the rudder
Ready for adjustment.   5
Erect stood He, scanning His work proudly.
Then—at fateful time—a wrong called,
And God turned, heeding.
Lo, the ship, at this opportunity, slipped slyly,
Making cunning noiseless travel down the ways.   10
So that, for ever rudderless, it went upon the seas
Going ridiculous voyages,
Making quaint progress,
Turning as with serious purpose
Before stupid winds.   15
And there were many in the sky
Who laughed at this thing.

—1895

War Is Kind

XXI

A man said to the universe:
"Sir, I exist!"
"However," replied the universe,
"The fact has not created in me
A sense of obligation."   5

—1899

Paul Laurence Dunbar 1872–1906

A native of Dayton, Ohio, Dunbar was one of the first black poets to make a mark in American literature. Many of his dialect poems reflect a sentimentalized view of life in the South, which he did not know directly. However, he was also capable of powerful expressions of racial protest.

We Wear the Mask

We wear the mask that grins and lies,
It hides our cheeks and shades our eyes,—
This debt we pay to human guile;
With torn and bleeding hearts we smile,
And mouth with myriad subtleties.   5

Why should the world be over-wise,
In counting all our tears and sighs?
Nay, let them only see us, while
    We wear the mask.

We smile, but, O great Christ, our cries   10
To thee from tortured souls arise.
We sing, but oh the clay is vile
Beneath our feet, and long the mile;
But let the world dream otherwise,
    We wear the mask!   15

—1896

Robert Frost 1874–1963

During the second half of his long life, Frost was a public figure who attained a popularity unmatched by any American poet of this century. His reading at the inauguration of John F. Kennedy in 1961 capped an impressive career that included four Pulitzer Prizes. Unattracted by the more exotic aspects of modernism, Frost nevertheless remains a poet who speaks eloquently to contemporary uncertainties about humanity's place in a universe that does not seem to care much for its existence. While Frost is rarely directly an autobiographical poet ("The Road Not Taken" was intended to be about a friend, English poet Edward Thomas), his work always bears the stamp of his powerful personality and identification with the New England landscape.

Acquainted with the Night

I have been one acquainted with the night.
I have walked out in rain—and back in rain.
I have outwalked the furthest city light.

I have looked down the saddest city lane.
I have passed by the watchman on his beat   5
And dropped my eyes, unwilling to explain.

I have stood still and stopped the sound of feet
When far away an interrupted cry
Came over houses from another street,

But not to call me back or say good-bye;   10
And further still at an unearthly height
One luminary clock against the sky

Proclaimed the time was neither wrong nor right.
I have been one acquainted with the night.

                                                      —1928

After Apple-Picking

My long two-pointed ladder's sticking through a tree
Toward heaven still,
And there's a barrel that I didn't fill
Beside it, and there may be two or three
Apples I didn't pick upon some bough.   5
But I am done with apple-picking now.
Essence of winter sleep is on the night,
The scent of apples: I am drowsing off.
I cannot rub the strangeness from my sight
I got from looking through a pane of glass   10
I skimmed this morning from the drinking trough
And held against the world of hoary grass.
It melted, and I let it fall and break.
But I was well
Upon my way to sleep before it fell,   15
And I could tell
What form my dreaming was about to take.
Magnified apples appear and disappear,
Stem end and blossom end,
And every fleck of russet showing clear.   20

My instep arch not only keeps the ache,
It keeps the pressure of a ladder-round.
I feel the ladder sway as the boughs bend.
And I keep hearing from the cellar bin
The rumbling sound   25
Of load on load of apples coming in.
For I have had too much
Of apple-picking: I am overtired
Of the great harvest I myself desired.
There were ten thousand thousand fruit to touch,   30
Cherish in hand, lift down, and not let fall.
For all
That struck the earth,
No matter if not bruised or spiked with stubble,
Went surely to the cider-apple heap   35
As of no worth.
One can see what will trouble
This sleep of mine, whatever sleep it is.
Were he not gone,
The woodchuck could say whether it's like his   40
Long sleep, as I describe its coming on,
Or just some human sleep.

                                                        —1914

Come In

As I came to the edge of the woods,
Thrush music—hark!
Now if it was dusk outside,
Inside it was dark.

Too dark in the woods for a bird   5
By sleight of wing
To better its perch for the night,
Though it still could sing.

The last of the light of the sun
That had died in the west   10
Still lived for one song more
In a thrush's breast.

Far in the pillared dark
Thrush music went—
Almost like a call to come in   15
To the dark and lament.

But no, I was out for stars:
I would not come in.
I meant not even if asked,
And I hadn't been.

                                                    —1941

Design

I found a dimpled spider, fat and white,
On a white heal-all,° holding up a moth
Like a white piece of rigid satin cloth—
Assorted characters of death and blight
Mixed ready to begin the morning right,   5
Like the ingredients of a witches' broth—
A snow-drop spider, a flower like a froth,
And dead wings carried like a paper kite.

What had that flower to do with being white,
The wayside blue and innocent heal-all?   10
What brought the kindred spider to that height,
Then steered the white moth thither in the night?
What but design of darkness to appall?—
If design govern in a thing so small.

                                                    —1936

Home Burial

He saw her from the bottom of the stairs
Before she saw him. She was starting down,
Looking back over her shoulder at some fear.
She took a doubtful step and then undid it
To raise herself and look again. He spoke   5
Advancing toward her: "What is it you see
From up there always?—for I want to know."
She turned and sank upon her skirts at that,
And her face changed from terrified to dull.
He said to gain time: "What is it you see?"   10
Mounting until she cowered under him.
"I will find out now—you must tell me, dear."
She, in her place, refused him any help,
With the least stiffening of her neck and silence.
She let him look, sure that he wouldn't see,   15
Blind creature; and awhile he didn't see.
But at last he murmured, "Oh," and again, "Oh."

---

2 **heal-all** a wildflower, usually blue

"What is it—what?" she said.

"Just that I see."

"You don't," she challenged. "Tell me what it is."

"The wonder is I didn't see at once   20
I never noticed it from here before.
I must be wonted to it—that's the reason.
The little graveyard where my people are!
So small the window frames the whole of it.
Not so much larger than a bedroom, is it?   25
There are three stones of slate and one of marble,
Broad-shouldered little slabs there in the sunlight
On the sidehill. We haven't to mind *those*.
But I understand: it is not the stones,
But the child's mound—"

                         "Don't, don't, don't, don't," she cried.   30

She withdrew, shrinking from beneath his arm
That rested on the banister, and slid downstairs;
And turned on him with such a daunting look,
He said twice over before he knew himself:
"Can't a man speak of his own child he's lost?"   35

"Not you!—Oh, where's my hat? Oh, I don't need it!
I must get out of here. I must get air.—
I don't know rightly whether any man can."

"Amy! Don't go to someone else this time.
Listen to me. I won't come down the stairs."   40
He sat and fixed his chin between his fists.
"There's something I should like to ask you, dear."

"You don't know how to ask it."

                         "Help me, then."

Her fingers moved the latch for all reply.

"My words are nearly always an offense.   45
I don't know how to speak of anything
So as to please you. But I might be taught,
I should suppose. I can't say I see how.
A man must partly give up being a man

With womenfolk. We could have some arrangement   50
By which I'd bind myself to keep hands off
Anything special you're a-mind to name.
Though I don't like such things 'twixt those that love.
Two that don't love can't live together without them.
But two that do can't live together with them."   55
She moved the latch a little. "Don't—don't go.
Don't carry it to someone else this time.
Tell me about it if it's something human.
Let me into your grief. I'm not so much
Unlike other folks as your standing there   60
Apart would make me out. Give me my chance.
I do think, though, you overdo it a little.
What was it brought you up to think it the thing
To take your mother-loss of a first child
So inconsolably—in the face of love.   65
You'd think his memory might be satisfied—"

"There you go sneering now!"

                    "I'm not, I'm not!
You make me angry. I'll come down to you.
God, what a woman! And it's come to this,
A man can't speak of his own child that's dead."   70

"You can't because you don't know how to speak.
If you had any feelings, you that dug
With your own hand—how could you?—his little grave;
I saw you from that very window there,
Making the gravel leap and leap in air,   75
Leap up, like that, like that, and land so lightly
And roll back down the mound beside the hole.
I thought, Who is that man? I didn't know you.
And I crept down the stairs and up the stairs
To look again, and still your spade kept lifting.   80
Then you came in. I heard your rumbling voice
Out in the kitchen, and I don't know why,
But I went near to see with my own eyes.
You could sit there with the stains on your shoes
Of the fresh earth from your own baby's grave   85
And talk about your everyday concerns.
You had stood the spade up against the wall
Outside there in the entry, for I saw it."

"I shall laugh the worst laugh I ever laughed.
I'm cursed. God, if I don't believe I'm cursed."   90

"I can repeat the very words you were saying:
'Three foggy mornings and one rainy day
Will rot the best birch fence a man can build.'
Think of it, talk like that at such a time!
What had how long it takes a birch to rot   95
To do with what was in the darkened parlor?
You *couldn't* care! The nearest friends can go
With anyone to death, comes so far short
They might as well not try to go at all.
No, from the time when one is sick to death,   100
One is alone, and he dies more alone.
Friends make pretense of following to the grave,
But before one is in it, their minds are turned
And making the best of their way back to life
And living people, and things they understand.   105
But the world's evil. I won't have grief so
If I can change it. Oh, I won't, I won't!"

"There, you have said it all and you feel better.
You won't go now. You're crying. Close the door.
The heart's gone out of it: why keep it up?   110
Amy! There's someone coming down the road!"

"*You*—oh, you think the talk is all. I must go—
Somewhere out of this house. How can I make you—"

"If—you—do!" She was opening the door wider.
"Where do you mean to go? First tell me that.   115
I'll follow and bring you back by force. I *will!*—"

                                                     —1914

Stopping by Woods on a Snowy Evening

Whose woods these are I think I know.
His house is in the village though;
He will not see me stopping here
To watch his woods fill up with snow.

My little horse must think it queer   5
To stop without a farmhouse near
Between the woods and frozen lake
The darkest evening of the year.

He gives his harness bells a shake
To ask if there is some mistake.   10
The only other sound's the sweep
Of easy wind and downy flake.

The woods are lovely, dark and deep,
But I have promises to keep,
And miles to go before I sleep,   15
And miles to go before I sleep.

                                                    —1923

WALLACE STEVENS   1879-1955

A lawyer specializing in surety bonds, Stevens rose to be a vice-president of the Hartford Accident and Indemnity Company. His poetry was collected for the first time in *Harmonium* when he was forty-five, and, while he published widely during his lifetime, his poetry was only slowly recognized as the work of a major modernist whose originality has not been surpassed. Stevens's idea of poetry as a force taking the place of religion has had a profound influence on poets and critics of this century.

Anecdote of the Jar

I placed a jar in Tennessee,
And round it was, upon a hill.
It made the slovenly wilderness
Surround that hill.

The wilderness rose up to it,   5
And sprawled around, no longer wild.
The jar was round upon the ground
And tall and of a port in air.

It took dominion everywhere.
The jar was gray and bare.   10
It did not give of bird or bush,
Like nothing else in Tennessee.

                                                    —1923

Disillusionment of Ten O'Clock

The houses are haunted
By white night-gowns.

None are green,
Or purple with green rings,
Or green with yellow rings,   5
Or yellow with blue rings.
None of them are strange,
With socks of lace
And beaded ceintures.°
People are not going   10
To dream of baboons and periwinkles.°
Only, here and there, an old sailor,
Drunk and asleep in his boots,
Catches tigers
In red weather.   15

                                              —1923

The Snow Man

One must have a mind of winter
To regard the frost and the boughs
Of the pine-trees crusted with snow;

And have been cold a long time
To behold the junipers shagged with ice,   5
The spruces rough in the distant glitter

Of the January sun; and not to think
Of any misery in the sound of the wind,
In the sound of a few leaves,

Which is the sound of the land   10
Full of the same wind
That is blowing in the same bare place

For the listener, who listens in the snow,
And, nothing himself, beholds
Nothing that is not there and the nothing that is.   15

                                              —1923

Sunday Morning

I

Complacencies of the peignoir,° and late
Coffee and oranges in a sunny chair,

---

9 **ceintures** sashes   11 **periwinkles** either wildflowers or small mollusks
1 **peignoir** woman's dressing gown

And the green freedom of a cockatoo
Upon a rug mingle to dissipate
The holy hush of ancient sacrifice.   5
She dreams a little, and she feels the dark
Encroachment of that old catastrophe,
As a calm darkens among water-lights.
The pungent oranges and bright, green wings
Seem things in some procession of the dead,   10
Winding across wide water, without sound.
The day is like wide water, without sound,
Stilled for the passing of her dreaming feet
Over the seas, to silent Palestine,
Dominion of the blood and sepulchre.   15

II
Why should she give her bounty to the dead?
What is divinity if it can come
Only in silent shadows and in dreams?
Shall she not find in comforts of the sun,
In pungent fruit and bright, green wings, or else   20
In any balm or beauty of the earth,
Things to be cherished like the thought of heaven?
Divinity must live within herself:
Passions of rain, or moods in falling snow;
Grievings in loneliness, or unsubdued   25
Elations when the forest blooms; gusty
Emotions on wet roads on autumn nights;
All pleasures and all pains, remembering
The bough of summer and the winter branch.
These are the measures destined for her soul.   30

III
Jove° in the clouds had his inhuman birth.
No mother suckled him, no sweet land gave
Large-mannered motions to his mythy mind.
He moved among us, as a muttering king,
Magnificent, would move among his hinds,°   35
Until our blood, commingling, virginal,
With heaven, brought such requital to desire
The very hinds discerned it, in a star.
Shall our blood fail? Or shall it come to be
The blood of paradise? And shall the earth   40
Seem all of paradise that we shall know?

---

31 **Jove** Roman name of Zeus   35 **hinds** inferiors or shepherds (see 1. 38)

The sky will be much friendlier then than now,
A part of labor and a part of pain,
And next in glory to enduring love,
Not this dividing and indifferent blue.   45

IV

She says, "I am content when wakened birds,
Before they fly, test the reality
Of misty fields, by their sweet questionings;
But when the birds are gone, and their warm fields
Return no more, where, then, is paradise?"   50
There is not any haunt of prophecy,
Nor any old chimera° of the grave,
Neither the golden underground, nor isle
Melodious, where spirits gat them home,
Nor visionary south, nor cloudy palm   55
Remote on heaven's hill, that has endured
As April's green endures; or will endure
Like her remembrance of awakened birds,
Or her desire for June and evening, tipped
By the consummation of the swallow's wings.   60

V

She says, "But in contentment I still feel
The need of some imperishable bliss."
Death is the mother of beauty; hence from her,
Alone, shall come fulfilment to our dreams
And our desires. Although she strews the leaves   65
Of sure obliteration on our paths,
The path sick sorrow took, the many paths
Where triumph rang its brassy phrase, or love
Whispered a little out of tenderness,
She makes the willow shiver in the sun   70
For maidens who were wont to sit and gaze
Upon the grass, relinquished to their feet.
She causes boys to pile new plums and pears
On disregarded plate. The maidens taste
And stray impassioned in the littering leaves.   75

VI

Is there no change of death in paradise?
Does ripe fruit never fall? Or do the boughs
Hang always heavy in that perfect sky,

---

52 chimera imagined monster

Unchanging, yet so like our perishing earth,
With rivers like our own that seek for seas   80
They never find, the same receding shores
That never touch with inarticulate pang?
Why set the pear upon those river-banks
Or spice the shores with odors of the plum?
Alas, that they should wear our colors there,   85
The silken weavings of our afternoons,
And pick the strings of our insipid lutes!
Death is the mother of beauty, mystical,
Within whose burning bosom we devise
Our earthly mothers waiting, sleeplessly.   90

VII

Supple and turbulent, a ring of men
Shall chant in orgy on a summer morn
Their boisterous devotion to the sun,
Not as a god, but as a god might be,
Naked among them, like a savage source.   95
Their chant shall be a chant of paradise,
Out of their blood, returning to the sky;
And in their chant shall enter, voice by voice,
The windy lake wherein their lord delights,
The trees, like serafin,° and echoing hills,   100
That choir among themselves long afterward.
They shall know well the heavenly fellowship
Of men that perish and of summer morn.
And whence they came and whither they shall go
The dew upon their feet shall manifest.   105

VIII

She hears, upon that water without sound,
A voice that cries, "The tomb in Palestine
Is not the porch of spirits lingering.
It is the grave of Jesus, where he lay."
We live in an old chaos of the sun,   110
Or old dependency of day and night,
Or island solitude, unsponsored, free,
Of that wide water, inescapable.
Deer walk upon our mountains, and the quail
Whistle about us their spontaneous cries;   115
Sweet berries ripen in the wilderness;
And, in the isolation of the sky,

---

100 serafin seraphim, a type of angel

At evening, casual flocks of pigeons make
Ambiguous undulations as they sink,
Downward to darkness, on extended wings.   120

                                              —1923

WILLIAM CARLOS WILLIAMS   1883-1963

Like his friend Wallace Stevens, Williams followed an unconventional career, working until his death as a pediatrician in Rutherford, New Jersey. Williams is modern poetry's greatest proponent of the American idiom. His plainspoken poems have been more widely imitated than those of any other American poet of this century, perhaps because he represents a homegrown modernist alternative to the intellectualized Europeanism of Eliot and Ezra Pound (a friend of his from college days). In his later years Williams assisted many younger poets, among them Allen Ginsberg, for whose controversial book *Howl* he wrote an introduction.

The Last Words of My English Grandmother

There were some dirty plates
and a glass of milk
beside her on a small table
near the rank, disheveled bed—

Wrinkled and nearly blind   5
she lay and snored
rousing with anger in her tones
to cry for food,

Gimme something to eat—
They're starving me—   10
I'm all right—I won't go
to the hospital. No, no, no

Give me something to eat!
Let me take you
to the hospital, I said   15
and after you are well

you can do as you please.
She smiled, Yes

you do what you please first
then I can do what I please—   20

Oh, oh, oh! she cried
as the ambulance men lifted
her to the stretcher—
Is this what you call

making me comfortable?   25
By now her mind was clear—
Oh you think you're smart
you young people,

she said, but I'll tell you
you don't know anything.   30
Then we started.
On the way

We passed a long row
of elms. She looked at them
awhile out of   35
the ambulance window and said,

What are all those
fuzzy-looking things out there?
Trees? Well, I'm tired
of them and rolled her head away.   40

                                        —1920

The Red Wheelbarrow

so much depends
upon

a red wheel
barrow

glazed with rain   5
water

beside the white
chickens.

                                        —1923

Spring and All

By the road to the contagious hospital°
under the surge of the blue
mottled clouds driven from the
northeast—a cold wind. Beyond, the
waste of broad, muddy fields   5
brown with dried weeds, standing and fallen

patches of standing water
the scattering of tall trees

All along the road the reddish
purplish, forked, upstanding, twiggy   10
stuff of bushes and small trees
with dead, brown leaves under them
leafless vines—

Lifeless in appearance, sluggish
dazed spring approaches—   15

They enter the new world naked,
cold, uncertain of all
save that they enter. All about them
the cold, familiar wind—

Now the grass, tomorrow   20
the stiff curl of wildcarrot leaf
One by one objects are defined—
It quickens: clarity, outline of leaf

But now the stark dignity of
entrance—Still, the profound change   25
has come upon them: rooted, they
grip down and begin to awaken

                                               —1923

E zra P ound   1885–1972

Pound was the greatest international proponent of modern poetry.
Born in Idaho and reared in Philadelphia, he emigrated to England

---

1 **contagious hospital** a hospital for quarantined patients

in 1909, where he befriended Yeats, promoted the early work of Frost, and discovered Eliot. Pound's early promotion of the Imagist movement assisted a number of important poetic principles and reputations, including those of H. D. (Hilda Doolittle) and, later, William Carlos Williams. Pound's support of Mussolini during World War II, expressed in controversial radio broadcasts, caused him to be held for over a decade after the war as a mental patient in the United States, after which he returned to Italy for the final years of his long and controversial life.

In a Station of the Metro

The apparition of these faces in the crowd;
Petals on a wet, black bough.

—1916

The River-Merchant's Wife: A Letter°

While my hair was still cut straight across my forehead
I played about the front gate, pulling flowers.
You came by on bamboo stilts, playing horse,
You walked about my seat, playing with blue plums.
And we went on living in the village of Chokan: 5
Two small people, without dislike or suspicion.
At fourteen I married My Lord you.
I never laughed, being bashful.
Lowering my head, I looked at the wall.
Called to, a thousand times, I never looked back.   10

At fifteen I stopped scowling,
I desired my dust to be mingled with yours
Forever and forever and forever.
Why should I climb the lookout?

At sixteen you departed,   15
You went into far Ku-to-yen, by the river of swirling eddies,
And you have been gone five months.
The monkeys make sorrowful noise overhead.

You dragged your feet when you went out.
By the gate now, the moss is grown, the different mosses,   20
Too deep to clear them away!

The River-Merchant's Wife: A Letter translation of a poem by Li-Po (A.D. 701-762)

The leaves fall early this autumn, in wind.
The paired butterflies are already yellow with August
Over the grass in the West garden;
They hurt me. I grow older.   25
If you are coming down through the narrows of the river Kiang,
Please let me know beforehand,
And I will come out to meet you
    As far as Cho-Fu-Sa.

                                                            —1915

Sestina: Altaforte

LOQUITUR:° En Bertrans de Born.°
Dante Alighieri put this man in hell for that he was a stirrer up of strife.
Eccovi!°
Judge ye!
Have I dug him up again?
The scene is at his castle, Altaforte. "Papiols" is his jongleur.°
"The Leopard," the device of Richard Cœur de Lion.°

I
Damn it all! all this our South stinks peace.
You whoreson dog, Papiols, come! Let's to music!
I have no life save when the swords clash.
But ah! when I see the standards gold, vair,° purple, opposing
And the broad fields beneath them turn crimson,   5
Then howl I my heart nigh mad with rejoicing.

II
In hot summer have I great rejoicing
When the tempests kill the earth's foul peace,
And the lightnings from black heav'n flash crimson,
And the fierce thunders roar me their music   10
And the winds shriek through the clouds mad, opposing,
And through all the riven skies God's swords clash.

III
Hell grant soon we hear again the swords clash!
And the shrill neighs of destriers° in battle rejoicing,
Spiked breast to spiked breast opposing!   15
Better one hour's stour° than a year's peace
With fat boards, bawds, wine and frail music!
Bah! there's no wine like the blood's crimson!

Loquitur speaker Bertrans de Born Provençal poet and soldier (1140-1209) Eccovi! Behold!
jongleur minstrel Richard Cœur de Lion Richard I of England, the Lion-Hearted (1157-
1199) 4 vair fur used in heraldry 14 destriers war-horses 16 stour combat

IV

And I love to see the sun rise blood-crimson.
And I watch his spears through the dark clash   20
And it fills all my heart with rejoicing
And pries wide my mouth with fast music
When I see him so scorn and defy peace,
His lone might 'gainst all darkness opposing.

V

The man who fears war and squats opposing   25
My words for stour, hath no blood of crimson
But is fit only to rot in womanish peace
Far from where worth's won and the swords clash
For the death of such sluts I go rejoicing;
Yea, I fill all the air with my music.   30

VI

Papiols, Papiols, to the music!
There's no sound like to swords swords opposing,
No cry like the battle's rejoicing
When our elbows and swords drip the crimson
And our charges 'gainst "The Leopard's" rush clash.   35
May God damn for ever all who cry "Peace!"

VII

And let the music of the swords make them crimson!
Hell grant soon we hear again the swords clash!
Hell blot black for alway the thought "Peace"!

—1909

ELINOR WYLIE   1885–1928

The considerable lyrical skills of Elinor Wylie, which found wide
popularity during her relatively brief career, have only recently come
to the notice of the present generation. For many readers in the post-
World War I era, Wylie, along with her slightly younger contemporary Edna St. Vincent Millay, helped to define the literary role of the
New Woman of the 1920s. A poetic traditionalist whose lifestyle was
thoroughly modern, Wylie now seems overdue for a serious reassess-
ment of her place in the development of twentieth-century women's
poetry.

Let No Charitable Hope

Now let no charitable hope
Confuse my mind with images

Of eagle and of antelope:
I am in nature none of these.

I was, being human, born alone;   5
I am, being woman, hard beset;
I live by squeezing from a stone
The little nourishment I get.

In masks outrageous and austere
The years go by in single file;   10
But none has merited my fear,
And none has quite escaped my smile.

                                                    —1923

H. D. (HILDA DOOLITTLE)   1886–1961

Born in Bethlehem, Pennsylvania, Hilda Doolittle was a college
friend of both Williams and Pound, and moved to Europe permanently in 1911. With her husband Richard Aldington, H. D. was
an important member of the Imagist group promoted by Pound.

Pear Tree

Silver dust,
lifted from the earth,
higher than my arms reach,
you have mounted,
O, silver,   5
higher than my arms reach,
you front us with great mass;

no flower ever opened
so staunch a white leaf,
no flower ever parted silver   10
from such rare silver;

O, white pear,
your flower-tufts
thick on the branch
bring summer and ripe fruits   15
in their purple hearts.

                                                    —1916

SIEGFRIED SASSOON   1886-1967

A decorated hero who publicly denounced World War I, Sassoon was a friend and supporter of other British war poets, including Robert Graves and Wilfred Owen. His sardonic, anti-heroic war poems owe much to Thomas Hardy, whom he acknowledged as his chief poetic influence.

Dreamers

Soldiers are citizens of death's grey land,
    Drawing no dividend from time's tomorrows.
In the great hour of destiny they stand,
    Each with his feuds, and jealousies, and sorrows.

Soldiers are sworn to action; they must win   5
    Some flaming, fatal climax with their lives.
Soldiers are dreamers, when the guns begin
    They think of firelit homes, clean beds, and wives.

I see them in foul dug-outs, gnawed by rats,
    And in the ruined trenches, lashed with rain,   10
Dreaming of things they did with balls and bats,
    And mocked by hopeless longing to regain
Bank-holidays, and picture shows, and spats,
    And going to the office in the train.

                                                      —1918

ROBINSON JEFFERS   1887-1962

Jeffers lived with his wife and children for many years in Carmel, California, in a rock tower that he built himself by the sea. Many of his ideas about man's small place in the larger world of nature have gained in relevance through the years since his death. Largely forgotten for many years, his poetry, particularly his book-length verse narratives, is once more regaining the attention of serious readers.

The Purse-Seine°

Our sardine fishermen work at night in the dark of the moon;
    daylight or moonlight

Purse-Seine large circular fishing net; the bottom is closed (or pursed) before it is hauled in

They could not tell where to spread the net, unable to see the
    phosphorescence of the shoals of fish.
They work northward from Monterey, coasting Santa Cruz; off
    New Year's Point or off Pigeon Point
The look-out man will see some lakes of milk-color light on the
    sea's night-purple; he points, and the helmsman
Turns the dark prow, the motorboat circles the gleaming shoal and
    drifts out her seine-net. They close the circle   5
and purse the bottom of the net, then with great labor haul it in.

                                            I cannot tell you
How beautiful the scene is, and a little terrible, then, when the
    crowded fish
Know they are caught, and wildly beat from one wall to the other
    of their closing destiny the phosphorescent
Water to a pool of flame, each beautiful slender body sheeted with
    flame, like a live rocket   10
A comet's tail wake of clear yellow flame; while outside the
    narrowing
Floats and cordage of the net great sea-lions come up to watch,
    sighing in the dark; the vast walls of night
Stand erect to the stars.

                        Lately I was looking from a night mountain-top
On a wide city, the colored splendor, galaxies of light: how could
    I help but recall the seine-net   15
Gathering the luminous fish? I cannot tell you how beautiful the
    city appeared, and a little terrible.
I thought, We have geared the machines and locked all together
    into interdependence; we have built the great cities; now
There is no escape. We have gathered vast populations incapable
    of free survival, insulated
From the strong earth, each person in himself helpless, on all
    dependent. The circle is closed, and the net
Is being hauled in. They hardly feel the cords drawing, yet they
    shine already. The inevitable mass-disasters   20
Will not come in our time nor in our children's, but we and our
    children
Must watch the net draw narrower, government take all powers—
    or revolution, and the new government
Take more than all, add to kept bodies kept souls—or anarchy,
    the mass-disasters.

                        These things are Progress;
Do you marvel our verse is troubled or frowning, while it keeps
    its reason? Or it lets go, lets the mood flow   25

In the manner of the recent young men into mere hysteria, splin-
tered gleams, crackled laughter. But they are quite wrong.
There is no reason for amazement: surely one always knew that
cultures decay, and life's end is death.

                                                          —1937

Marianne Moore   1887–1972

Moore called her own work poetry—unconventional and marked
with the stamp of a rare personality—because, as she put it, there was
no other category for it. For four years she was editor of the *Dial*, one
of the chief modernist periodicals. Moore's wide range of reference,
which can leap from the commonplace to the wondrous in a single
poem, reflects her unique set of personal interests—which can range
from natural species to baseball in a single poem.

Poetry

I, too, dislike it: there are things that are important beyond all
         this fiddle.
   Reading it, however, with a perfect contempt for it, one
         discovers in
   it after all, a place for the genuine.   5
      Hands that can grasp, eyes
      that can dilate, hair that can rise
         if it must, these things are important not because a

high-sounding interpretation can be put upon them but because
         they are   10
   useful. When they become so derivative as to become
         unintelligible,
   the same thing may be said for all of us, that we
      do not admire what
      we cannot understand: the bat   15
         holding on upside down or in quest of something to

eat, elephants pushing, a wild horse taking a roll, a tireless wolf
         under
   a tree, the immovable critic twitching his skin like a horse that
         feels a flea, the base-   20
      ball fan, the statistician—
      nor is it valid
         to discriminate against 'business documents and

school-books'; all these phenomena are important. One must make
        a distinction   25
    however: when dragged into prominence by half poets, the
        result is not poetry,
    nor till the poets among us can be
        'literalists of
        the imagination'—above   30
            insolence and triviality and can present

for inspection, 'imaginary gardens with real toads in them,' shall
        we have
    it. In the meantime, if you demand on the one hand,
    the raw material of poetry in   35
        all its rawness and
        that which is on the other hand
            genuine, you are interested in poetry.

                                                            —1921

Silence

My father used to say,
"Superior people never make long visits,
have to be shown Longfellow's grave
or the glass flowers at Harvard.
Self-reliant like the cat—   5
that takes its prey to privacy,
the mouse's limp tail hanging like a shoelace from its mouth—
they sometimes enjoy solitude
and can be robbed of speech
by speech which has delighted them.   10
The deepest feeling always shows itself in silence;
not in silence, but restraint."
Nor was he insincere in saying, "Make my house your inn."
Inns are not residences.

                                                            —1935

T. S. ELIOT   1888-1965

As the author of The Waste Land, one of the most famous and difficult modernist poems, Eliot became an international figure. Born in
St. Louis and educated at Harvard, he moved to London in 1914,
where he remained for the rest of his life, becoming a British subject
in 1927. This chief prophet of modern despair turned to the Church
of England in later life, and wrote successful dramas on religious
themes. As a critic and influential editor, Eliot dominated poetic

taste in England and America for over twenty-five years. He was
awarded the Nobel Prize in 1948.

Journey of the Magi°

'A cold coming we had of it,
Just the worst time of the year
For a journey, and such a long journey:
The ways deep and the weather sharp,
The very dead of winter.'°   5
And the camels galled, sore-footed, refractory,
Lying down in the melting snow.
There were times we regretted
The summer palaces on slopes, the terraces,
And the silken girls bringing sherbet.   10
Then the camel men cursing and grumbling
And running away, and wanting their liquor and women,
And the night-fires going out, and the lack of shelters,
And the cities hostile and the towns unfriendly
And the villages dirty and charging high prices: 15
A hard time we had of it.
At the end we preferred to travel all night,
Sleeping in snatches,
With the voices singing in our ears, saying
That this was all folly.   20

Then at dawn we came down to a temperate valley,
Wet, below the snow line, smelling of vegetation;
With a running stream and a water-mill beating the darkness,
And three trees on the low sky.
And an old white horse galloped away in the meadow.   25
Then we came to a tavern with vine-leaves over the lintel,
Six hands at an open door dicing for pieces of silver,
And feet kicking the empty wine-skins.
But there was no information, and so we continued
And arrived at evening, not a moment too soon   30
Finding the place; it was (you may say) satisfactory.

All this was a long time ago, I remember,
And I would do it again, but set down
This° set down
This: were we led all that way for   35

Magi Wise Men mentioned in Matthew 2:1-2   **1-5** 'A cold . . . winter' The quotation marks
indicated Eliot's source, a sermon by Lancelot Andrewes (1555-1626).   **33-34** set down . . .
This The Magus is dictating his memoirs to a scribe

Birth or Death? There was a Birth, certainly,
We had evidence and no doubt. I had seen birth and death,
But had thought they were different; this Birth was
Hard and bitter agony for us, like Death, our death.
We returned to our places, these Kingdoms,   40
But no longer at ease here, in the old dispensation,°
With an alien people clutching their gods.
I should be glad of another death.

                                                          —1927

The Love Song of J. Alfred Prufrock

> S'io credesse che mia risposta fosse
> A persona che mai tornasse al mondo,
> Questa fiamma staria senza più scosse.
> Ma perciocche giammai di questo fondo
> Non tornò vivo alcun, s'i'odo il vero,
> Senza tema d'infamia ti rispondo.°

Let us go then, you° and I,
When the evening is spread out against the sky
Like a patient etherised upon a table;
Let us go, through certain half-deserted streets,
The muttering retreats   5
Of restless nights in one-night cheap hotels
And sawdust restaurants with oyster-shells:
Streets that follow like a tedious argument
Of insidious intent
To lead you to an overwhelming question . . .   10
Oh, do not ask, "What is it?"
Let us go and make our visit.

In the room the women come and go
Talking of Michelangelo.°

The yellow fog that rubs its back upon the window-panes,   15
The yellow smoke that rubs its muzzle on the window-panes,
Licked its tongue into the corners of the evening,
Lingered upon the pools that stand in drains,

---

41 old dispensation world before the birth of Christ
S'io credesse . . . rispondo From Dante's *Inferno* (Canto 27). The speaker is Guido da
Montefeltro: "If I thought I spoke to someone who would return to the world, this flame
would tremble no longer. But, if what I hear is true, since no one has ever returned alive from
this place I can answer you without fear of infamy."   **1 you** Eliot said that the auditor of the
poem was a male companion of Prufrock.   **14 Michelangelo** Italian painter and sculptor
(1475-1564)

Let fall upon its back the soot that falls from chimneys,
Slipped by the terrace, made a sudden leap,   20
And seeing that it was a soft October night,
Curled once about the house, and fell asleep.

And indeed there will be time
For the yellow smoke that slides along the street,
Rubbing its back upon the window-panes;   25
There will be time, there will be time
To prepare a face to meet the faces that you meet;
There will be time to murder and create,
And time for all the works and days of hands
That lift and drop a question on your plate: 30
Time for you and time for me,
And time yet for a hundred indecisions,
And for a hundred visions and revisions,
Before the taking of a toast and tea.

In the room the women come and go   35
Talking of Michelangelo.

And indeed there will be time
To wonder, "Do I dare?" and, "Do I dare?"—
Time to turn back and descend the stair,
With a bald spot in the middle of my hair—   40
(They will say: "How his hair is growing thin!")
My morning coat, my collar mounting firmly to the chin,
My necktie rich and modest, but asserted by a simple pin—
(They will say: "But how his arms and legs are thin!")
Do I dare   45
Disturb the universe?
In a minute there is time
For decisions and revisions which a minute will reverse.

For I have known them all already, known them all:
Have known the evenings, mornings, afternoons,   50
I have measured out my life with coffee spoons;
I know the voices dying with a dying fall
Beneath the music from a farther room.
          So how should I presume?

And I have known the eyes already, known them all—   55
The eyes that fix you in a formulated phrase,
And when I am formulated, sprawling on a pin,

When I am pinned and wriggling on the wall,
Then how should I begin
To spit out all the butt-ends of my days and ways?   60
        And how should I presume?

And I have known the arms already, known them all—
Arms that are braceleted and white and bare
(But in the lamplight, downed with light brown hair!)
Is it perfume from a dress   65
That makes me so digress?
Arms that lie along a table, or wrap about a shawl.
        And should I then presume?
        And how should I begin?
            . . . . .
Shall I say, I have gone at dusk through narrow streets,   70
And watched the smoke that rises from the pipes
Of lonely men in shirtsleeves, leaning out of windows? . . .

I should have been a pair of ragged claws
Scuttling across the floors of silent seas.
            . . . . .
And the afternoon, the evening, sleeps so peacefully!   75
Smoothed by long fingers,
Asleep . . . tired . . . or it malingers,
Stretched on the floor, here beside you and me.
Should I, after tea and cakes and ices,
Have the strength to force the moment to its crisis?   80
But though I have wept and fasted, wept and prayed,
Though I have seen my head (grown slightly bald) brought in upon a
    platter,
I am no prophet°—and here's no great matter;
I have seen the moment of my greatness flicker,
And I have seen the eternal Footman hold my coat, and snicker,   85
        And in short, I was afraid.

And would it have been worth it, after all,
After the cups, the marmalade, the tea,
Among the porcelain, among some talk of you and me,
Would it have been worth while,   90
To have bitten off the matter with a smile,
To have squeezed the universe into a ball
To roll it towards some overwhelming question,
To say: "I am Lazarus,° come from the dead,

82-83 my head . . . no prophet allusion to John the Baptist   94 Lazarus raised from the
dead in John 11:1-44

Come back to tell you all, I shall tell you all"—   95
If one, settling a pillow by her head,
    Should say: "That is not what I meant at all;
    That is not it, at all."

And would it have been worth it, after all,
Would it have been worth while,   100
After the sunsets and the dooryards and the sprinkled streets,
After the novels, after the teacups, after the skirts that trail along
    the floor—
And this, and so much more?—
It is impossible to say just what I mean!
But as if a magic lantern° threw the nerves in patterns on
    a screen: 105
Would it have been worth while
If one, settling a pillow or throwing off a shawl,
And turning toward the window, should say:
    "That is not it at all,
    That is not what I meant, at all."   110
    . . . . .
No! I am not Prince Hamlet, nor was meant to be;
Am an attendant lord, one that will do
To swell a progress, start a scene or two,
Advise the prince; no doubt, an easy tool,
Deferential, glad to be of use,   115
Politic, cautious, and meticulous;
Full of high sentence, but a bit obtuse;
At times, indeed, almost ridiculous—
Almost, at times, the Fool.°

I grow old . . . I grow old . . .   120
I shall wear the bottoms of my trousers rolled.

Shall I part my hair behind? Do I dare to eat a peach?
I shall wear white flannel trousers, and walk upon the beach.
I have heard the mermaids singing, each to each.

I do not think that they will sing to me.   125

I have seen them riding seaward on the waves
Combing the white hair of the waves blown back
When the wind blows the water white and black.

---

105 magic lantern old-fashioned slide projector   **111-119 not Prince Hamlet . . . the Fool**
The allusion is probably to Polonius, a character in *Hamlet*.

We have lingered in the chambers of the sea
By sea-girls wreathed with seaweed red and brown   130
Till human voices wake us, and we drown.

                                                                —1917

JOHN CROWE RANSOM   1888–1974

As a professor at Vanderbilt University in Nashville, Ransom began
a little magazine called the *Fugitive*, which lent its name to a group
of young southern poets who published in it. Later he moved to
Kenyon College, where he was editor of the *Kenyon Review* for many
years. Ransom was influential as both a poet and a critic.

Bells for John Whiteside's Daughter

There was such speed in her little body,
And such lightness in her footfall,
It is no wonder her brown study°
Astonishes us all.

Her wars were bruited° in our high window.   5
We looked among orchard trees and beyond
Where she took arms against her shadow,
Or harried unto the pond

The lazy geese, like a snow cloud
Dripping their snow on the green grass,   10
Tricking and stopping, sleepy and proud,
Who cried in goose, Alas,

For the tireless heart within the little
Lady with rod that made them rise
From their noon apple-dreams and scuttle   15
Goose-fashion under the skies!

But now go the bells, and we are ready,
In one house we are sternly stopped
To say we are vexed at her brown study,
Lying so primly propped.   20

                                                                —1924

---

3 brown study appearance of deep concentration   **5 bruited** shouted

Piazza° Piece

—I am a gentleman in a dustcoat° trying
To make you hear. Your ears are soft and small
And listen to an old man not at all.
They want the young men's whispering and sighing.
But see the roses on your trellis dying   5
And hear the spectral singing of the moon;
For I must have my lovely lady soon,
I am a gentleman in a dustcoat trying.

—I am a lady young in beauty waiting
Until my truelove comes, and then we kiss.   10
But what grey man among the vines is this
Whose words are dry and faint as in a dream?
Back from my trellis, Sir, before I scream!
I am a lady young in beauty waiting.

—1927

EDNA ST. VINCENT MILLAY   1892-1950

Millay's poetry was extremely popular in the 1920s, when her sonnets seemed the ultimate expression of the liberated sexuality of
what was then called the New Woman. Neglected for many years, her
poems have recently generated renewed interest, and it seems likely
that she will eventually regain her status as one of the most important female poets of the century.

If I Should Learn, in Some Quite Casual Way

If I should learn, in some quite casual way,
That you were gone, not to return again—
Read from the back-page of a paper, say,
Held by a neighbor in a subway train,
How at the corner of this avenue   5
And such a street (so are the papers filled)
A hurrying man, who happened to be you,
At noon today had happened to be killed—
I should not cry aloud—I could not cry
Aloud, or wring my hands in such a place—   10

Piazza courtyard   **1 dustcoat** old-fashioned coat worn while driving an open car

I should but watch the station lights rush by
With a more careful interest on my face;
Or raise my eyes and read with greater care
Where to store furs and how to treat the hair.

—1917

Not in a Silver Casket

Not in a silver casket cool with pearls
Or rich with red corundum or with blue,
Locked, and the key withheld, as other girls
Have given their loves, I give my love to you;
Not in a lovers'-knot, not in a ring   5
Worked in such fashion, and the legend plain—
Semper fidelis, where a secret spring
Kennels a drop of mischief for the brain:
Love in the open hand, no thing but that,
Ungemmed, unhidden, wishing not to hurt,   10
As one should bring you cowslips in a hat
Swung from the hand, or apples in her skirt,
I bring you, calling out as children do:
"Look what I have!—And these are all for you."

—1931

Oh, Oh, You Will Be Sorry for that Word

Oh, oh, you will be sorry for that word!
Give back my book and take my kiss instead.
Was it my enemy or my friend I heard,
"What a big book for such a little head!"
Come, I will show you now my newest hat,   5
And you may watch me purse my mouth and prink!°
Oh, I shall love you still, and all of that.
I never again shall tell you what I think.
I shall be sweet and crafty, soft and sly;
You will not catch me reading any more: 10
I shall be called a wife to pattern by;
And some day when you knock and push the door,
Some sane day, not too bright and not too stormy,
I shall be gone, and you may whistle for me.

—1923

---

6 prink primp

What Lips My Lips Have Kissed, and Where, and Why

What lips my lips have kissed, and where, and why,
I have forgotten, and what arms have lain
Under my head till morning; but the rain
Is full of ghosts tonight, that tap and sigh
Upon the glass and listen for reply,   5
And in my heart there stirs a quiet pain
For unremembered lads that not again
Will turn to me at midnight with a cry.
Thus in the winter stands the lonely tree,
Nor knows what birds have vanished one by one,   10
Yet knows its boughs more silent than before:
I cannot say what loves have come and gone,
I only know that summer sang in me
A little while, that in me sings no more.

—1923

Archibald MacLeish   1892–1982

MacLeish was both a poet and a public servant, serving as an under-
secretary of state during the Roosevelt administration. He won
Pulitzer Prizes, both for his poetry and for his play *J.B.*, a modern
retelling of the Old Testament story of Job.

The End of the World

Quite unexpectedly as Vasserot
The armless ambidextrian was lighting
A match between his great and second toe,
And Ralph the lion was engaged in biting
The neck of Madame Sossman while the drum   5
Pointed, and Teeny was about to cough
In waltz-time swinging Jocko by the thumb—
Quite unexpectedly the top blew off:

And there, there overhead, there, there hung over
Those thousands of white faces, those dazed eyes,   10
There in the starless dark the poise, the hover,
There with vast wings across the canceled skies,
There in the sudden blackness the black pall
Of nothing, nothing, nothing—nothing at all.

—1926

WILFRED OWEN   1893–1918

Killed in the trenches only a few days before the armistice that ended
World War I, Owen showed more promise than any other English
poet of his generation. A decorated officer whose nerves broke down
after exposure to battle, he met Siegfried Sassoon at Craiglockhart
military hospital. His work was posthumously collected by his friend.
A recent novel by Pat Barker, *Regeneration*, deals with their poetic and
personal relationship.

Dulce et Decorum Est°

Bent double, like old beggars under sacks,
Knock-kneed, coughing like hags, we cursed through sludge,
Till on the haunting flares we turned our backs
And towards our distant rest began to trudge.
Men marched asleep. Many had lost their boots   5
But limped on, blood-shod. All went lame; all blind;
Drunk with fatigue; deaf even to the hoots
Of tired, outstripped Five-Nines° that dropped behind.

Gas! Gas! Quick, boys!—An ecstasy of fumbling
Fitting the clumsy helmets just in time;   10
But someone still was yelling out and stumbling
And flound'ring like a man in fire or lime . . .
Dim, through the misty panes and thick green light,°
As under a green sea, I saw him drowning.

In all my dreams, before my helpless sight,   15
He plunges at me, guttering, choking, drowning.

If in some smothering dreams you too could pace
Behind the wagon that we flung him in,
And watch the white eyes writhing in his face,
His hanging face, like a devil's sick of sin;   20
If you could hear, at every jolt, the blood
Come gargling from the froth-corrupted lungs,
Obscene as cancer, bitter as the cud
Of vile, incurable sores on innocent tongues,—
My friend,° you would not tell with such high zest   25

Dulce et Decorum Est (pro patria mori) from the Roman poet Horace: "It is sweet and
proper to die for one's country" **8 Five-Nines** German artillery shells (59 mm) **13 misty
panes and thick green light** i.e., through the gas mask **25 my friend** The poem was originally addressed to Jessie Pope, a writer of patriotic verse.

To children ardent for some desperate glory,
The old Lie: Dulce et decorum est
Pro patria mori.

—1920

DOROTHY PARKER   1893–1967

Humorist, journalist, and poet, Parker was for many years associated with the *New Yorker* as both author and critic. Along with Robert Benchley, James Thurber, and E. B. White, she epitomizes the hard-edged humor that made that magazine unique among American periodicals.

One Perfect Rose

A single flow'r he sent me, since we met.
All tenderly his messenger he chose;
Deep-hearted, pure, with scented dew still wet—
One perfect rose.

I knew the language of the floweret;   5
"My fragile leaves," it said, "his heart enclose."
Love long has taken for his amulet
One perfect rose.

Why is it no one sent me yet
One perfect limousine, do you suppose?   10
Ah no, it's always just my luck to get
One perfect rose.

—1926

Résumé

Razors pain you;
Rivers are damp;
Acids stain you;
And drugs cause cramp.
Guns aren't lawful;   5
Nooses give;
Gas smells awful;
You might as well live.

—1926

E. E. Cummings   1894–1962

The son of a Harvard professor and Unitarian clergyman, Edward
Estlin Cummings served as a volunteer ambulance driver in France
during World War I. Cummings's experimentation with the typo-
graphical aspects of poetry reveals his serious interest in cubist painting, which he studied in Paris in the 1920s. A brilliant satirist, he
also excelled as a writer of lyrical poems whose unusual appearance
and idiosyncratic grammar, spelling, and punctuation often overshadow their traditional themes.

in Just-

in Just-
spring   when the world is mud-
luscious the little
lame balloonman

whistles   far   and wee   5

and eddieandbill come
running from marbles and
piracies and it's
spring

when the world is puddle-wonderful   10

the queer
old balloonman whistles
far   and   wee
and bettyandisbel come dancing

from hop-scotch and jump-rope and   15

it's
spring
and
    the

        goat-footed°   20

balloonMan   whistles
far
and
wee

                                                          —1923

---

20 goat-footed allusion to Pan, Roman god of spring

pity this busy monster,manunkind

pity this busy monster,manunkind,

not. Progress is a comfortable disease:
your victim (death and life safely beyond)

plays with the bigness of his littleness
—electrons° deify one razorblade   5
into a mountainrange; lenses extend

unwish through curving wherewhen till unwish
returns on its unself.
                            A world of made
is not a world of born—pity poor flesh   10

and trees,poor stars and stones,but never this
fine specimen of hypermagical

ultraomnipotence. We doctors know

a hopeless case if—listen: there's a hell
of a good universe next door; let's go   15

                                            —1944

r-p-o-p-h-e-s-s-a-g-r

                         r-p-o-p-h-e-s-s-a-g-r
              who
a)s w(e loo)k
upnowgath
        PPEGORHRASS   5
              eringint(o-
aThe):l
   eA
   !p:
S   a   10
           (r
rIvInG   .gRrEaPsPhOs)
                  to
rea(be)rran(com)gi(e)ngly
,grasshopper; 15

                                          —1932

---

5 electrons in an electron microscope

Jean Toomer   1894–1967

Toomer was born in Washington, D.C., the grandson of a black man who served as governor of Louisiana during Reconstruction. His only book, *Cane* (1923), is a mixed collection of prose and verse based on his observations of life in rural Georgia, where he was a schoolteacher. A complete edition of his poetry, most of it unpublished during his life, was assembled over twenty years after his death.

Reapers

Black reapers with the sound of steel on stones
Are sharpening scythes. I see them place the hones
In their hip-pockets as a thing that's done,
And start their silent swinging, one by one.
Black horses drive a mower through the weeds,   5
And there, a field rat, startled, squealing bleeds,
His belly close to ground. I see the blade,
Blood-stained, continue cutting weeds and shade.

                                                        —1923

Louise Bogan   1897–1970

Bogan was for many years the poetry editor and resident critic of the *New Yorker*, and the opinions expressed in her many book reviews have held up well in the years since her death. In her later years Bogan suffered from severe bouts of clinical depression and wrote little poetry, but her relatively slim output reveals a unique poetic voice.

Women

Women have no wilderness in them,
They are provident instead,
Content in the tight hot cell of their hearts
To eat dusty bread.

They do not see cattle cropping red winter grass,   5
They do not hear
Snow water going down under culverts
Shallow and clear.

They wait, when they should turn to journeys,
They stiffen, when they should bend.   10
They use against themselves that benevolence
To which no man is friend.

They cannot think of so many crops to a field
Or of clean wood cleft by an axe.
Their love is an eager meaninglessness   15
Too tense, or too lax.

They hear in every whisper that speaks to them
A shout and a cry.
As like as not, when they take life over their door-sills
They should let it go by.   20

         —1923

H ART C RANE   1899–1933

> Crane is one of the first modernists to make extensive poetic use of
> the artifacts—advertising slogans, motion picture lore, trade names—
> of American popular culture. Much of this material surfaces in *The
> Bridge* (1930), his book-length attempt to write an epic sequence
> about modern America. Crane committed suicide by leaping from a
> ship returning from the Yucatán, where he spent his last year on a
> Guggenheim Fellowship, attempting to write an epic poem about
> the conquest of Mexico.

Chaplinesque°

We make our meek adjustments,
Contented with such random consolations
As the wind deposits
In slithered and too ample pockets.

For we can still love the world, who find   5
A famished kitten on the step, and know
Recesses for it from the fury of the street,
Or warm torn elbow coverts.

We will sidestep, and to the final smirk
Dally the doom of that inevitable thumb   10

Chaplinesque after Charlie Chaplin, silent-film comedian

That slowly chafes its puckered index toward us,
Facing the dull squint with what innocence
And what surprise!

And yet these fine collapses are not lies
More than the pirouettes of any pliant cane;   15
Our obsequies are in a way, no enterprise.
We can evade you, and all else but the heart:
What blame to us if the heart live on.

The game enforces smirks; but we have seen
The moon in lonely alleys make   20
A grail of laughter of an empty ash can,
And through all sound of gaiety and quest
Have heard a kitten in the wilderness.

                                                                    —1926

LANGSTON HUGHES   1902–1967

As a leading figure in the Harlem Renaissance of the 1920s, Hughes
became the most famous black writer of his day. Phrases from his
poems and other writings have become deeply ingrained in the
American consciousness. An important experimenter with poetic
form, Hughes is credited with incorporating the rhythms of jazz into
poetry.

Dream Boogie

Good morning, daddy!
Ain't you heard
The boogie-woogie rumble
Of a dream deferred?

Listen closely: 5
You'll hear their feet
Beating out and beating out a—

        You think
        It's a happy beat?

Listen to it closely: 10
Ain't you heard
something underneath
like a—

What did I say?
Sure,   15
I'm happy!
Take it away!

   Hey, pop!
   Re-bop!
   Mop!   20

     Y-e-a-h!

               —1951

The Negro Speaks of Rivers

I've known rivers:
I've known rivers ancient as the world and older than the flow of
   human blood in human veins.

My soul has grown deep like the rivers.

I bathed in the Euphrates when dawns were young.
I built my hut near the Congo and it lulled me to sleep.   5
I looked upon the Nile and raised the pyramids above it.
I heard the singing of the Mississippi when Abe Lincoln went
   down to New Orleans, and I've seen its muddy bosom turn
   all golden in the sunset.

I've known rivers:
Ancient, dusky rivers.

My soul has grown deep like the rivers.   10

               —1926

COUNTEE CULLEN   1903–1946

Among black writers of the first half of the century, Cullen's poetry
represents a more conservative style than that of his contemporary
Hughes. Although he wrote a number of lyrics on poetic themes, he
is best remembered for his eloquent poems on racial subjects.

Incident

Once riding in old Baltimore,
   Heart-filled, head-filled with glee,

I saw a Baltimorean
   Keep looking straight at me.

Now I was eight and very small,   5
   And he was no whit bigger,
And so I smiled, but he poked out
   His tongue, and called me, "Nigger."

I saw the whole of Baltimore
   From May until December;   10
Of all the things that happened there
   That's all that I remember.

                                  —1963

Yet Do I Marvel

I doubt not God is good, well-meaning, kind,
And did He stoop to quibble could tell why
The little buried mole continues blind,
Why flesh that mirrors Him must some day die,
Make plain the reason tortured Tantalus°   5
Is baited by the fickle fruit, declare
If merely brute caprice dooms Sisyphus°
To struggle up a never-ending stair.
Inscrutable His ways are, and immune
To catechism by a mind too strewn   10
With petty cares to slightly understand
What awful brain compels His awful hand.
Yet do I marvel at this curious thing:
To make a poet black and bid him sing!

                                  —1963

RICHARD EBERHART   B. 1904

Born in Austin, Minnesota, and educated at the University of
Minnesota, Dartmouth College, and Cambridge, Eberhart has
worked in business and as a teacher. During World War II, he served
as a naval gunnery instructor. His *Collected Poems*, containing work
from seven decades, was published in 1988.

---

5 Tantalus mythological character tortured by unreachable fruit   **7 Sisyphus** figure in myth
who endlessly rolls a boulder uphill

The Fury of Aerial Bombardment

You would think the fury of aerial bombardment
Would rouse God to relent; the infinite spaces
Are still silent. He looks on shock-pried faces.
History, even, does not know what is meant.

You would feel that after so many centuries   5
God would give man to repent; yet he can kill
As Cain could, but with multitudinous will,
No farther advanced than in his ancient furies.

Was man made stupid to see his own stupidity?
Is God by definition indifferent, beyond us all?   10
Is the eternal truth man's fighting soul
Wherein the Beast ravens° in its own avidity?

Of Van Wettering I speak, and Averill,
Names on a list, whose faces I do not recall
But they are gone to early death, who late in school   15
Distinguished the belt feed lever from the belt holding pawl.°

—1947

A. D. HOPE   B. 1907

The first unquestionably major poet to emerge from Australia, Hope
waited until he was almost fifty to publish his first collection of poetry. Even then, the sexual frankness of poems like "Imperial Adam"
proved controversial in the conservative climate of mid-1950s
Australia. A poet who strongly rejects most of the tendencies of modernism (most prominently free verse), Hope seems closer in spirit to
eighteenth-century satirists like Swift and Pope, whom he obviously
admires, and to his exact contemporary, W. H. Auden.

Imperial Adam

Imperial Adam, naked in the dew,
Felt his brown flanks and found the rib was gone.
Puzzled he turned and saw where, two and two,
The mighty spoor of Jahweh marked the lawn.

---

12 **ravens** devours greedily   16 **belt feed . . . holding pawl** parts of a .50 caliber machine
gun; the poet was a naval gunner instructor during World War II

Then he remembered through mysterious sleep   5
The surgeon fingers probing at the bone,
The voice so far away, so rich and deep:
"It is not good for him to live alone."

Turning once more he found Man's counterpart
In tender parody breathing at his side.   10
He knew her at first sight, he knew by heart
Her allegory of sense unsatisfied.

The pawpaw drooped its golden breasts above
Less generous than the honey of her flesh;
The innocent sunlight showed the place of love;   15
The dew on its dark hairs winked crisp and fresh.

This plump gourd severed from his virile root,
She promised on the turf of Paradise
Delicious pulp of the forbidden fruit;
Sly as the snake she loosed her sinuous thighs,   20

And waking, smiled up at him from the grass;
Her breasts rose softly and he heard her sigh—
From all the beasts whose pleasant task it was
In Eden to increase and multiply

Adam had learned the jolly deed of kind: 25
He took her in his arms and there and then,
Like the clean beasts, embracing from behind,
Began in joy to found the breed of men.

Then from the spurt of seed within her broke
Her terrible and triumphant female cry,   30
Split upward by the sexual lightning stroke.
It was the beasts now who stood watching by:

The gravid elephant, the calving hind,
The breeding bitch, the she-ape big with young
Were the first gentle midwives of mankind;   35
The teeming lioness rasped her with her tongue;

The proud vicuña nuzzled her as she slept
Lax on the grass; and Adam watching too
Saw how her dumb breasts at their ripening wept,
The great pod of her belly swelled and grew,   40

And saw its water break, and saw, in fear,
Its quaking muscles in the act of birth,
Between her legs a pigmy face appear,
And the first murderer lay upon the earth.

—1955

W. H. Auden   1907–1973

Auden was already established as an important younger British poet
before he moved to America in 1939 (he later became a U.S. citizen).
As an important transatlantic link between two literary cultures,
Auden was one of the most important literary figures and cultural
spokespersons in the English-speaking world for almost forty years,
giving a name to the postwar era when he dubbed it "The Age of
Anxiety" in a poem. In his last years he returned briefly to Oxford,
where he occupied the poetry chair.

As I Walked Out One Evening

As I walked out one evening,
    Walking down Bristol Street,
The crowds upon the pavement
    Were fields of harvest wheat.

And down by the brimming river   5
    I heard a lover sing
Under an arch of the railway:
    "Love has no ending.

"I'll love you, dear, I'll love you
    Till China and Africa meet,   10
And the river jumps over the mountain
    And the salmon sing in the street.

"I'll love you till the ocean
    Is folded and hung up to dry,
And the seven stars go squawking   15
    Like geese about the sky.

"The years shall run like rabbits,
    For in my arms I hold
The Flower of the Ages,
    And the first love of the world."   20

But all the clocks in the city
    Began to whirr and chime:
"O let not Time deceive you,
    You cannot conquer Time.

"In the burrows of the Nightmare   25
    Where Justice naked is,
Time watches from the shadow
    And coughs when you would kiss.

"In headaches and in worry
    Vaguely life leaks away,   30
And Time will have his fancy
    Tomorrow or to-day.

"Into many a green valley
    Drifts the appalling snow;
Time breaks the threaded dances   35
    And the diver's brilliant bow.

"O plunge your hands in water,
    Plunge them in up to the wrist;
Stare, stare in the basin
    And wonder what you've missed.   40

"The glacier knocks in the cupboard,
    The desert sighs in the bed,
And the crack in the tea-cup opens
    A lane to the land of the dead.

"Where the beggars raffle the banknotes   45
    And the Giant is enchanting to Jack,
And the Lily-white Boy is a Roarer,
    And Jill goes down on her back.

"O look, look in the mirror,
    O look in your distress;   50
Life remains a blessing
    Although you cannot bless.

"O stand, stand at the window
    As the tears scald and start;
You shall love your crooked neighbor   55
    With your crooked heart."

It was late, late in the evening,
        The lovers they were gone;
The clocks had ceased their chiming,
        And the deep river ran on.   60

                                                    —1940

Musée des Beaux Arts°

About suffering they were never wrong,
The Old Masters: how well they understood
Its human position; how it takes place
While someone else is eating or opening a window or just walking
        dully along;
How, when the aged are reverently, passionately waiting   5
For the miraculous birth, there always must be
Children who did not specially want it to happen, skating
On a pond at the edge of the wood:
They never forgot
That even the dreadful martyrdom must run its course   10
Anyhow in a corner, some untidy spot
Where the dogs go on with their doggy life and the torturer's horse
Scratches its innocent behind on a tree.

In Brueghel's *Icarus*,° for instance: how everything turns away
Quite leisurely from the disaster; the ploughman may   15
Have heard the splash, the forsaken cry,
But for him it was not an important failure; the sun shone
As it had to on the white legs disappearing into the green
Water; and the expensive delicate ship that must have seen
Something amazing, a boy falling out of the sky,   20
Had somewhere to get to and sailed calmly on.

                                                    —1938

The Unknown Citizen

To JS/07/M/378
This Marble Monument Is Erected by the State

He was found by the Bureau of Statistics to be
One against whom there was no official complaint,
And all the reports on his conduct agree

Musée des Beaux Arts Museum of Fine Arts   14 **Brueghel's** *Icarus* In this painting
(c. 1550) the famous event from Greek myth is almost inconspicuous among the other details
Auden mentions.

That, in the modern sense of an old-fashioned word, he was a
    saint,
For in everything he did he served the Greater Community.   5
Except for the War till the day he retired
He worked in a factory and never got fired,
But satisfied his employers, Fudge Motors Inc.
Yet he wasn't a scab or odd in his views,
For his Union reports that he paid his dues,   10
(Our report on his Union shows it was sound)
And our Social Psychology workers found
That he was popular with his mates and liked a drink.
The Press are convinced that he bought a paper every day
And that his reactions to advertisements were normal in every
    way.   15
Policies taken out in his name prove that he was fully insured,
And his Health-card shows he was once in hospital but left it
    cured.
Both Producers Research and High-Grade Living declare
He was fully sensible to the advantages of the Installment Plan
And had everything necessary to the Modern Man,   20
A phonograph, a radio, a car and a frigidaire.
Our researchers into Public Opinion are content
That he held the proper opinions for the time of year;
When there was peace, he was for peace; when there was war, he
    went.
He was married and added five children to the population,   25
Which our Eugenist says was the right number for a parent of his
    generation,
And our teachers report that he never interfered with their
    education.
Was he free? Was he happy? The question is absurd:
Had anything been wrong, we should certainly have heard.

                                                            —1939

THEODORE ROETHKE   1908–1963

Born in Michigan, Roethke was an influential teacher of poetry at
the University of Washington for many years. His father was the
owner of a greenhouse, and Roethke's childhood closeness to nature
was an important influence on his mature poetry. His periodic nervous breakdowns, the result of bipolar manic-depression, presaged
his early death.

Dolor°

I have known the inexorable sadness of pencils,
Neat in their boxes, dolor of pad and paper-weight,
All of the misery of manilla folders and mucilage,
Desolation in immaculate public places,
Lonely reception room, lavatory, switchboard,   5
The unalterable pathos of basin and pitcher,
Ritual of multigraph, paper-clip, comma,
Endless duplication of lives and objects.
And I have seen dust from the walls of institutions,
Finer than flour, alive, more dangerous than silica,°   10
Sift, almost invisible, through long afternoons of tedium,
Dropping a fine film on nails and delicate eyebrows,
Glazing the pale hair, the duplicate grey standard faces.

                                                         —1948

My Papa's Waltz

The whiskey on your breath
Could make a small boy dizzy;
But I hung on like death:
Such waltzing was not easy.

We romped until the pans   5
Slid from the kitchen shelf;
My mother's countenance
Could not unfrown itself.

The hand that held my wrist
Was battered on one knuckle;   10
At every step you missed
My right ear scraped a buckle.

You beat time on my head
With a palm caked hard by dirt,
Then waltzed me off to bed   15
Still clinging to your shirt.

                                                         —1948

Dolor sadness   **10 silica** rock dust, a cause of silicosis, an occupational disease of miners and
quarry workers

Root Cellar

Nothing would sleep in that cellar, dank as a ditch,
Bulbs broke out of boxes hunting for chinks in the dark,
Shoots dangled and drooped,
Lolling obscenely from mildewed crates,
Hung down long yellow evil necks, like tropical snakes.   5
And what a congress of stinks!—
Roots ripe as old bait,
Pulpy stems, rank, silo-rich,
Leaf-mold, manure, lime, piled against slippery planks.
Nothing would give up life: 10
Even the dirt kept breathing a small breath.

                                                    —1948

ELIZABETH BISHOP   1911–1979

During most of her life, Bishop was highly regarded as a "poet's
poet," winning the Pulitzer Prize for *North and South* in 1956, but in
the years since her death she has gained a wider readership. She traveled widely and lived in Brazil for a number of years before returning to the United States to teach at Harvard during the last years of
her life.

The Fish

I caught a tremendous fish
and held him beside the boat
half out of water, with my hook
fast in a corner of his mouth.
He didn't fight.   5
He hadn't fought at all.
He hung a grunting weight,
battered and venerable
and homely. Here and there
his brown skin hung in strips   10
like ancient wallpaper,
and its pattern of darker brown
was like wallpaper:
shapes like full-blown roses
stained and lost through age.   15
He was speckled with barnacles,
fine rosettes of lime,

and infested
with tiny white sea-lice,
and underneath two or three   20
rags of green weed hung down.
While his gills were breathing in
the terrible oxygen
—the frightening gills,
fresh and crisp with blood,   25
that can cut so badly—
I thought of the coarse white flesh
packed in like feathers,
the big bones and the little bones,
the dramatic reds and blacks   30
of his shiny entrails,
and the pink swim-bladder
like a big peony.
I looked into his eyes
which were far larger than mine   35
but shallower, and yellowed,
the irises backed and packed
with tarnished tinfoil
seen through the lenses
of old scratched isinglass.°   40
They shifted a little, but not
to return my stare.
—It was more like the tipping
of an object toward the light.
I admired his sullen face,   45
the mechanism of his jaw,
and then I saw
that from his lower lip
—if you could call it a lip—
grim, wet, and weapon-like,   50
hung five old pieces of fish-line,
or four and a wire leader
with the swivel still attached,
with all their five big hooks
grown firmly in his mouth.   55
A green line, frayed at the end
where he broke it, two heavier lines,
and a fine black thread
still crimped from the strain and snap
when it broke and he got away.   60

---

40 isinglass semi-transparent material made from fish bladders

Like medals with their ribbons
frayed and wavering,
a five-haired beard of wisdom
trailing from his aching jaw.
I stared and stared   65
and victory filled up
the little rented boat,
from the pool of bilge
where oil had spread a rainbow
around the rusted engine   70
to the bailer° rusted orange,
the sun-cracked thwarts,
the oarlocks on their strings,
the gunnels°—until everything
was rainbow, rainbow, rainbow!   75
and I let the fish go.

                                                   —1946

One Art

The art of losing isn't hard to master;
so many things seem filled with the intent
to be lost that their loss is no disaster.

Lose something every day. Accept the fluster
of lost door keys, the hour badly spent.   5
The art of losing isn't hard to master.

Then practice losing farther, losing faster:
places, and names, and where it was you meant
to travel. None of these will bring disaster.

I lost my mother's watch. And look! my last, or   10
next-to-last, of three loved houses went.
The art of losing isn't hard to master.

I lost two cities, lovely ones. And, vaster,
some realms I owned, two rivers, a continent.
I miss them, but it wasn't a disaster.   15

—Even losing you (the joking voice, a gesture
I love) I shan't have lied. It's evident
the art of losing's not too hard to master
though it may look like (Write it!) like disaster.

                                                   —1976

---

71 **bailer** bucket   74 **gunnels** gunwales

MAY SARTON   1912–1995

Born in Belgium, Sarton succeeded equally in poetry and prose.
The journals and memoirs she produced in her last two decades
added considerably to the literature of aging and won her readers
perhaps more numerous than the many admirers of her poetry. Her
feminism and lesbianism, made public long before doing so was
either fashionable or prudent, rarely overshadow her skills at evok-
ing the New England landscape she passionately loved.

A Guest

My woods belong to woodcock and to deer;
For them, it is an accident I'm here.

If, for the plump raccoon, I represent
An ash can that was surely heaven-sent,

The bright-eyed mask, the clever little paws   5
Obey not mine, but someone else's laws.

The young buck takes me in with a long glance
That says that I, not he, am here by chance.

And they all go their ways, as I must do,
Up through the green and down again to snow,   10

No one of us responsible or near,
But each himself and in the singular.

When we do meet, I am the one to stare
As if an angel had me by the hair,

As I am flooded by some ancient bliss   15
Before all I possess and can't possess.

So when a stranger knocks hard at the door,
He cannot know what I am startled for—

To see before me an unfurry face,
A creature like myself in this wild place.   20

Our wilderness gets wilder every day
And we intend to keep the tamed at bay.

Robert Hayden   1913–1980

Hayden named Countee Cullen as one of the chief early influences
on his poetry. A native of Michigan, he taught for many years at Fisk
University in Nashville and at the University of Michigan. Although
many of Hayden's poems are on black subjects, he wished to be considered a poet with strong links to the mainstream English tradition.

Those Winter Sundays

Sundays too my father got up early
and put his clothes on in the blueblack cold,
then with cracked hands that ached
from labor in the weekday weather made
banked fires blaze. No one ever thanked him.   5

I'd wake and hear the cold splintering, breaking.
When the rooms were warm, he'd call,
and slowly I would rise and dress,
fearing the chronic angers of that house,

Speaking indifferently to him,   10
who had driven out the cold
and polished my good shoes as well.
What did I know, what did I know
of love's austere and lonely offices?°

                                                        —1962

Dudley Randall   b. 1914

Randall is the founder of Broadside Press, a black-owned publishing
firm that eventually attracted important black writers like Gwendolyn Brooks and Don L. Lee. For most of his life a resident of
Detroit, Randall spent many years working in that city's library system before taking a similar position at the University of Detroit.

Ballad of Birmingham

(On the Bombing of a Church in
Birmingham, Alabama, 1963)°

"Mother dear, may I go downtown
Instead of out to play,

---

14 offices daily religious ceremonies
Birmingham, Alabama, 1963 during the height of the civil rights movement

And march the streets of Birmingham
In a Freedom March today?"

"No, baby, no, you may not go,   5
For the dogs are fierce and wild,
And clubs and hoses, guns and jail
Aren't good for a little child."

"But, mother, I won't be alone.
Other children will go with me,   10
And march the streets of Birmingham
To make our country free."

"No, baby, no, you may not go,
For I fear those guns will fire.
But you may go to church instead   15
And sing in the children's choir."

She has combed and brushed her night-dark hair,
And bathed rose petal sweet,
And drawn white gloves on her small brown hands,
And white shoes on her feet.   20

The mother smiled to know her child
Was in the sacred place,
But that smile was the last smile
To come upon her face.

For when she heard the explosion,   25
Her eyes grew wet and wild.
She raced through the streets of Birmingham
Calling for her child.

She clawed through bits of glass and brick,
Then lifted out a shoe.   30
"O, here's the shoe my baby wore,
But, baby, where are you?"

—1969

WILLIAM STAFFORD   1914–1993

One of the most prolific poets of the postwar era, Stafford published
in virtually every magazine in the United States. Raised in Kansas as
a member of the pacifist Church of the Brethren, Stafford served in

a camp for conscientious objectors during World War II. His first
book did not appear until he was in his forties, but he published
over thirty collections before his death at 79.

Traveling through the Dark

Traveling through the dark I found a deer
dead on the edge of the Wilson River road.
It is usually best to roll them into the canyon:
that road is narrow; to swerve might make more dead.

By glow of the tail-light I stumbled back of the car   5
and stood by the heap, a doe, a recent killing;
she had stiffened already, almost cold.
I dragged her off; she was large in the belly.

My fingers touching her side brought me the reason—
her side was warm; her fawn lay there waiting,   10
alive, still, never to be born.
Beside that mountain road I hesitated.

The car aimed ahead its lowered parking lights;
under the hood purred the steady engine.
I stood in the glare of the warm exhaust turning red;   15
around our group I could hear the wilderness listen.

I thought hard for us all—my only swerving—
then pushed her over the edge into the river.

—1960

DYLAN THOMAS   1914–1953

Thomas was a legendary performer of his and others' poetry, and his
popularity in the United States led to several collegiate reading tours,
punctuated with outrageous behavior and self-destructive drinking
that led to his early death in New York City, the victim of what the
autopsy report labeled "insult to the brain." The Wales of his childhood remained a constant source of inspiration for his poetry and
for radio dramas like Under Milk Wood, which was turned into a film
by fellow Welshman Richard Burton and his then-wife, Elizabeth
Taylor.

Do Not Go Gentle into That Good Night

Do not go gentle into that good night,
Old age should burn and rave at close of day;
Rage, rage against the dying of the light.

Though wise men at their end know dark is right,
Because their words had forked no lightning they
Do not go gentle into that good night.

Good men, the last wave by, crying how bright
Their frail deeds might have danced in a green bay,
Rage, rage against the dying of the light.

Wild men who caught and sang the sun in flight,
And learn, too late, they grieved it on its way,
Do not go gentle into that good night.

Grave men, near death, who see with blinding sight
Blind eyes could blaze like meteors and be gay,
Rage, rage against the dying of the light.

And you, my father, there on the sad height,
Curse, bless, me now with your fierce tears, I pray,
Do not go gentle into that good night.
Rage, rage against the dying of the light.

—1952

Fern Hill

Now as I was young and easy under the apple boughs
About the lilting house and happy as the grass was green,
    The night above the dingle starry,
        Time let me hail and climb
    Golden in the heydays of his eyes,
And honored among wagons I was prince of the apple towns
And once below a time I lordly had the trees and leaves
        Trail with daisies and barley
    Down the rivers of the windfall light.

And as I was green and carefree, famous among the barns
About the happy yard and singing as the farm was home,

In the sun that is young once only,
    Time let me play and be
  Golden in the mercy of his means,
And green and golden I was huntsman and herdsman, the calves   15
Sang to my horn, the foxes on the hills barked clear and cold,
    And the sabbath rang slowly
  In the pebbles of the holy streams.

All the sun long it was running, it was lovely, the hay
Fields high as the house, the tunes from the chimneys, it was air   20
    And playing, lovely and watery
      And fire green as grass.
    And nightly under the simple stars
As I rode to sleep the owls were bearing the farm away,
All the moon long I heard, blessed among stables, the night-jars   25
    Flying with the ricks, and the horses
      Flashing into the dark.

And then to awake, and the farm, like a wanderer white
With the dew, come back, the cock on his shoulder: it was all
    Shining, it was Adam and maiden,   30
      The sky gathered again
    And the sun grew round that very day.
So it must have been after the birth of the simple light
In the first, spinning place, the spellbound horses walking warm
    Out of the whinnying green stable   35
      On to the fields of praise.

And honored among foxes and pheasants by the gay house
Under the new made clouds and happy as the heart was long,
    In the sun born over and over,
      I ran my heedless ways,
    My wishes raced through the house high hay   40
And nothing I cared, at my sky blue trades, that time allows
In all his tuneful turning so few and such morning songs
    Before the children green and golden
      Follow him out of grace,   45

Nothing I cared, in the lamb white days, that time would take me
Up to the swallow thronged loft by the shadow of my hand,
    In the moon that is always rising,
      Nor that riding to sleep
    I should hear him fly with the high fields   50
And wake to the farm forever fled from the childless land.

Oh as I was young and easy in the mercy of his means,
    Time held me green and dying
Though I sang in my chains like the sea.

—1946

WELDON KEES   1914–1955

Kees was a multi-talented poet, painter, jazz musician, and filmmaker
who went from the University of Nebraska to New York to
California. His reputation, aided by posthumous publication of his
stories, criticism, letters, and novels, has grown steadily since his
apparent suicide by leaping from the Golden Gate Bridge.

For My Daughter

Looking into my daughter's eyes I read
Beneath the innocence of morning flesh
Concealed, hintings of death she does not heed.
Coldest of winds have blown this hair, and mesh
Of seaweed snarled these miniatures of hands;   5
The night's slow poison, tolerant and bland,
Has moved her blood. Parched years that I have seen
That may be hers appear; foul, lingering
Death in certain war, the slim legs green.
Or, fed on hate, she relishes the sting   10
Of others' agony; perhaps the cruel
Bride of a syphilitic or a fool.
These speculations sour in the sun.
I have no daughter. I desire none.

—1943

RANDALL JARRELL   1914–1965

Jarrell excelled as both a poet and a (sometimes brutally honest)
reviewer of poetry. Ironically, the author of what is perhaps the best-
known poem to have emerged from World War II did not see combat during the war: he served as a control tower officer in stateside
bases. A native of Nashville, Kentucky, Jarrell studied at Vanderbilt
University and followed his mentor, John Crowe Ransom, to
Kenyon College in 1937, where he befriended another student,
Robert Lowell.

The Death of the Ball Turret° Gunner

From my mother's sleep I fell into the State,
And I hunched in its belly till my wet fur froze.
Six miles from earth, loosed from its dream of life,
I woke to black flak and the nightmare fighters.
When I died they washed me out of the turret with a hose.   5

—1945

Margaret Walker   B. 1915

As a female African-American poet, Walker has perhaps been
overshadowed by Gwendolyn Brooks, even though Walker's receipt
of the Yale Younger Poets Award in 1942 for *For My People* came
some years before Brooks's own recognition. A longtime teacher at
Jackson State University, she has influenced several generations of
young writers.

For Malcolm X

All you violated ones with gentle hearts;
You violent dreamers whose cries shout heartbreak;
Whose voices echo clamors of our cool capers,
And whose black faces have hollowed pits for eyes.
All you gambling sons and hooked children and bowery bums   5
Hating white devils and black bourgeoisie,
Thumbing your noses at your burning red suns,
Gather round this coffin and mourn your dying swan.

Snow-white moslem head-dress around a dead black face!
Beautiful were your sand-papering words against our skins!   10
Our blood and water pour from your flowing wounds.
You have cut open our breasts and dug scalpels in our brains.
When and Where will another come to take your holy place?
Old man mumbling in his dotage, or crying child, unborn?

—1970

Ball Turret A Plexiglas sphere set into the belly of a heavy bomber; Jarrell noted the similarity between the gunner and a fetus in the womb.

Gwendolyn Brooks   B. 1917

The first African-American poet to win a Pulitzer Prize for poetry,
Brooks has reflected many changes in black culture during her long
career, and she has written about the stages of her own life and
career candidly in *From the Mecca*, her literary autobiography. The
last Poetry Consultant of the Library of Congress before that position became Poet Laureate of the United States, Brooks is among the
most honored of living American poets.

the mother

Abortions will not let you forget.
You remember the children you got that you did not get,
The damp small pulps with a little or with no hair,
The singers and workers that never handled the air.
You will never neglect or beat   5
them, or silence or buy with a sweet.
You will never wind up the sucking-thumb
Or scuttle off ghosts that come.
You will never leave them, controlling your luscious sigh,
Return for a snack of them, with gobbling mother-eye.   10

I have heard in the voices of the wind the voices of my dim killed
    children.
I have contracted. I have eased
My dim dears at the breasts they could never suck.
I have said, Sweets, if I sinned, if I seized
Your luck   15
And your lives from your unfinished reach,
If I stole your births and your names,
Your straight baby tears and your games,
Your stilted or lovely loves, your tumults, your marriages, aches,
    and your deaths,
If I poisoned the beginnings of your breaths,   20
Believe that even in my deliberateness I was not deliberate.
Though why should I whine,
Whine that the crime was other than mine?—
Since anyhow you are dead.
Or rather, or instead,   25
You were never made.
But that too, I am afraid,
Is faulty: oh, what shall I say, how is the truth to be said?
You were born, you had body, you died.
It is just that you never giggled or planned or cried.   30

Believe me, I loved you all.
Believe me, I knew you, though faintly, and I loved, I loved you
All.

—1945

We Real Cool

The Pool Players.
Seven at the Golden Shovel.

We real cool. We
Left school. We

Lurk late. We
Strike straight. We

Sing sin. We   5
Thin gin. We

Jazz June. We
Die soon.

—1960

CHARLES CAUSLEY   B. 1917

Except for service in the British Royal Navy in World War II,
Causley has spent most of his life teaching in his native Cornwall.
He has written extensively for children, and many of his ballads
display the influence of the popular song. Causley was virtually
unknown in the United States until *Secret Destinations*, a volume of
his selected poems, was published in 1989.

Eden Rock

They are waiting for me somewhere beyond Eden Rock:
My father, twenty-five, in the same suit
Of Genuine Irish Tweed, his terrier Jack
Still two years old and trembling at his feet.

My mother, twenty-three, in a sprigged dress   5
Drawn at the waist, ribbon in her straw hat,
Has spread the stiff white cloth over the grass.
Her hair, the colour of wheat, takes on the light.

She pours tea from a Thermos, the milk straight
From an old H.P. sauce-bottle, a screw   10
Of paper for a cork; slowly sets out
The same three plates, the tin cups painted blue.

The sky whitens as if lit by three suns.
My mother shades her eyes and looks my way
Over the drifted stream. My father spins   15
A stone along the water. Leisurely,

They beckon to me from the other bank.
I hear them call, 'See where the stream-path is!
Crossing is not as hard as you might think.'

I had not thought that it would be like this.   20

                                                                    —1989

R OBERT L OWELL   1917–1977

Because of the immense influence of his nakedly autobiographical
collection of 1959, *Life Studies*, Lowell is noted as one of the chief
confessional poets. His literary career covered many bases—complex,
formal early work; poetic dramas and translations; public figure—and
he had, as the scion of one of Boston's oldest families, a ready-made
stature that made him a public figure for most of his adult life.

For the Union Dead

"Relinquunt Omnia Servare Rem Publicam"°

The old South Boston Aquarium stands
in a Sahara of snow now. Its broken windows are boarded.
The bronze weathervane cod has lost half its scales.
The airy tanks are dry.

Once my nose crawled like a snail on the glass;   5
my hand tingled
to burst the bubbles
drifting from the noses of the cowed, compliant fish.

My hand draws back. I often sigh still
for the dark downward and vegetating kingdom   10

Relinquunt . . . Publicam "They sacrificed everything to serve the state"

of the fish and reptile. One morning last March,
I pressed against the new barbed and galvanized

fence on the Boston Common. Behind their cage,
yellow dinosaur steamshovels were grunting
as they cropped up tons of mush and grass   15
to gouge their underworld garage.

Parking spaces luxuriate like civic
sandpiles in the heart of Boston.
A girdle of orange, Puritan-pumpkin colored girders
braces the tingling Statehouse,   20

shaking over the excavations, as it faces Colonel Shaw°
and his bell-cheeked Negro infantry
on St. Gaudens'° shaking Civil War relief,
propped by a plank splint against the garage's earthquake.

Two months after marching through Boston,   25
half the regiment was dead;
at the dedication,
William James° could almost hear the bronze Negroes breathe.

Their monument sticks like a fishbone
in the city's throat.   30
Its Colonel is as lean
as a compass-needle.

He has an angry wrenlike vigilance,
a greyhound's gentle tautness;
he seems to wince at pleasure,   35
and suffocate for privacy.

He is out of bounds now. He rejoices in man's lovely,
peculiar power to choose life and die—
when he leads his black soldiers to death,
he cannot bend his back.   40

On a thousand small town New England greens,
the old white churches hold their air

---

21 **Colonel Shaw** Robert Gould Shaw (1837-1863) led the black troops of the Massachusetts 54th regiment and died with many of them during the attack on Fort Wagner, S.C. *Glory,* a recent film, was based on these events.   23 **St. Gaudens** American sculptor (1848-1907) 28 **William James** American philosopher (1842-1910) who gave a dedication speech for the monument

of sparse, sincere rebellion; frayed flags
quilt the graveyards of the Grand Army of the Republic.

The stone statues of the abstract Union Soldier   45
grow slimmer and younger each year—
wasp-waisted, they doze over muskets
and muse through their sideburns . . .

Shaw's father wanted no monument
except the ditch,   50
where his son's body was thrown
and lost with his "niggers."

The ditch is nearer.
There are no statues for the last war here;
on Boylston Street, a commercial photograph   55
shows Hiroshima boiling

over a Mosler Safe, the "Rock of Ages"
that survived the blast. Space is nearer.
When I crouch to my television set,
the drained faces of Negro school-children° rise like balloons.   60

Colonel Shaw
is riding on his bubble,
he waits
for the blessèd break.

The Aquarium is gone. Everywhere,   65
giant finned cars nose forward like fish;
a savage servility
slides by on grease.

                                                          —1959

Lawrence Ferlinghetti   b. 1919

As owner of a literary landmark, San Francisco's City Lights
Bookstore, Ferlinghetti has promoted and published the voice of the
American avant-garde since the early 1950s. His own output has
been relatively small, but Ferlinghetti's A Coney Island of the Mind
remains one of the quintessential documents of the Beat
Generation.

---

60 **Negro school-children** refers to protesters during the early days of the civil rights movement

A Coney Island of the Mind, #15

Constantly risking absurdity
                    and death
        whenever he performs
                    above the heads
                        of his audience
    the poet like an acrobat
                    climbs on rime
                        to a high wire of his own making
    and balancing on eyebeams
                        above a sea of faces
            paces his way
                    to the other side of day
        performing entrechats
                    and sleight-of-foot tricks
        and other high theatrics
                    and all without mistaking
                any thing
                    for what it may not be

        For he's the super realist
                        who must perforce perceive
            taut truth
                        before the taking of each stance or step
    in his supposed advance
                        toward that still higher perch
    where Beauty stands and waits
                    with gravity
                        to start her death-defying leap
        And he
            a little charleychaplin man
                        who may or may not catch
    her fair eternal form
                spreadeagled in the empty air
        of existence
                                                    —1958

MAY SWENSON   1919–1989

The inventiveness of May Swenson's poetry ranges from traditional formalism to many spatial or concrete poems. A careful observer of the natural world, Swenson often attempts to mimic directly the rhythms of the physical universe in her self-labeled "iconographs."

How Everything Happens

(BASED ON A STUDY OF THE WAVE)

                                                                happen.
                                                       to
                                               up
                                       stacking
                                   is
                           something
When nothing is happening

When it happens
                       something
                               pulls
                                       back
                                           not
                                               to
                                                   happen.

When   has happened.
        pulling back   stacking up
                        happens

            has happened   stacks up.
When it   something   nothing
                            pulls back while

Then nothing is happening

                                               happens.
                                           and
                                   forward
                           pushes
                       up
                   stacks
            something
Then

                                                       —1967

H OWARD N EMEROV   1920–1991

Nemerov served as Poet Laureate of the United States during 1988
and 1989. A poet of brilliant formal inventiveness, he was also a

skilled satirist and observer of the American scene. His sister, Diane
Arbus, was a famous photographer. His *Collected Poems* won the
Pulitzer Prize in 1978.

A Primer of the Daily Round

A peels an apple, while B kneels to God,
C telephones to D, who has a hand
On E's knee, F coughs, G turns up the sod
For H's grave, I do not understand
But J is bringing one clay pigeon down   5
While K brings down a nightstick on L's head,
And M takes mustard, N drives into town,
O goes to bed with P, and Q drops dead,
R lies to S, but happens to be heard
By T, who tells U not to fire V   10
For having to give W the word
That X is now deceiving Y with Z,
    Who happens just now to remember A
    Peeling an apple somewhere far away.

—1958

Richard Wilbur   b. 1921

Posterity will remember Wilbur as perhaps the most skillful metricist
and exponent of wit that American poetry has produced. His highly
polished poetry—against the grain of much contemporary writing—is
a monument to his craftsmanship and intelligence. Perhaps the most
honored of all living American poets, Wilbur served as Poet Laureate
of the United States in 1987. His translations of the verse dramas of
Molière and Racine are regularly performed throughout the world.

Hamlen Brook

    At the alder-darkened brink
  Where the stream slows to a lucid jet
I lean to the water, dinting its top with sweat,
    And see, before I can drink,

    A startled inchling trout   5
  Of spotted near-transparency,
Trawling a shadow solider than he.
    He swerves now, darting out

To where, in a flicked slew
Of sparks and glittering silt, he weaves   10
Through stream-bed rocks, disturbing foundered leaves,
And butts then out of view

Beneath a sliding glass
Crazed by the skimming of a brace
Of burnished dragon-flies across its face,   15
In which deep cloudlets pass

And a white precipice
Of mirrored birch-trees plunges down
Toward where the azures of the zenith drown.
How shall I drink all this?   20

Joy's trick is to supply
Dry lips with what can cool and slake,
Leaving them dumbstruck also with an ache
Nothing can satisfy.

—1987

Playboy

High on his stockroom ladder like a dunce
The stock-boy sits, and studies like a sage
The subject matter of one glossy page,
As lost in curves as Archimedes° once.

Sometimes, without a glance, he feeds himself.   5
The left hand, like a mother-bird in flight,
Brings him a sandwich for a sidelong bite,
And then returns it to a dusty shelf.

What so engrosses him? The wild décor
Of this pink-papered alcove into which   10
A naked girl has stumbled, with its rich
Welter of pelts and pillows on the floor,

Amidst which, kneeling in a supple pose,
She lifts a goblet in her farther hand,
As if about to toast a flower-stand   15
Above which hovers an exploding rose

---

4 **Archimedes** Greek mathematician (287-212 B.C.)

Fired from a long-necked crystal vase that rests
Upon a tasseled and vermillion cloth
One taste of which would shrivel up a moth?
Or is he pondering her perfect breasts?   20

Nothing escapes him of her body's grace
Or of her floodlit skin, so sleek and warm
And yet so strangely like a uniform,
But what now grips his fancy is her face.

And how the cunning picture holds her still   25
At just that smiling instant when her soul,
Grown sweetly faint, and swept beyond control,
Consents to his inexorable will.

                                                    —1969

The Writer

In her room at the prow of the house
Where light breaks, and the windows are tossed with linden,
My daughter is writing a story.

I pause in the stairwell, hearing
From her shut door a commotion of typewriter-keys   5
Like a chain hauled over a gunwale.

Young as she is, the stuff
Of her life is a great cargo, and some of it heavy:
I wish her a lucky passage.

But now it is she who pauses,   10
As if to reject my thought and its easy figure.
A stillness greatens, in which

The whole house seems to be thinking,
And then she is at it again with a bunched clamor
Of strokes, and again is silent.   15

I remember the dazed starling
Which was trapped in that very room, two years ago;
How we stole in, lifted a sash

And retreated, not to affright it;
And how for a helpless hour, through the crack of the door, 20
We watched the sleek, wild, dark

And iridescent creature
Batter against the brilliance, drop like a glove
To the hard floor, or the desk-top.

And wait then, humped and bloody,   25
For the wits to try it again; and how our spirits
Rose when, suddenly sure,

It lifted off from a chair-back,
Beating a smooth course for the right window
And clearing the sill of the world.   30

It is always a matter, my darling,
Of life or death, as I had forgotten. I wish
What I wished you before, but harder.

                                                      −1976

Year's End

Now winter downs the dying of the year,
And night is all a settlement of snow;
From the soft street the rooms of houses show
A gathered light, a shapen atmosphere,
Like frozen-over lakes whose ice is thin   5
And still allows some stirring down within.

I've known the wind by water banks to shake
The late leaves down, which frozen where they fell
And held in ice as dancers in a spell
Fluttered all winter long into a lake;   10
Graved on the dark in gestures of descent,
They seemed their own most perfect monument.

There was perfection in the death of ferns
Which laid their fragile cheeks against the stone
A million years. Great mammoths overthrown   15
Composedly have made their long sojourns,
Like palaces of patience, in the gray
And changeless lands of ice. And at Pompeii°

The little dog lay curled and did not rise
But slept the deeper as the ashes rose   20
And found the people incomplete, and froze

18 **Pompeii** Roman city destroyed by volcanic eruption in A.D. 79

The random hands, the loose unready eyes
Of men expecting yet another sun
To do the shapely thing they had not done.

These sudden ends of time must give us pause. 25
We fray into the future, rarely wrought
Save in the tapestries of afterthought.
More time, more time. Barrages of applause
Come muffled from a buried radio.
The New-year bells are wrangling with the snow. 30

—1950

PHILIP LARKIN 1922–1985

After W. H. Auden, Larkin was perhaps the last British poet to estab-
lish a significant body of readers in the United States. The general
pessimism of his work is mitigated by a wry sense of irony and brilliant formal control. For many years he was a librarian at the
University of Hull, and he was also a dedicated fan and critic of jazz.

Next, Please

Always too eager for the future, we
Pick up bad habits of expectancy.
Something is always approaching; every day
Till then we say,

Watching from a bluff the tiny, clear, 5
Sparkling armada of promises draw near.
How slow they are! And how much time they waste,
Refusing to make haste!

Yet still they leave us holding wretched stalks
Of disappointment, for, though nothing balks 10
Each big approach, leaning with brasswork prinked,
Each rope distinct,

Flagged, and the figurehead with golden tits
Arching our way, it never anchors; it's
No sooner present than it turns to past. 15
Right to the last

We think each one will heave to and unload
All good into our lives, all we are owed

For waiting so devoutly and so long.
But we are wrong: 20

Only one ship is seeking us, a black-
Sailed unfamiliar, towing at her back
A huge and birdless silence. In her wake
No waters breed or break.

                                                —1951

Aubade

I work all day, and get half drunk at night.
Waking at four to soundless dark, I stare.
In time the curtain-edges will grow light.
Till then I see what's really always there:
Unresting death, a whole day nearer now,   5
Making all thought impossible but how
And where and when I shall myself die.
Arid interrogation: yet the dread
Of dying, and being dead,
Flashes afresh to hold and horrify.   10

The mind blanks at the glare. Not in remorse
—The good not done, the love not given, time
Torn off unused—nor wretchedly because
An only life can take so long to climb
Clear of its wrong beginnings, and may never;   15
But at the total emptiness for ever,
The sure extinction that we travel to
And shall be lost in always. Not to be here,
Not to be anywhere,
And soon; nothing more terrible, nothing more true.   20

This is a special way of being afraid
No trick dispels. Religion used to try,
That vast moth-eaten musical brocade
Created to pretend we never die,
And specious stuff that says No rational being   25
Can fear a thing it will not feel, not seeing
That this is what we fear—no sight, no sound,
No touch or taste or smell, nothing to think with,
Nothing to love or link with,
The anaesthetic from which none come round.   30

And so it stays just on the edge of vision,
A small unfocused blur, a standing chill

That slows each impulse down to indecision.
Most things may never happen: this one will,
And realization of it rages out   35
In furnace-fear when we are caught without
People or drink. Courage is no good:
It means not scaring others. Being brave
Lets no one off the grave.
Death is no different whined at than withstood.   40

Slowly light strengthens, and the room takes shape.
It stands plain as a wardrobe, what we know,
Have always known, know that we can't escape,
Yet can't accept. One side will have to go.
Meanwhile telephones crouch, getting ready to ring   45
In locked-up offices, and all the uncaring
Intricate rented world begins to rouse.
The sky is white as clay, with no sun.
Work has to be done.
Postmen like doctors go from house to house.   50

                                                        —1977

This Be The Verse

They fuck you up, your mum and dad.
    They may not mean to, but they do.
They fill you with the faults they had
    And add some extra, just for you.

But they were fucked up in their turn   5
    By fools in old-style hats and coats,
Who half the time were soppy-stern
    And half at one another's throats.

Man hands on misery to man.
    It deepens like a coastal shelf.   10
Get out as early as you can,
    And don't have any kids yourself.

                                                        —1971

JAMES DICKEY   1923–1997

Dickey became a national celebrity with the success of his novel
Deliverance (1970) and the celebrated film version. There was a long
background to Dickey's success, with years spent in the advertising
business before he devoted himself fully to writing. Born in Atlanta

and educated at Clemson, Vanderbilt, and Rice Universities, Dickey
rarely strayed long from the South and taught at the University of
South Carolina for over two decades.

Cherrylog Road

Off Highway 106
At Cherrylog Road I entered
The '34 Ford without wheels,
Smothered in kudzu,°
With a seat pulled out to run   5
Corn whiskey down from the hills,

And then from the other side
Crept into an Essex
With a rumble seat of red leather
And then out again, aboard   10
A blue Chevrolet, releasing
The rust from its other color,

Reared up on three building blocks
None had the same body heat;
I changed with them inward, toward   15
The weedy heart of the junkyard,
For I knew that Doris Holbrook
Would escape from her father at noon

And would come from the farm
To seek parts owned by the sun   20
Among the abandoned chassis,
Sitting in each in turn
As I did, leaning forward
As in a wild stock-car race

In the parking lot of the dead.   25
Time after time, I climbed in
And out the other side, like
An envoy or movie star
Met at the station by crickets.
A radiator cap raised its head,   30

Become a real toad or a kingsnake
As I neared the hub of the yard,
Passing through many states,
Many lives, to reach

---

4 kudzu prolific Asian vine widespread in the South

Some grandmother's long Pierce-Arrow   35
Sending platters of blindness forth

From its nickel hubcaps
And spilling its tender upholstery
On sleepy roaches,
The glass panel in between   40
Lady and colored driver
Not all the way broken out,

The back-seat phone
Still on its hook.
I got in as though to exclaim,   45
"Let us go to the orphan asylum,
John; I have some old toys
For children who say their prayers."

I popped with sweat as I thought
I heard Doris Holbrook scrape   50
Like a mouse in the southern-state sun
That was eating the paint in blisters
From a hundred car tops and hoods
She was tapping like code,

Loosening the screws,   55
Carrying off headlights,
Sparkplugs, bumpers,
Cracked mirrors and gear-knobs,
Getting ready, already,
To go back with something to show   60

Other than her lips' new trembling
I would hold to me soon, soon,
Where I sat in the ripped back seat
Talking over the interphone,
Praying for Doris Holbrook   65
To come from her father's farm

And to get back there
With no trace of me on her face
To be seen by her red-haired father
Who would change, in the squalling barn   70
Her back's pale skin with a strop,
Then lay for me

In a bootlegger's roasting car
With a string-triggered 12-gauge shotgun

To blast the breath from the air.   75
Not cut by the jagged windshields,
Through the acres of wrecks she came
With a wrench in her hand,

Through dust where the blacksnake dies
Of boredom, and the beetle knows   80
The compost has no more life.
Someone outside would have seen
The oldest car's door inexplicably
Close from within:

I held her and held her and held her,   85
Convoyed at terrific speed
By the stalled, dreaming traffic around us,
So the blacksnake, stiff
With inaction, curved back
Into life, and hunted the mouse   90

With deadly overexcitement,
The beetles reclaimed their field
As we clung, glued together,
With the hooks of the seat springs
Working through to catch us red-handed   95
Amidst the gray breathless batting

That burst from the seat at our backs.
We left by separate doors
Into the changed, other bodies
Of cars, she down Cherrylog Road   100
And I to my motorcycle
Parked like the soul of the junkyard

Restored, a bicycle fleshed
With power, and tore off
Up Highway 106, continually   105
Drunk on the wind in my mouth,
Wringing the handlebar for speed,
Wild to be wreckage forever.

                                                          —1964

Alan Dugan   b. 1923

Dugan received the 1961 Yale Younger Poets Award, leading to the
publication of his first collection as he neared forty. His plainspoken
poetic voice, often with sardonic overtones, is appropriate for the

anti-romantic stance of his most characteristic poems. For many
years Dugan has been associated with the Fine Arts Work Center in
Provincetown, Massachusetts, on Cape Cod.

Love Song: I and Thou

Nothing is plumb, level or square:
    the studs are bowed, the joists
are shaky by nature, no piece fits
    any other piece without a gap
or pinch, and bent nails   5
    dance all over the surfacing
like maggots. By Christ
    I am no carpenter. I built
the roof for myself, the walls
    for myself, the floors   10
for myself, and got
    hung up in it myself. I
danced with a purple thumb
    at this house-warming, drunk
with my prime whiskey: rage.   15
    Oh I spat rage's nails
into the frame-up of my work:
    it held. It settled plumb,
level, solid, square and true
    for that great moment. Then   20
it screamed and went on through,
    skewing as wrong the other way.
God damned it. This is hell,
    but I planned it, I sawed it,
I nailed it, and I   25
    will live in it until it kills me.
I can nail my left palm
    to the left-hand cross-piece but
I can't do everything myself.
    I need a hand to nail the right,   30
a help, a love, a you, a wife.

                                                              —1961

ANTHONY HECHT   B. 1923

Hecht is most often linked with Richard Wilbur as one of the
American poets of the postwar era who have most effectively utilized

traditional poetic forms. The brilliance of Hecht's technique, however, must be set beside the powerful moral intelligence that informs his poetry. *The Hard Hours*, his second collection, won the Pulitzer Prize for 1968.

"More Light! More Light!"°

FOR HEINRICH BLÜCHER AND HANNAH ARENDT°

Composed in the Tower before his° execution
These moving verses, and being brought at that time
Painfully to the stake, submitted, declaring thus:
"I implore my God to witness that I have made no crime."

Nor was he forsaken of courage, but the death was horrible,   5
The sack of gunpowder failing to ignite.
His legs were blistered sticks on which the black sap
Bubbled and burst as he howled for the Kindly Light.

And that was but one, and by no means one of the worst;
Permitted at least his pitiful dignity;   10
And such as were by made prayers in the name of Christ,
That shall judge all men, for his soul's tranquillity.

We move now to outside a German wood.°
Three men are there commanded to dig a hole
In which the two Jews are ordered to lie down   15
And be buried alive by the third, who is a Pole.

Not light from the shrine at Weimar° beyond the hill
Nor light from heaven appeared. But he did refuse.
A Lüger° settled back deeply in its glove.
He was ordered to change places with the Jews.   20

Much casual death had drained away their souls.
The thick dirt mounted toward the quivering chin.
When only the head was exposed the order came
To dig him out again and to get back in.

No light, no light in the blue Polish eye.   25
When he finished a riding boot packed down the earth.

"**More Light! More Light!**" reputed last words of Johann Wolfgang von Goethe (1749-1832), greatest German poet   **Heinrich Blücher and Hannah Arendt** husband and wife who escaped from Germany in 1941; Arendt wrote several books on the Holocaust   **1 his** a fictional English religious martyr (c. 1550), a composite of several actual cases   **13 German wood** Buchenwald ("beechen wood") was the site of a concentration camp.   **17 shrine at Weimar** Goethe's home   **19 Lüger** German military pistol

The Lüger hovered lightly in its glove.
He was shot in the belly and in three hours bled to death.

No prayers or incense rose up in those hours
Which grew to be years, and every day came mute   30
Ghosts from the ovens, sifting through crisp air,
And settled upon his eyes in a black soot.

                                            —1967

D<small>ENISE</small> L<small>EVERTOV</small>   B. 1923

Levertov was as an outspoken opponent of U.S. involvement in the
Vietnam War, an activity that has tended to overshadow her accom-
plishments as a lyric poet. Born of Jewish and Welsh parents in
England, she emigrated to the United States during World War II.

The Ache of Marriage

The ache of marriage:

thigh and tongue, beloved,
are heavy with it,
it throbs in the teeth

We look for communion   5
and are turned away, beloved,
each and each

It is leviathan° and we
in its belly
looking for joy, some joy   10
not to be known outside it

two by two in the ark of
the ache of it.

                                            —1964

L<small>OUIS</small> S<small>IMPSON</small>   B. 1923

Born in Jamaica to a colonial lawyer and an American mother,
Simpson came to the United States in his teens and served in the
U.S. Army in World War II. He won the Pulitzer Prize in 1964 for

---

8 leviathan great sea-creature mentioned in book of Job

At the End of the Open Road, a volume that attempts to reexamine
Walt Whitman's nineteenth-century definitions of the American
experience. Subsequent collections have continued to demonstrate
Simpson's unsentimental view of American suburban life.

American Classic

It's a classic American scene—
a car stopped off the road
and a man trying to repair it.

The woman who stays in the car
in the classic American scene   5
stares back at the freeway traffic.

They look surprised, and ashamed
to be so helpless . . .
let down in the middle of the road!

To think that their car would do this!   10
They look like mountain people
whose son has gone against the law.

But every night they set out food
and the robber goes skulking back to the trees.
That's how it is with the car . . .   15

it's theirs, they're stuck with it.
Now they know what it's like to sit
and see the world go whizzing by.

In the fume of carbon monoxide and dust
they are not such good Americans   20
as they thought they were.

The feeling of being left out
through no fault of your own, is common.
That's why I say, an American classic.

                                                        —1980

My Father in the Night Commanding No

My father in the night commanding No
Has work to do. Smoke issues from his lips;

He reads in silence.
The frogs are croaking and the street lamps glow.

And then my mother winds the gramophone: 5
The Bride of Lammermoor° begins to shriek—
  Or reads a story
About a prince, a castle, and a dragon.

The moon is glittering above the hill.
I stand before the gateposts of the King—   10
  So runs the story—
Of Thule, at midnight when the mice are still.

And I have been in Thule! It has come true—
The journey and the danger of the world,
  All that there is   15
To bear and to enjoy, endure and do.

Landscapes, seascapes . . . Where have I been led?
The names of cities—Paris, Venice, Rome—
  Held out their arms.
A feathered god, seductive, went ahead.   20

Here is my house. Under a red rose tree
A child is swinging; another gravely plays.
  They are not surprised
That I am here; they were expecting me.

And yet my father sits and reads in silence,   25
My mother sheds a tear, the moon is still,
  And the dark wind
Is murmuring that nothing ever happens.

Beyond his jurisdiction as I move,
Do I not prove him wrong? And yet, it's true   30
  They will not change
There, on the stage of terror and of love.

The actors in that playhouse always sit
In fixed positions—father, mother, child
  With painted eyes.   35
How sad it is to be a little puppet!

---

6 **Bride of Lammermoor** *Lucia di Lammermoor*, opera by Donizetti

Their heads are wooden. And you once pretended
To understand them! Shake them as you will,
     They cannot speak.
Do what you will, the comedy is ended.   40

Father, why did you work? Why did you weep,
Mother? Was the story so important?
          "*Listen!*" the wind
Said to the children, and they fell asleep.

                                                         —1963

V<small>ASSAR</small> M<small>ILLER</small>   B. 1924

A lifelong resident of Houston, Texas, and a victim of cerebral palsy
since birth, Miller has published both traditional devotional verse
and a large amount of poetry in open form. *If I Had Wheels or Love,*
her collected poems, appeared in 1990.

Subterfuge

I remember my father, slight,
staggering in with his Underwood,°
bearing it in his arms like an awkward bouquet

for his spastic child who sits down
on the floor, one knee on the frame   5
of the typewriter, and holding her left wrist

with her right hand, in that precision known
to the crippled, pecks at the keys
with a sparrow's preoccupation.

Falling by chance on rhyme, novel and curious bubble   10
blown with a magic pipe, she tries them over and over,
spellbound by life's clashing in accord or against itself,

pretending pretense and playing at playing,
she does her childhood backward as children do,
her fun a delaying action against what she knows.   15

---

2 **Underwood** popular brand of manual typewriter

My father must lose her, his runaway on her treadmill,
will lose the terrible favor that life has done him
as she toils at tomorrow, tensed at her makeshift toy.

                                                    —1981

DONALD JUSTICE   B. 1925

Justice has published more selectively than most of his contemporaries. His Pulitzer Prize-winning volume of selected poems displays
considerable literary sophistication and reveals the poet's familiarity
with the traditions of contemporary European and Latin American
poetry. As an editor, he is responsible for rescuing the important
work of Weldon Kees from obscurity.

In Bertram's Garden

Jane looks down at her organdy skirt
As if it somehow were the thing disgraced,
For being there, on the floor, in the dirt,
And she catches it up about her waist,
Smooths it out along one hip,   5
And pulls it over the crumpled slip.

On the porch, green-shuttered, cool,
Asleep is Bertram, that bronze boy,
Who, having wound her around a spool,
Sends her spinning like a toy   10
Out to the garden, all alone,
To sit and weep on a bench of stone.

Soon the purple dark will bruise
Lily and bleeding-heart and rose,
And the little Cupid lose   15
Eyes and ears and chin and nose,
And Jane lie down with others soon
Naked to the naked moon.

                                                    —1960

CAROLYN KIZER   B. 1925

Kizer's fascinating career includes a year's study in Taiwan and
another year in Pakistan, where she worked for the U.S. State

Department. Her first collection, *The Ungrateful Garden* (1961), demonstrates an equal facility with formal and free verse, but her subsequent books (including the Pulitzer Prize-winning *Yin* of 1985) have tended more toward the latter. A committed feminist, Kizer anticipated many of today's women's issues as early as the mid-1950s, just as the poem "The Ungrateful Garden" was published a decade before "ecology" became a household word.

The Ungrateful Garden

Midas watched the golden crust
That formed over his streaming sores,
Hugged his agues, loved his lust,
But damned to hell the out-of-doors

Where blazing motes of sun impaled   5
The serried° roses, metal-bright.
"Those famous flowers," Midas wailed,
"Have scorched my retina with light."

This gift, he'd thought, would gild his joys,
Silt up the waters of his grief;   10
His lawns a wilderness of noise,
The heavy clang of leaf on leaf.

Within, the golden cup is good
To heft, to sip the yellow mead.
Outside, in summer's rage, the rude   15
Gold thorn has made his fingers bleed.

"I strolled my halls in golden shift,
As ruddy as a lion's meat.
Then I rushed out to share my gift,
And golden stubble cut my feet."   20

Dazzled with wounds, he limped away
To climb into his golden bed.
Roses, roses can betray.
"Nature is evil," Midas said.

—1961

MAXINE KUMIN   B. 1925

Born in Philadelphia and educated at Radcliffe, Kumin was an early literary ally and friend of Anne Sexton, with whom she co-authored

---

6 **serried** crowded in rows

several children's books. The winner of the 1973 Pulitzer Prize, Kumin has preferred a rural life raising horses for some years. Her increased interest in the natural world has paralleled the environmental awareness of many of her readers.

Noted in the New York Times

LAKE BUENA VISTA, FLORIDA, JUNE 16, 1987

Death claimed the last pure dusky seaside sparrow
today, whose coastal range was narrow,
as narrow as its two-part buzzy song.
From hummocks lost to Cape Canaveral
this mouselike skulker in the matted grass,   5
a six-inch bird, plain brown, once thousands strong,
sang *toodle-raeee azhee*, ending on a trill
before the air gave way to rocket blasts.

It laid its dull white eggs (brown specked) in small
neat cups of grass on plots of pickleweed,   10
bulrushes, or salt hay. It dined
on caterpillars, beetles, ticks, the seeds
of sedges. Unremarkable
the life it lead with others of its kind.

Tomorrow we can put it on a stamp,   15
a first-day cover with Key Largo rat,
Schaus swallowtail, Florida swamp
crocodile, and fading cotton mouse.
How simply symbols replace habitat!
The tower frames of Aerospace   20
quiver in the flush of another shot
where, once indigenous, the dusky sparrow
soared trilling twenty feet above its burrow.

                                                            —1989

ROBERT CREELEY   B. 1926

Educated at Harvard, Creeley is one of several important contemporary poets (Denise Levertov is another) to be associated with Black Mountain College, a small experimental school in North Carolina that attracted writers and artists during the 1950s.

I Know a Man

As I sd to my
friend, because I am
always talking,—John, I

sd, which was not his
name, the darkness sur-   5
rounds us, what

can we do against
it, or else, shall we &
why not, buy a goddamn big car,

drive, he sd, for   10
christ's sake, look
out where yr going.

                                                    —1962

Oh No

If you wander far enough
you will come to it
and when you get there
they will give you a place to sit

for yourself only, in a nice chair,   5
and all your friends will be there
with smiles on their faces
and they will likewise all have places.

                                                    —1962

ALLEN GINSBERG   1926–1997

Ginsberg, the chief poetic spokesman of the Beat Generation, was a
force—as poet and celebrity—who continued to outrage and delight
four decades after the appearance of *Howl*, the monumental poem
describing how Ginsberg saw: "the best minds of my generation
destroyed by madness." Ginsberg's poems are cultural documents
key to understanding the radical changes in American life, particularly among youth, that began in the mid-1950s.

A Supermarket in California

What thoughts I have of you tonight, Walt Whitman, for I
walked down the sidestreets under the trees with a headache self-
conscious looking at the full moon.
    In my hungry fatigue, and shopping for images, I went into
the neon fruit supermarket, dreaming of your enumerations!
    What peaches and what penumbras?° Whole families shopping

---

3 penumbras shadows

at night! Aisles full of husbands! Wives in the avocados, babies
in the tomatoes!—and you, García Lorca,° what were you doing
down by the watermelons?

I saw you, Walt Whitman, childless, lonely old grubber,
poking among the meats in the refrigerator and eyeing the
grocery boys.
I heard you asking questions of each: Who killed the pork
chops? What price bananas? Are you my Angel?   5
I wandered in and out of the brilliant stacks of cans following you, and followed in my imagination by the store detective.
We strode down the open corridors together in our solitary
fancy tasting artichokes, possessing every frozen delicacy, and
never passing the cashier.

Where are we going, Walt Whitman? The doors close in an
hour. Which way does your beard point tonight?
(I touch your book and dream of our odyssey in the supermarket and feel absurd.)
Will we walk all night through solitary streets? The trees add
shade to shade, lights out in the houses, we'll both be lonely.   10
Will we stroll dreaming of the lost America of love past blue
automobiles in driveways, home to our silent cottage?
Ah, dear father, graybeard, lonely old courage-teacher, what
America did you have when Charon° quit poling his ferry and
you got out on a smoking bank and stood watching the boat
disappear on the black waters of Lethe?°

—1956

JAMES MERRILL   1926-1995

Merrill's The "Changing Light at Sandover," a long poem that
resulted from many years of sessions with a Ouija board, is Merrill's
major work and, among many other things, a remarkable memoir of
a long-term gay relationship. Merrill's shorter poems reveal meticulous craftsmanship and a play of wit unequaled among contemporary American poets.

Casual Wear

Your average tourist: Fifty. 2.3
Times married. Dressed, this year, in Ferdi Plinthbower°

---

3 **García Lorca** Federico García Lorca, Spanish poet (1899-1936)   12 **Charon** ferryman of
Hades   **Lethe** river in Hades, means forgetfulness
2 **Ferdi Plinthbower** a fictional designer

Originals. Odds 1 to $9^{10°}$
Against her strolling past the Embassy

Today at noon. Your average terrorist: 5
Twenty-five. Celibate. No use for trends,
At least in clothing. Mark, though, where it ends.
People have come forth made of colored mist

Unsmiling on one hundred million screens
To tell of his prompt phone call to the station,   10
"Claiming responsibility"—devastation
Signed with a flourish, like the dead wife's jeans.

                                              —1984

Charles on Fire

Another evening we sprawled about discussing
Appearances. And it was the consensus
That while uncommon physical good looks
Continued to launch one, as before, in life
(Among its vaporous eddies and false calms),   5
Still, as one of us said into his beard,
"Without your intellectual and spiritual
Values, man, you are sunk." No one but squared
The shoulders of his own unloveliness.
Long-suffering Charles, having cooked and served the meal,   10
Now brought out little tumblers finely etched
He filled with amber liquor and then passed.
"Say," said the same young man, "in Paris, France,
They do it this way"—bounding to his feet
And touching a lit match to our host's full glass.   15
A blue flame, gentle, beautiful, came, went
Above the surface. In a hush that fell
We heard the vessel crack. The contents drained
As who should step down from a crystal coach.
Steward of spirits, Charles's glistening hand   20
All at once gloved itself in eeriness.
The moment passed. He made two quick sweeps and
Was flesh again. "It couldn't matter less,"
He said, but with a shocked, unconscious glance
Into the mirror. Finding nothing changed,   25
He filled a fresh glass and sank down among us.

                                              —1966

---

3 **1 to 9^{10}** pronounced "one to nine to the tenth power"

W. D. SNODGRASS B. 1926

Snodgrass won the Pulitzer Prize for his first collection, *Heart's Needle,* and is generally considered one of the first important con-fessional poets. However, in his later career he has turned away from autobiographical subjects, writing a long sequence of dramatic monologues spoken by leading Nazis during the final days of the Hitler regime.

Mementos, I

Sorting out letters and piles of my old
    Canceled checks, old clippings, and yellow note cards
That meant something once, I happened to find
    Your picture. *That* picture. I stopped there cold,
Like a man raking piles of dead leaves in his yard   5
    Who has turned up a severed hand.

Still, that first second, I was glad: you stand
    Just as you stood—shy, delicate, slender,
In that long gown of green lace netting and daisies
    That you wore to our first dance. The sight of you stunned   10
Us all. Well, our needs were different, then,
    And our ideals came easy.

Then through the war and those two long years
    Overseas, the Japanese dead in their shacks
Among dishes, dolls, and lost shoes; I carried   15
    This glimpse of you, there, to choke down my fear,
Prove it had been, that it might come back.
    That was before we got married.

—Before we drained out one another's force
    With lies, self-denial, unspoken regret   20
And the sick eyes that blame; before the divorce
    And the treachery. Say it: before we met. Still,
I put back your picture. Someday, in due course,
    I will find that it's still there.

—1968

FRANK O'HARA 1926–1966

O'Hara's untimely death in a dune buggy accident on Fire Island robbed American poetry of one its most refreshing talents. An

authority on modern art, O'Hara incorporates many of the spontaneous techniques of abstract painting in his own poetry, which was
often written as an immediate reaction to the events of his daily life.

The Day Lady° Died

It is 12:20 in New York a Friday
three days after Bastille day,° yes
it is 1959 and I go get a shoeshine
because I will get off the 4:19 in Easthampton
at 7:15 and then go straight to dinner   5
and I don't know the people who will feed me

I walk up the muggy street beginning to sun
and have a hamburger and a malted and buy
an ugly NEW WORLD WRITING to see what the poets
in Ghana are doing these days   10
                                 I go on to the bank
and Miss Stillwagon (first name Linda I once heard)
doesn't even look up my balance for once in her life
and in the GOLDEN GRIFFIN I get a little Verlaine
for Patsy with drawings by Bonnard although I do   15
think of Hesiod, trans. Richard Lattimore or
Brendan Behan's new play or *Le Balcon* or *Les Nègres*
of Genet, but I don't, I stick with Verlaine
after practically going to sleep with quandariness

and for Mike I just stroll into the PARK LANE   20
Liquor Store and ask for a bottle of Strega and
then I go back where I came from to 6th Avenue
and the tobacconist in the Ziegfeld Theatre and
casually ask for a carton of Gauloises and a carton
of Picayunes, and a NEW YORK POST with her face on it   25

and I am sweating a lot by now and thinking of
leaning on the john door in the 5 SPOT
while she whispered a song along the keyboard
to Mal Waldron° and everyone and I stopped breathing.

                                                    —1964

Lady Billie Holiday (1915-1959), blues singer   2 Bastille day July 14   29 Mal Waldron
Holiday's accompanist.

JOHN ASHBERY   B. 1927

Ashbery was born in Rochester, New York, and educated at Harvard University. His first full-length book, *Some Trees*, was chosen by W. H. Auden as winner of the Yale Younger Poets Award in 1956. His enigmatic poems have intrigued readers for so long that much contemporary literary theory seems to have been created expressly for explicating his poems. Impossible to dismiss, Ashbery is now seen as the chief inheritor of the symbolist tradition brought to American locales by Wallace Stevens.

Farm Implements and Rutabagas in a Landscape

The first of the undecoded messages read: "Popeye sits in thunder,
Unthought of. From that shoebox of an apartment,
From livid curtain's hue, a tangram emerges: a country."
Meanwhile the Sea Hag was relaxing on a green couch: "How pleasant
To spend one's vacation *en la casa de Popeye*," she scratched   5
Her cleft chin's solitary hair. She remembered spinach

And was going to ask Wimpy if he had bought any spinach.
"M'love," he intercepted, "the plains are decked out in thunder
Today, and it shall be as you wish." He scratched
The part of his head under his hat. The apartment   10
Seemed to grow smaller. "But what if no pleasant
Inspiration plunge us now to the stars? *For this is my country.*"

Suddenly they remembered how it was cheaper in the country.
Wimpy was thoughtfully cutting open a number 2 can of spinach
When the door opened and Swee'pea crept in. "How pleasant!"   15
But Swee'pea looked morose. A note was pinned to his bib.
    "Thunder
And tears are unavailing," it read. "Henceforth shall Popeye's apartment
Be but remembered space, toxic or salubrious, whole or scratched."

Olive came hurtling through the window; its geraniums scratched
Her long thigh. "I have news!" she gasped. "Popeye, forced as you
    know to flee the country   20
One musty gusty evening, by the schemes of his wizened, duplicate
    father, jealous of the apartment
And all that it contains, myself and spinach

In particular, heaves bolts of loving thunder
At his own astonished becoming, rupturing the pleasant

Arpeggio of our years. No more shall pleasant   25
Rays of the sun refresh your sense of growing old, nor the
    scratched
Tree-trunks and mossy foliage, only immaculate darkness and
    thunder."
She grabbed Swee'pea. "I'm taking the brat to the country."
"But you can't do that—he hasn't even finished his spinach,"
Urged the Sea Hag, looking fearfully around at the apartment.   30

But Olive was already out of earshot. Now the apartment
Succumbed to a strange new hush. "Actually it's quite pleasant
Here," thought the Sea Hag. "If this is all we need fear from spinach
Then I don't mind so much. Perhaps we could invite Alice the
    Goon over"——she scratched
One dug pensively——"but Wimpy is such a country   35
Bumpkin, always burping like that." Minute at first, the thunder

Soon filled the apartment. It was domestic thunder,
The color of spinach. Popeye chuckled and scratched
His balls: it sure was pleasant to spend a day in the country.
                                                        —1966

Paradoxes and Oxymorons

The poem is concerned with language on a very plain level.
Look at it talking to you. You look out a window
Or pretend to fidget. You have it but you don't have it.
You miss it, it misses you. You miss each other.

The poem is sad because it wants to be yours, and cannot.   5
What's a plain level? It is that and other things,
Bringing a system of them into play. Play?
Well, actually, yes, but I consider play to be

A deeper outside thing, a dreamed role-pattern,
As in the division of grace these long August days   10
Without proof. Open-ended. And before you know
It gets lost in the steam and chatter of typewriters.

It has been played once more. I think you exist only
To tease me into doing it, on your level, and then you aren't there
Or have adopted a different attitude. And the poem   15
Has set me softly down beside you. The poem is you.
                                                        —1981

W. S. MERWIN   B. 1927

In recent years Merwin's environmental concerns have come to dom-
inate his poetry, but even in earlier work his fears of the results of
uncontrolled destruction of the environment are presented allegori-
cally. Born in New York City, he currently resides in Hawaii.

For the Anniversary of My Death

Every year without knowing it I have passed the day
When the last fires will wave to me
And the silence will set out
Tireless traveller
Like the beam of a lightless star   5

Then I will no longer
find myself in life as in a strange garment
surprised at the earth
And the love of one woman
And then shamelessness of men   10
As today writing after three days of rain
Hearing the wren sing and the falling cease
And bowing not knowing to what

                                                          —1969

The Last One

Well they'd make up their minds to be everywhere because why not.
Everywhere was theirs because they thought so.
They with two leaves they whom the birds despise.
In the middle of stones they made up their minds.
They started to cut.   5

Well they cut everything because why not.
Everything was theirs because they thought so.
It fell into its shadows and they took both away.
Some to have some for burning.

Well cutting everything they came to the water.   10
They came to the end of the day there was one left standing.
They would cut it tomorrow they went away.
The night gathered in the last branches.
The shadow of the night gathered in the shadow on the water.
The night and the shadow put on the same head.   15
And it said Now.

Well in the morning they cut the last one.
Like the others the last one fell into its shadow.
It fell into its shadow on the water.
They took it away its shadow stayed on the water.   20

Well they shrugged they started trying to get the shadow away.
They cut right to the ground the shadow stayed whole.
They laid boards on it the shadow came out on top.
They shone lights on it the shadow got blacker and clearer.
They exploded the water the shadow rocked.   25
They built a huge fire on the roots.
They sent up black smoke between the shadow and the sun.
The new shadow flowed without changing the old one.
They shrugged they went away to get stones.

They came back the shadow was growing.   30
They started setting up stones it was growing.
They looked the other way it went on growing.
They decided they would make a stone out of it.
They took stones to the water they poured them into the shadow.
They poured them in they poured them in the stones vanished.   35
The shadow was not filled it went on growing.
That was one day.

The next day was just the same it went on growing.
They did all the same things it was just the same.
They decided to take its water from under it.   40
They took away water they took it away the water went down.
The shadow stayed where it was before.
It went on growing it grew onto the land.
They started to scrape the shadow with machines.
When it touched the machines it stayed on them.   45
They started to beat the shadow with sticks.
Where it touched the sticks it stayed on them.
They started to beat the shadow with hands.
Where it touched the hands it stayed on them.
That was another day.   50

Well the next day started about the same it went on growing.
They pushed lights into the shadow.
Where the shadow got onto them they went out.
They began to stomp on the edge it got their feet.
And when it got their feet they fell down.   55
It got into eyes the eyes went blind.
The ones that fell down it grew over and they vanished.

The ones that went blind and walked into it vanished.
The ones that could see and stood still
It swallowed their shadows.   60
Then it swallowed them too and they vanished.
Well the others ran.

The ones that were left went away to live if it would let them.
They went as far as they could.
The lucky ones with their shadows.   65

                                                    —1969

J AMES W RIGHT   1927–1980

Wright's compassion for losers and underdogs of all types is everywhere in his poetry. A native of Martins Ferry, Ohio, he often
described lives of quiet desperation in the blue-collar towns of his
youth. Like many poets of his generation, Wright wrote formal verse
in his early career and shifted to open forms during the 1960s.

A Blessing

Just off the highway to Rochester, Minnesota,
Twilight bounds softly forth on the grass.
And the eyes of those two Indian ponies
Darken with kindness.
They have come gladly out of the willows   5
To welcome my friend and me.
We step over the barbed wire into the pasture
Where they have been grazing all day, alone.
They ripple tensely, they can hardly contain their happiness
That we have come.   10
They bow shyly as wet swans. They love each other.
There is no loneliness like theirs.
At home once more,
They begin munching the young tufts of spring in the darkness.
I would like to hold the slenderer one in my arms,   15
For she has walked over to me
And nuzzled my left hand.
She is black and white,
Her mane falls wild on her forehead,
And the light breeze moves me to caress her long ear   20
That is delicate as the skin over a girl's wrist.
Suddenly I realize
That if I stepped out of my body I would break
Into blossom.

                                                    —1963

Saint Judas

When I went out to kill myself, I caught
A pack of hoodlums beating up a man.
Running to spare his suffering, I forgot
My name, my number, how my day began,
How soldiers milled around the garden stone   5
And sang amusing songs; how all that day
Their javelins measured crowds; how I alone
Bargained the proper coins, and slipped away.

Banished from heaven, I found this victim beaten,
Stripped, kneed, and left to cry. Dropping my rope   10
Aside, I ran, ignored the uniforms:
Then I remembered bread my flesh had eaten,
The kiss that ate my flesh. Flayed without hope,
I held the man for nothing in my arms.

                                              —1959

PHILIP LEVINE   B. 1928

Born in Detroit, Michigan, Levine is one of many contemporary
poets to hold a degree from the University of Iowa Writers'
Workshop. The gritty urban landscapes and characters trapped in
dead-end industrial jobs that provide Levine subjects for many
poems match exactly with his unadorned, informal idiom. Like the
deceptively simple William Carlos Williams, Levine has influenced
many younger poets.

Genius

Two old dancing shoes my grandfather
gave the Christian Ladies,
an unpaid water bill, the rear license
of a dog that messed on your lawn,
a tooth I saved for the good fairy   5
and which is stained with base metals
and plastic filler. With these images
and your black luck and my bad breath
a bright beginner could make a poem
in fourteen rhyming lines about the purity   10
of first love or the rose's many thorns
or dew that won't wait long enough
to stand my little gray wren a drink.

                                              —1981

Donald Petersen   B. 1928

Born in Minneapolis, Minnesota, Petersen taught for many years at the State University College in Oneonta, New York. One of Petersen's first appearances was in *New Poets of England and America*, a popular and influential anthology of the early 1960s.

The Ballad of Dead Yankees

Where's Babe Ruth,° the King of Swat,
Who rocked the heavens with his blows?
Grabowski, Pennock, and Malone—
Mother of mercy, where are those?

Where's Tony (Poosh 'em up) Lazzeri,   5
The quickest man that ever played?
Where's the gang that raised the roof
In the house that Colonel Ruppert made?

Where's Lou Gehrig, strong and shy,
who never missed a single game?   10
Where's Tiny Bonham, where's Jake Powell
And many another peerless name?

Where's Steve Sundra, good but late,
Who for a season had his fling?
Where are the traded, faded ones?   15
Lord, can they tell us anything?

Where's the withered nameless dwarf
Who sold us pencils at the gate?
Hurled past the clamor of our cheers?
Gone to rest with the good and great?   20

Where's the swagger, where's the strut,
Where's the style that was the hitter?
Where's the pitcher's swanlike motion?
What in God's name turned life bitter?

For strong-armed Steve, who lost control   25
And weighed no more than eighty pounds,

---

1 **Babe Ruth** This and the names that follow are those of former players for the New York Yankees.

No sooner benched than in his grave,
Where's the cleverness that confounds?

For Lou the man, erect and clean,
Wracked with a cruel paralysis,   30
Gone in his thirty-seventh year,
Where's the virtue that was his?

For nimble Tony, cramped in death,
God knows why and God knows how,
Shut in a dark and silent house,   35
Where's the squirrel quickness now?

For big brash Babe in an outsize suit,
Himself grown thin and hoarse with cancer,
Still autographing balls for boys,
Mother of mercy, what's the answer?   40

Is there a heaven with rainbow flags,
Silver trophies hung on walls,
A horseshoe grandstand, mobs of fans,
Webbed gloves and official balls?

Is there a power in judgment there   45
To stand behind the body's laws,
A stern-faced czar whose slightest word
Is righteous as Judge Kenesaw's?°

And if there be no turnstile gate
At that green park, can we get in?   50
Is the game suspended or postponed,
And do the players play to win?

Mother of mercy, if you're there,
Pray to the high celestial czar
For all of these, the early dead,   55
Who've gone where no ovations are.

                                                            —1964

ANNE SEXTON   1928–1974

Sexton, with her tortured history of mental illness and family troubles, is the model of the confessional poet. A housewife with two
small daughters, she began writing poetry as the result of a program

---

48 **Judge Kenesaw** Kenesaw Mountain Landis (1866-1945), the first commissioner of organized
baseball

on public television, later taking a workshop from Robert Lowell in
which Sylvia Plath was a fellow student. For fifteen years until her
suicide, she was a vibrant, exciting presence in American poetry. A
controversial biography of Sexton by Diane Wood Middlebrook
appeared in 1991.

Cinderella

You always read about it:
the plumber with twelve children
who wins the Irish Sweepstakes.
From toilets to riches.
That story.   5

Or the nursemaid,
some luscious sweet from Denmark
who captures the oldest son's heart.
From diapers to Dior.
That story.   10

Or a milkman who serves the wealthy,
eggs, cream, butter, yogurt, milk,
the white truck like an ambulance
who goes into real estate
and makes a pile.   15
From homogenized to martinis at lunch.

Or the charwoman
who is on the bus when it cracks up
and collects enough from the insurance.
From mops to Bonwit Teller.   20
That story.

Once
the wife of a rich man was on her deathbed
and she said to her daughter Cinderella:
Be devout. Be good. Then I will smile   25
down from heaven in the seam of a cloud.
The man took another wife who had
two daughters, pretty enough
but with hearts like blackjacks.
Cinderella was their maid.   30
She slept on the sooty hearth each night
and walked around looking like Al Jolson.
Her father brought presents home from town,
jewels and gowns for the other women

but the twig of a tree for Cinderella.   35
She planted that twig on her mother's grave
and it grew to a tree where a white dove sat.
Whenever she wished for anything the dove
would drop it like an egg upon the ground.
The bird is important, my dears, so heed him.   40

Next came the ball, as you all know.
It was a marriage market.
The prince was looking for a wife.
All but Cinderella were preparing
and gussying up for the big event.   45
Cinderella begged to go too.
Her stepmother threw a dish of lentils
into the cinders and said: Pick them
up in an hour and you shall go.
The white dove brought all his friends;   50
all the warm wings of the fatherland came,
and picked up the lentils in a jiffy.
No, Cinderella, said the stepmother,
you have no clothes and cannot dance.
That's the way with stepmothers.   55

Cinderella went to the tree at the grave
and cried forth like a gospel singer:
Mama! Mama! My turtledove,
send me to the prince's ball!
The bird dropped down a golden dress   60
and delicate little gold slippers.
Rather a large package for a simple bird.
So she went. Which is no surprise.
Her stepmother and sisters didn't
recognize her without her cinder face   65
and the prince took her hand on the spot
and danced with no other the whole day.

As nightfall came she thought she'd
better get home. The prince walked her home
and she disappeared into the pigeon house   70
and although the prince took an axe and broke
it open she was gone. Back to her cinders.
These events repeated themselves for three days.
However on the third day the prince
covered the palace steps with cobbler's wax   75
And Cinderella's gold shoe stuck upon it.

Now he would find whom the shoe fit
and find his strange dancing girl for keeps.
He went to their house and the two sisters
were delighted because they had lovely feet.   80
The eldest went into a room to try the slipper on
but her big toe got in the way so she simply
sliced it off and put on the slipper.
The prince rode away with her until the white dove
told him to look at the blood pouring forth.   85
That is the way with amputations.
They don't just heal up like a wish.
The other sister cut off her heel
but the blood told as blood will.
The prince was getting tired.   90
He began to feel like a shoe salesman.
But he gave it one last try.
This time Cinderella fit into the shoe
like a love letter into its envelope.

At the wedding ceremony   95
the two sisters came to curry favor
and the white dove pecked their eyes out.
Two hollow spots were left
like soup spoons.

Cinderella and the prince   100
lived, they say, happily ever after,
like two dolls in a museum case
never bothered by diapers or dust,
never arguing over the timing of an egg,
never telling the same story twice,   105
never getting a middle-aged spread,
their darling smiles pasted on for eternity
Regular Bobbsey Twins.
That story.

                                                    —1970

Thom Gunn   B. 1929

An expatriate who has lived in San Francisco for over four decades, Gunn has managed to retain his ties to the traditions of British literature while writing about motorcycle gangs, surfers, gay bars, and drug experiences. *The Man with Night Sweats*, his 1992 collection,

contains a number of forthright poems on AIDS, of which
"Terminal" is one.

From the Wave

It mounts at sea, a concave wall
    Down-ribbed with shine,
And pushes forward, building tall
    Its steep incline.

Then from their hiding rise to sight   5
    Black shapes on boards
Bearing before the fringe of white
    It mottles towards.

Their pale feet curl, they poise their weight
    With a learn'd skill.   10
It is the wave they imitate
    Keeps them so still.

The marbling bodies have become
    Half wave, half men,
Grafted it seems by feet of foam   15
    Some seconds, then,

Late as they can, they slice the face
    In timed procession:
Balance is triumph in this place,
    Triumph possession.   20

The mindless heave of which they rode
    A fluid shelf
Breaks as they leave it, falls and, slowed,
    Loses itself.

Clear, the sheathed bodies slick as seals   25
    Loosen and tingle;
And by the board the bare foot feels
    The suck of shingle.

They paddle in the shallows still;
    Two splash each other;   30
Then all swim out to wait until
    The right waves gather.

                        —1971

Terminal

The eight years difference in age seems now
Disparity so wide between the two
That when I see the man who armoured stood
Resistant to all help however good
Now helped through day itself, eased into chairs,   5
Or else led step by step down the long stairs
With firm and gentle guidance by his friend,
Who loves him, through each effort to descend,
Each wavering, each attempt made to complete
An arc of movement and bring down the feet   10
As if with that spare strength he used to enjoy,
I think of Oedipus, old, led by a boy.

                                                    —1992

JOHN HOLLANDER   B. 1929

A prolific author of poetry and criticism, Hollander's wit and formal
originality mark him as one of the chief contemporary heirs of W. H.
Auden. A native of New York City, he was educated at Columbia
and served as a Junior Fellow at Harvard University. He has taught
at Yale University for many years.

Adam's Task

*"And Adam gave names to all cattle, and to the fowl of the air, and to every beast
of the field . . ."–Gen. 2:20*

Thou, paw-paw-paw; thou, glurd; thou, spotted
    Glurd; thou, whitestap, lurching through
The high-grown brush; thou, pliant-footed,
    Implex; thou, awagabu.

Every burrower, each flier   5
    Came for the name he had to give:
Gay, first work, ever to be prior,
    Not yet sunk to primitive.

Thou, verdle; thou, McFleery's pomma;
    Thou; thou; thou—three types of grawl;   10
Thou, flisket; thou, kabasch; thou, comma-
    Eared mashawk; thou, all; thou, all.

Were, in a fire of becoming,
   Laboring to be burned away,
Then work, half-measuring, half-humming,   15
   Would be as serious as play.

Thou, pambler; thou, rivarn; thou, greater
   Wherret, and thou, lesser one;
Thou, sproal; thou, zant; thou, lily-eater.
   Naming's over. Day is done.   20

                    −1971

X. J. KENNEDY   B. 1929

Kennedy is one the few contemporary American poets who has not
been attracted by free verse, preferring to remain what he calls a
"dinosaur," one of those poets who continue to write in meter. He is
also rare among his contemporaries in his commitment to writing
poems with strong ties to song. Kennedy is also the author of
Literature: An Introduction to Fiction, Poetry, and Drama, perhaps the
most widely used college literature text ever written.

In a Prominent Bar in Secaucus One Day

TO THE TUNE OF "THE OLD ORANGE FLUTE"
OR THE TUNE OF "SWEET BETSY FROM PIKE"

In a prominent bar in Secaucus one day
Rose a lady in skunk with a topheavy sway,
Raised a knobby red finger—all turned from their beer—
While with eyes bright as snowcrust she sang high and clear:

"Now who of you'd think from an eyeload of me   5
That I once was a lady as proud as could be?
Oh I'd never sit down by a tumbledown drunk
If it wasn't, my dears, for the high cost of junk.

"All the gents used to swear that the white of my calf
Beat the down of the swan by a length and a half.   10
In the kerchief of linen I caught to my nose
Ah, there never fell snot, but a little gold rose.

"I had seven gold teeth and a toothpick of gold,
My Virginia cheroot° was a leaf of it rolled
And I'd light it each time with a thousand in cash—   15
Why the bums used to fight if I flicked them an ash.

"Once the toast of the Biltmore, the belle of the Taft,
I would drink bottle beer at the Drake, never draft,
And dine at the Astor on Salisbury steak
With a clean tablecloth for each bite I did take.   20

"In a car like the Roxy I'd roll to the track,
A steel-guitar trio, a bar in the back,
And the wheels made no noise, they turned over so fast,
Still it took you ten minutes to see me go past.

"When the horses bowed down to me that I might choose,   25
I bet on them all, for I hated to lose.
Now I'm saddled each night for my butter and eggs
And the broken threads race down the backs of my legs.

"Let you hold in mind, girls, that your beauty must pass
Like a lovely white clover that rusts with its grass.   30
Keep your bottoms off barstools and marry you young
Or be left—an old barrel with many a bung.

"For when time takes you out for a spin in his car
You'll be hard-pressed to stop him from going too far
And be left by the roadside, for all your good deeds,   35
Two toadstools for tits and a face full of weeds."

All the house raised a cheer, but the man at the bar
Made a phonecall and up pulled a red patrol car
And she blew us a kiss as they copped her away
From that prominent bar in Secaucus, N.J.   40

                                                    —1961

ADRIENNE RICH   B. 1929

A winner of the Yale Younger Poets competition for her first book,
Rich has evolved over the years from a careful formalist to one of the
chief spokespersons of the feminist movement. Her support of various social causes is apparent in her poetry, and she often seems well
in advance of her readers in the turns her life has taken. Oddly,
some of the nation's major awards have eluded her, a reflection perhaps of the controversy that her words often engender.

---

14 cheroot a thin cigar

Aunt Jennifer's Tigers

Aunt Jennifer's tigers prance across a screen,
Bright topaz denizens of a world of green.
They do not fear the men beneath the tree;
They pace in sleek chivalric certainty.

Aunt Jennifer's fingers fluttering through her wool   5
Find even the ivory needle hard to pull.
The massive weight of Uncle's wedding band
Sits heavily upon Aunt Jennifer's hand.

When Aunt is dead, her terrified hands will lie
Still ringed with ordeals she was mastered by.   10
The tigers in the panel that she made
Will go on prancing, proud and unafraid.

                                        —1950

Diving into the Wreck

First having read the book of myths,
and loaded the camera,
and checked the edge of the knife-blade,
I put on
the body-armor of black rubber   5
the absurd flippers
the grave and awkward mask.
I am having to do this
not like Cousteau° with his
assiduous team   10
aboard the sun-flooded schooner
but here alone.

There is a ladder.
The ladder is always there
hanging innocently   15
close to the side of the schooner.
We know what it is for,
we who have used it.
Otherwise
it is a piece of maritime floss   20
some sundry equipment.

---

9 **Cousteau** Jacques-Yves Cousteau (b. 1910), underwater explorer and inventor of the scuba tank

I go down.
Rung after rung and still
the oxygen immerses me
the blue light   25
the clear atoms
of our human air.
I go down.
My flippers cripple me,
I crawl like an insect down the ladder   30
and there is no one
to tell me when the ocean
will begin.

First the air is blue and then
it is bluer and then green and then   35
black I am blacking out and yet
my mask is powerful
it pumps my blood with power
the sea is another story
the sea is not a question of power   40
I have to learn alone
to turn my body without force
in the deep element.

And now: it is easy to forget
what I came for   45
among so many who have always
lived here
swaying their crenellated fans
between the reefs
and besides   50
you breathe differently down here.

I came to explore the wreck.
The words are purposes.
The words are maps.
I came to see the damage that was done   55
and the treasures that prevail.
I stroke the beam of my lamp
slowly along the flank
of something more permanent
than fish or weed   60

the thing I came for:
the wreck and not the story of the wreck

the thing itself and not the myth
the drowned face always staring
toward the sun   65
the evidence of damage
worn by salt and sway into this threadbare beauty
the ribs of the disaster
curving their assertion
among the tentative haunters.   70

This is the place.
And I am here, the mermaid whose dark hair
streams black, the merman in his armored body.
We circle silently
about the wreck   75
we dive into the hold.
I am she: I am he

whose drowned face sleeps with open eyes
whose breasts still bear the stress
whose silver, copper, vermeil cargo lies   80
obscurely inside barrels
half-wedged and left to rot
we are the half-destroyed instruments
that once held to a course
the water-eaten log   85
the fouled compass

We are, I am, you are
by cowardice or courage
the one who find our way
back to this scene   90
carrying a knife, a camera
a book of myths
in which
our names do not appear.

                                        —1972

Rape

There is a cop who is both prowler and father:
he comes from your block, grew up with your brothers,
had certain ideals.
You hardly know him in his boots and silver badge,
on horseback, one hand touching his gun.   5

You hardly know him but you have to get to know him:
he has access to machinery that could kill you.
He and his stallion clop like warlords among the trash,
his ideals stand in the air, a frozen cloud
from between his unsmiling lips.   10

And so, when the time comes, you have to turn to him,
the maniac's sperm still greasing your thighs,
your mind whirling like crazy. You have to confess
to him, you are guilty of the crime
of having been forced.   15

And you see his blue eyes, the blue eyes of all the family
whom you used to know, grow narrow and glisten,
his hand types out the details
and he wants them all
but the hysteria in your voice pleases him best.   20

You hardly know him but now he thinks he knows you:
he has taken down your worst moment
on a machine and filed it in a file.
He knows, or thinks he knows, how much you imagined;
he knows, or thinks he knows, what you secretly wanted.   25

He has access to machinery that could get you put away;
and if, in the sickening light of the precinct,
and if, in the sickening light of the precinct,
your details sound like a portrait of your confessor,
will you swallow, will you deny them, will you lie your way home? 30
                                                          —1972

Ted Hughes   b. 1930

A native of Yorkshire, England, Hughes has never ventured far from
the natural world of his childhood for his subject matter. Hughes
was married to Sylvia Plath until her death in 1966, and has served
as her literary executor. He is currently Poet Laureate of England.

Pike

Pike, three inches long, perfect
Pike in all parts, green tigering the gold.
Killers from the egg: the malevolent aged grin.
They dance on the surface among the flies.

Or move, stunned by their own grandeur,   5
Over a bed of emerald, silhouette
Of submarine delicacy and horror.
A hundred feet long in their world.

In ponds, under the heat-struck lily pads—
Gloom of their stillness: 10
Logged on last year's black leaves, watching upwards.
Or hung in an amber cavern of weeds

The jaw's hooked clamp and fangs
Not to be changed at this date;
A life subdued to its instrument;   15
The gills kneading quietly, and the pectorals.

Three we kept behind glass,
Jungled in weed: three inches, four,
And four and a half: fed fry to them—
Suddenly there were two. Finally one   20

With a sag belly and the grin it was born with.
And indeed they spare nobody.
Two, six pounds each, over two feet long,
High and dry and dead in the willow-herb—

One jammed past its gills down the other's gullet: 25
The outside eye stared: as a vice locks—
The same iron in this eye
Though its film shrank in death.

A pond I fished, fifty yards across,
Whose lilies and muscular tench°   30
Had outlasted every visible stone
Of the monastery that planted them—

Stilled legendary depth:
It was as deep as England. It held
Pike too immense to stir, so immense and old   35
That past nightfall I dared not cast

But silently cast and fished
With the hair frozen on my head
For what might move, for what eye might move.
The still splashes on the dark pond,   40

---

30 tench European freshwater fish

Owls hushing the floating woods
Frail on my ear against the dream
Darkness beneath night's darkness had freed,
That rose slowly towards me, watching.

—1960

GARY SNYDER   B. 1930

Snyder was deeply involved in poetic activity in his hometown, San
Francisco, when that city became the locus of the Beat Generation
in the mid-1950s. Yet Snyder, whose studies in Zen Buddhism and
Oriental cultures preceded his acquaintance with Allen Ginsberg
and Jack Kerouac, has always exhibited a seriousness of purpose that
sets him apart from his peers. His long familiarity with the mountains of the Pacific Northwest date from his jobs with logging crews
during his college days.

A Walk

Sunday the only day we don't work:
Mules farting around the meadow,
    Murphy fishing,
The tent flaps in the warm
Early sun: I've eaten breakfast and I'll   5
    take a walk
To Benson Lake. Packed a lunch,
Goodbye. Hopping on creekbed boulders
Up the rock throat three miles
    Piute Creek—   10
In steep gorge glacier-slick rattlesnake country
Jump, land by a pool, trout skitter,
The clear sky. Deer tracks.
Bad place by a falls, boulders big as houses,
Lunch tied to belt,   15
I stemmed up a crack and almost fell
But rolled out safe on a ledge
    and ambled on.
Quail chicks freeze underfoot, color of stone
Then run cheep! away, hen quail fussing.   20
Craggy west end of Benson Lake—after edging
Past dark creek pools on a long white slope—
Lookt down in the ice-black lake
    lined with cliff

From far above: deep shimmering trout.   25
A lone duck in a gunsightpass
            steep side hill
Through slide-aspen and talus, to the east end
Down to grass, wading a wide smooth stream
Into camp. At last.   30
    By the rusty three-year-
Ago left-behind cookstove
Of the old trail crew,
Stoppt and swam and ate my lunch.

—1968

Derek Walcott   b. 1930

Walcott, a native of the tiny Caribbean island of St. Lucia in the
West Indies, combines a love of the tradition of English poetry with
the exotic surfaces of tropical life. In many ways, his life and career
have constituted a study in divided loyalties, which are displayed in
his ambivalent poems about life in the United States, where he has
lived and taught for many years. Walcott was awarded the Nobel
Prize in 1992.

Central America

Helicopters are cutlassing the wild bananas.
Between a nicotine thumb and forefinger
brittle faces crumble like tobacco leaves.
Children waddle in vests, their legs bowed,
little shrimps curled under their navels.   5
The old men's teeth are stumps in a charred forest.
Their skins grate like the iguana's.
Their gaze like slate stones.
Women squat by the river's consolations
where children wade up to their knees,   10
and a stick stirs up a twinkling of butterflies.
Up there, in the blue acres
of forest, flies circle their fathers.
In spring, in the upper provinces
of the Empire, yellow tanagers   15
float up through the bare branches.
There is no distinction in these distances.

—1987

Miller Williams   B. 1930

Williams won the Poets' Prize in 1990 for *Living on the Surface*, a volume of selected poems. A skillful translator of both Giuseppe Belli, a Roman poet of the early nineteenth century, and of Nicanor Parra, a contemporary Chilean, Williams has written many poems about his travels throughout the world yet has retained the relaxed idiom of his native Arkansas. He read a poem at the 1997 Presidential inauguration.

The Book

I held it in my hands while he told the story.

He had found it in a fallen bunker,
a book for notes with all the pages blank.
He took it to keep for a sketchbook and diary.

He learned years later, when he showed the book   5
to an old bookbinder, who paled, and stepped back
a long step and told him what he held,
what he had laid the days of his life in.
It's bound, the binder said, in human skin.

I stood turning it over in my hands,   10
turning it in my head. Human skin.

What child did this skin fit? What man, what woman?
Dragged still full of its flesh from what dream?

Who took it off the meat? Some other one
who stayed alive by knowing how to do this?   15

I stared at the changing book and a horror grew,
I stared and a horror grew, which was, which is,
how beautiful it was until I knew.

                                        —1989

Linda Pastan   B. 1932

Linda Pastan is Poet Laureate of Maryland, where she has lived and taught for many years. Her first book, *A Perfect Circle of Sun*, appeared in 1971, and four more collections have been published since.

Crocuses

They come
by stealth, spreading
the rumor of spring—
near the hedge . . .
by the gate . . .   5
at our chilly feet . . .
mothers of saffron, fathers
of insurrection, purple
and yellow scouts
of an army still massing   10
just to the south.

—1991

SYLVIA PLATH   1932–1963

Plath's troubled personal life is often difficult to separate from her
poetry, which is almost always read as autobiographical and confessional. A brilliant and precocious poet, she served a long apprenticeship to the tradition of modern poetry before attaining her mature
style in the final two years of her life. Only one collection, *The
Colossus*, appeared in her lifetime, and her fame has mainly rested on
her posthumous books of poetry and the success of her lone novel,
The Bell Jar. She committed suicide in 1963. Plath has been the subject of a half-dozen biographical studies, reflecting the intense interest that readers, especially women, have in her life and work.

Daddy

You do not do, you do not do
Any more, black shoe
In which I have lived like a foot
For thirty years, poor and white,
Barely daring to breathe or Achoo.   5

Daddy, I have had to kill you.
You died before I had time—
Marble-heavy, a bag full of God,
Ghastly statue with one gray toe
Big as a Frisco seal   10

And a head in the freakish Atlantic
Where it pours bean green over blue

In the waters off beautiful Nauset.
I used to pray to recover you.
Ach, du.°   15

In the German tongue, in the Polish town
Scraped flat by the roller
Of wars, wars, wars.
But the name of the town is common.
My Polack friend   20

Says there are a dozen or two.
So I never could tell where you
Put your foot, your root,
I never could talk to you.
The tongue stuck in my jaw.   25

It stuck in a barb wire snare.
Ich, ich, ich, ich,°
I could hardly speak.
I thought every German was you.
And the language obscene   30

An engine, an engine
Chuffing me off like a Jew.
A Jew to Dachau, Auschwitz, Belsen.°
I began to talk like a Jew.
I think I may well be a Jew.   35

The snows of the Tyrol, the clear beer of Vienna
Are not very pure or true.
With my gypsy ancestress and my weird luck
And my Taroc pack and my Taroc pack
I may be a bit of a Jew.   40

I have always been scared of *you*,
With your Luftwaffe,° your gobbledygoo.
And your neat mustache
And your Aryan eye, bright blue.
Panzer-man, panzer-man, O You—   45

Not God but a swastika
So black no sky could squeak through.

---

15 Ach, du "Oh, you"   **27 Ich, ich, ich, ich** "I, I, I, I"   **33 Dachau, Auschwitz, Belsen**
German concentration camps   **42 Luftwaffe** German Air Force

Every woman adores a Fascist,
The boot in the face, the brute
Brute heart of a brute like you.   50

You stand at the blackboard, daddy,
In the picture I have of you,
A cleft in your chin instead of your foot
But no less a devil for that, no not
Any less the black man who   55

Bit my pretty red heart in two.
I was ten when they buried you.
At twenty I tried to die
And get back, back, back to you.
I thought even the bones would do.   60

But they pulled me out of the sack,
And they stuck me together with glue.
And then I knew what to do.
I made a model of you,
A man in black with a Meinkampf° look   65

And a love of the rack and the screw.
And I said I do, I do.
So daddy, I'm finally through.
The black telephone's off at the root,
The voices just can't worm through.   70

If I've killed one man, I've killed two—
The vampire who said he was you
And drank my blood for a year,
Seven years, if you want to know.
Daddy, you can lie back now.   75

There's a stake in your fat black heart
And the villagers never liked you.
They are dancing and stamping on you.
They always *knew* it was you.
Daddy, daddy, you bastard, I'm through.   80

                                              —1966

---

65 **Meinkampf** title of Hitler's autobiography ("My Struggle")

Edge

The woman is perfected.
Her dead

Body wears the smile of accomplishment,
The illusion of a Greek necessity

Flows in the scrolls of her toga,   5
Her bare

Feet seem to be saying:
We have come so far, it is over.

Each dead child coiled, a white serpent,
One at each little   10

Pitcher of milk, now empty.
She has folded

Them back into her body as petals
Of a rose close when the garden

Stiffens and odors bleed   15
From the sweet, deep throats of the night flower.

The moon has nothing to be sad about,
Staring from her hood of bone.

She is used to this sort of thing.
Her blacks crackle and drag.   20

                                        —1965

Metaphors

I'm a riddle in nine syllables,
An elephant, a ponderous house,
A melon strolling on two tendrils.
O red fruit, ivory, fine timbers!
This loaf's big with its yeasty rising.   5
Money's new-minted in this fat purse.
I'm a means, a stage, a cow in calf.
I've eaten a bag of green apples,
Boarded the train there's no getting off.

                                        —1960

GERALD BARRAX   B. 1933

Gerald Barrax is the editor of *Obsidian II: Black Literature in Review*, one of the most influential journals of African-American writing. The author of four collections of poetry, he teaches at North Carolina State University.

"I had a terror—since September"

First a terror of choice, but that was done
By September—Renunciation my chosen word.
I hope she knows the troubles, what pools I wade,
What an old romantic ass I've become—
To remember each stage of that delirium   5
I bought the albums and use the music we heard
To keep us in time together out of handmade
Memories of loving and scrooving in double-tongue.
Double-stopped now, it's all I can do to hum
The tunes and hang on to what I can, less   10
Each September, channeling raw music into the wound—
Afraid when she appears in the room
As out of time as music from all this sound
I might say yes this time goddamn I'd say yes.

ANNE STEVENSON   B. 1933

Perhaps best known as the author of a controversial biography of Sylvia Plath, Stevenson was born in England of American parents and educated at the University of Michigan. She has lived in England since her twenties. Her *Selected Poems* appeared in 1987.

Sous-Entendu°

Don't think

that I don't know
that as you talk to me
the hand of your mind
is inconspicuously   5
taking off my stocking,
moving in resourceful blindness
up along my thigh.
Don't think

Sous-Entendu "hidden meaning"

that I don't know   10
that you know
everything I say
is a garment.

                    —1969

MARK STRAND   B. 1934

The deceptive simplicity of Strand's best poems reveals the influence of Spanish-language poets like Nicanor Parra, the father of "anti-poetry," and Rafael Alberti, whom Strand has translated. Strand was named U.S. Poet Laureate in 1990.

The Tunnel

A man has been standing
in front of my house
for days. I peek at him
from the living room
window and at night,   5
unable to sleep,
I shine my flashlight
down on the lawn.
He is always there.

After a while   10
I open the front door
just a crack and order
him out of my yard.
He narrows his eyes
and moans. I slam   15
the door and dash back
to the kitchen, then up
to the bedroom, then down.

I weep like a schoolgirl
and make obscene gestures   20
through the window. I
write large suicide notes
and place them so he
can read them easily.
I destroy the living   25
room furniture to prove
I own nothing of value.

When he seems unmoved
I decide to dig a tunnel
to a neighboring yard.   30
I seal the basement off
from the upstairs with
a brick wall. I dig hard
and in no time the tunnel
is done. Leaving my pick   35
and shovel below,

I come out in front of a house
and stand there too tired to
move or even speak, hoping
someone will help me.   40
I feel I'm being watched
and sometimes I hear
a man's voice,
but nothing is done
and I have been waiting for days.   45

                                                        —1968

MARY OLIVER   B. 1935

Mary Oliver was born in Cleveland, Ohio, and educated at Ohio State and Vassar. She has served as a visiting professor at a number of universities and at the Fine Arts Center in Provincetown, Massachusetts. She has won both the Pulitzer Prize and the National Book Award for her work, which first appeared in *No Voyage and Other Poems* in 1965.

The Black Walnut Tree

My mother and I debate:
we could sell
the black walnut tree
to the lumberman,
and pay off the mortgage.   5
Likely some storm anyway
will churn down its dark boughs,
smashing the house. We talk
slowly, two women trying
in a difficult time to be wise.   10
Roots in the cellar drains,

I say, and she replies
that the leaves are getting heavier
every year, and the fruit
harder to gather away.   15
But something brighter than money
moves in our blood—an edge
sharp and quick as a trowel
that wants us to dig and sow.
So we talk, but we don't do   20
anything. That night I dream
of my fathers out of Bohemia
filling the blue fields
of fresh and generous Ohio
with leaves and vines and orchards.   25
What my mother and I both know
is that we'd crawl with shame
in the emptiness we'd made
in our own and our fathers' backyard.
So the black walnut tree   30
swings through another year
of sun and leaping winds,
of leaves and bounding fruit,
and, month after month, the whip-
crack of the mortgage.   35

                                              —1979

FRED CHAPPELL   B. 1936

The immense achievement of Chappell's epic-length poem Midquest
(1981) was belatedly recognized when he was awarded the Bollingen
Prize in 1985. A four-part poem written over a decade, Midquest uses
the occasion of the poet's thirty-fifth birthday as a departure for a
complex sequence of autobiographical poems that are heavily indebt-
ed to Dante for their formal structure. A versatile writer of both
poetry and prose, Chappell displays his classical learning brilliantly
and in unusual contexts.

Narcissus and Echo°

Shall the water not remember   Ember
my hand's slow gesture, tracing above   of

Narcissus and Echo In the myth, the vain Narcissus drowned attempting to embrace his own
reflection in the water. Echo, a nymph who loved him, pined away until only her voice
remained.

its mirror my half-imaginary *airy*
portrait? My only belonging *longing*
is my beauty, which I take *ache*   5
away and then return as love *of*
teasing playfully the one being *unbeing.*

whose gratitude I treasure *Is your*
moves me. I live apart *heart*
from myself, yet cannot *not*   10
live apart. In the water's tone, *stone?*
that brilliant silence, a flower *Hour,*
whispers my name with such slight *light,*
moment, it seems filament of air, *fare*
the world become cloudswell. *well.*   15

                                            —1985

LUCILLE CLIFTON   B. 1936

Clifton, a native of Depew, New York, was educated at SUNY—
Fredonia and Howard University and has taught at several colleges,
including the American University in Washington, D.C. About her
own work, she has commented succinctly, "I am a Black woman
poet, and I sound like one."

to my last period

well girl, goodbye,
after thirty-eight years.
thirty-eight years and you
never arrived
splendid in your red dress   5
without trouble for me
somewhere, somehow.

now it is done,
and i feel just like
the grandmothers who,   10
after the hussy has gone,
sit holding her photograph
and sighing, *wasn't she*
beautiful? wasn't she beautiful?

MARGE PIERCY   B. 1936

A political radical during her student days at the University of
Michigan, Piercy has continued to be outspoken on political, cultural, and sexual issues. Her phrase "to be of use" has become a key
measure by which feminist writers and critics have gauged the meaning of their own life experiences.

Barbie Doll

This girlchild was born as usual
and presented dolls that did pee-pee
and miniature GE stoves and irons
and wee lipsticks the color of cherry candy.
Then in the magic of puberty, a classmate said: 5
You have a great big nose and fat legs.

She was healthy, tested intelligent
possessed strong arms and back,
abundant sexual drive and manual dexterity.
She went to and fro apologizing.   10
Everyone saw a fat nose on thick legs.

She was advised to play coy,
exhorted to come on hearty,
exercise, diet, smile and wheedle.
Her good nature wore out   15
like a fan belt.
So she cut off her nose and her legs
and offered them up.

In the casket displayed on satin she lay
with the undertaker's cosmetics painted on,   20
a turned-up putty nose,
dressed in a pink and white nightie.
Doesn't she look pretty? everyone said.
Consummation at last.
To every woman a happy ending.   25

—1982

NANCY WILLARD   B. 1936

The author of nine collections of poetry, Willard has also written a
novel and an award-winning book of poems for children, *A Visit to*

William Blake's Inn. About her whimsical work Donald Hall has said, "She imagines with a wonderful concreteness. But also, she takes real language and by literal-mindedness turns it into the structure of dream."

A Hardware Store as Proof of the Existence of God

I praise the brightness of hammers pointing east
like the steel woodpeckers of the future,
and dozens of hinges opening brass wings,
and six new rakes shyly fanning their toes,
and bins of hooks glittering into bees,   5

and a rack of wrenches like the long bones of horses,
and mailboxes sowing rows of silver chapels,
and a company of plungers waiting for God
to claim their thin legs in their big shoes
and put them on and walk away laughing.   10

In a world not perfect but not bad either
let there be glue, glaze, gum, and grabs,
caulk also, and hooks, shackles, cables, and slips,
and signs so spare a child may read them,
Men, Women, In, Out, No Parking, Beware the Dog.   15

In the right hands, they can work wonders.

                                        —1989

BETTY ADCOCK   B. 1938

Born in San Augustine, Texas, Adcock has lived for many years in Raleigh, North Carolina, where she is poet-in-residence at Meredith College. *The Different Wheel,* her fourth collection, appeared in 1995.

Digression on the Nuclear Age

In some difficult part of Africa, a termite tribe
builds elaborate tenements that might be called
cathedrals, were they for anything so terminal
as Milton's God. Who was it said
the perfect arch will always separate   5
the civilized from the not? Never mind.

These creatures are quite blind and soft
and hard at labor chemically induced.
Beginning with a dish-like hollow, groups
of workers pile up earthen pellets.   10
A few such piles will reach a certain height;
fewer still, a just proximity.
That's when direction changes, or a change
directs: the correct two bands of laborers
will make their towers bow toward each other.   15
Like saved and savior, they will meet in air.
It is unambiguously an arch and it will serve,
among the others rising and the waste,
an arch's purposes. Experts are sure
a specific moment comes when the very structure   20
triggers the response that will perfect it.

I've got this far and don't know what
termites can be made to mean. Or this poem:
a joke, a play on arrogance, nothing
but language? Untranslated, the world gets on   25
with dark, flawless constructions rising,
rising even where we think we are. And think
how we must hope convergences will fail this time,
that whatever it is we're working on won't work.

                                                         —1988

GARY GILDNER   B. 1938

Gildner was born in West Branch, Michigan, and attended
Michigan State University. He teaches at Drake University. "First
Practice" is the title poem of his first collection, published in 1969,
and a volume of Gildner's selected poems appeared in 1984.

First Practice

After the doctor checked to see
we weren't ruptured,
the man with the short cigar took us
under the grade school,
where we went in case of attack   5
or storm, and said
he was Clifford Hill, he was
a man who believed dogs
ate dogs, he had once killed
for his country, and if   10

there were any girls present
for them to leave now.
          No one
left. OK, he said, he said I take
that to mean you are hungry   15
men who hate to lose as much
as I do. OK. Then
he made two lines of us
facing each other,
and across the way, he said,   20
is the man you hate most
in the world,
and if we are to win
that title I want to see how.
But I don't want to see   25
any marks when you're dressed,
he said. He said, *Now.*

                                     —1969

Robert Phillips   B. 1938

Phillips labored for over thirty years as a New York advertising executive, a remarkable fact when one considers his many books of poetry, fiction, and criticism and the numerous books he has edited. He currently lives in Houston, where he teaches in the creative writing program at the University of Houston.

The Stone Crab: A Love Poem

*Joe's serves approximately 1000 pounds of crab claws
each day.—Florida Gold Coast Leisure Guide*

Delicacy of warm Florida waters,
his body is undesirable. One giant claw
is his claim to fame, and we claim it,

more than once. Meat sweeter than lobster,
less dear than his life, when grown that claw   5
is lifted, broken off at the joint.

Mutilated, the crustacean is thrown back
into the water, back upon his own resources.
One of nature's rarities, he replaces

an entire appendage as you or I   10

grow a nail. (No one asks how he survives
that crabby sea with just one claw;

two-fisted menaces real as night-
mares, ten-tentacled nights cold
as fright.) In time he grows another,   15

large, meaty, magnificent as the first.
And one astonished day, snap! it too
is twigged off, the cripple dropped

back into treachery. Unlike a twig,
it sprouts again. How many losses   20
can he endure? Well,

his shell is hard, the sea is wide.
Something vital broken off, he doesn't
nurse the wound; develops something new.

                                          —1994

CHARLES SIMIC   B. 1938

Simic was born in Yugoslavia and came with his parents to Chicago
in 1949. Educated at New York University, he teaches at the
University of New Hampshire. *The World Doesn't End*, a collection of
prose poems, won the Pulitzer Prize in 1990.

Stone

Go inside a stone
That would be my way.
Let somebody else become a dove
Or gnash with a tiger's tooth.
I am happy to be a stone.   5

From the outside the stone is a riddle:
No one knows how to answer it.
Yet within, it must be cool and quiet
Even though a cow steps on it full weight,
Even though a child throws it in a river;   10
The stone sinks, slow, unperturbed
To the river bottom
Where the fishes come to knock on it
And listen.

I have seen sparks fly out   15
When two stones are rubbed,
So perhaps it is not dark inside after all;
Perhaps there is a moon shining
From somewhere, as though behind a hill—
Just enough light to make out   20
The strange writings, the star-charts
On the inner walls.

                                                        —1971

Dabney Stuart   B. 1938

The supporting cast of the American family romance—parents, wives
and ex-wives, and children—are prominent in the work of Dabney
Stuart. A Virginian who has taught for many years at Washington
and Lee University, Stuart published *Light Years*, a volume of selected poems, in 1995.

Discovering My Daughter

Most of your life we have kept our separate places:
After I left your mother you knew an island,
Rented rooms, a slow coastal slide northward
To Boston, and, in summer, another island
Hung at the country's tip. Would you have kept going   5
All the way off the map, an absolute alien?

Sometimes I shiver, being almost forgetful enough
To have let that happen. We've come the longer way
Under such pressure, from one person to
Another. Our trip proves again the world is   10
Round, a singular island where people may come
Together, as we have, making a singular place.

                                                        —1987

Margaret Atwood   B. 1939

The leading woman writer of Canada, Atwood excels at both poetry
and prose fiction. Among her six novels, *The Handmaid's Tale* is perhaps the best known, becoming a best-seller in the United States and
the subject of a motion picture. Atwood's *Selected Poems* appeared in
1976.

Siren° Song

This is the one song everyone
would like to learn: the song
that is irresistible:

the song that forces men
to leap overboard in squadrons   5
even though they see the beached skulls

the song nobody knows
because anyone who has heard it
is dead, and the others can't remember.

Shall I tell you the secret   10
and if I do, will you get me
out of this bird suit?

I don't enjoy it here
squatting on this island
looking picturesque and mythical   15

with these two feathery maniacs,
I don't enjoy singing
this trio, fatal and valuable.

I will tell the secret to you,
to you, only to you.   20
Come closer. This song

is a cry for help: Help me!
Only you, only you can,
you are unique

at last. Alas   25
it is a boring song
but it works every time.

                                                      —1974

Stephen Dunn   B. 1939

A graduate of the creative writing program at Syracuse University,
Dunn teaches at Stockton State College in Pomona, New Jersey. His

---

Siren in Greek myth, one of the women whose irresistible song lured sailors onto the rocks

attempt to blend ordinary experience with larger significance is illus-
trated in the duality of his book titles like *Full of Lust and Good Usage*,
Work and Love, and *Between Angels*.

The Sacred

After the teacher asked if anyone had
    a sacred place
and the students fidgeted and shrank

in their chairs, the most serious of them all
    said it was his car,   5
being in it alone, his tape deck playing

things he'd chosen, and others knew the truth
    had been spoken
and began speaking about their rooms,

their hiding places, but the car kept coming up,   10
    the car in motion,
music filling it, and sometimes one other person

who understood the bright altar of the dashboard
    and how far away
a car could take him from the need   15

to speak, or to answer, the key
    in having a key
and putting it in, and going.

—1989

Seamus Heaney   B. 1939

Born in the troubled country of Northern Ireland, Heaney has largely avoided the type of political divisions that have divided his home-
land. Instead, he has chosen to focus on the landscape of the rural
Ireland he knew while growing up as a farmer's son. Since 1982,
Heaney has taught part of the year at Harvard University. He was
awarded the Nobel Prize for Literature in 1995.

Bogland

for T. P. Flanagan

We have no prairies
To slice a big sun at evening—

Everywhere the eye concedes to
Encroaching horizon,

Is wooed into the cyclops' eye   5
Of a tarn. Our unfenced country
Is bog that keeps crusting
Between the sights of the sun.

They've taken the skeleton
Of the Great Irish Elk   10
Out of the peat, set it up
An astounding crate full of air.

Butter sunk under
More than a hundred years
Was recovered salty and white.   15
The ground itself is kind, black butter

Melting and opening underfoot,
Missing its last definition
By millions of years.
They'll never dig coal here,   20

Only the waterlogged trunks
Of great firs, soft as pulp.
Our pioneers keep striking
Inwards and downwards,

Every layer they strip   25
Seems camped on before.
The bogholes might be Atlantic seepage.
The wet centre is bottomless.

                                                        —1969

Digging

Between my finger and my thumb
The squat pen rests; snug as a gun.

Under my window, a clean rasping sound
When the spade sinks into gravelly ground:
My father, digging. I look down   5

Till his straining rump among the flowerbeds
Bends low, comes up twenty years away

Stooping in rhythm through potato drills°
Where he was digging.

The coarse boot nestled on the lug, the shaft   10
Against the inside knee was levered firmly.
He rooted out tall tops, buried the bright edge deep
To scatter new potatoes that we picked
Loving their cool hardness in our hands.

By God, the old man could handle a spade.   15
Just like his old man.

My grandfather cut more turf in a day
Than any other man on Toner's bog.
Once I carried him milk in a bottle
Corked sloppily with paper. He straightened up   20
To drink it, then fell to right away

Nicking and slicing neatly, heaving sods
Over his shoulder, going down and down
For the good turf. Digging.

The cold smell of potato mould, the squelch and slap   25
Of soggy peat, the curt cuts of an edge
Through living roots awaken in my head.
But I've no spade to follow men like them.

Between my finger and my thumb
The squat pen rests.   30
I'll dig with it.

                                          —1980

Punishment

I can feel the tug
of the halter at the nape
of her neck, the wind
on her naked front.

It blows her nipples   5
to amber beads,
it shakes the frail rigging
of her ribs.

---

8 drills furrows

I can see her drowned
body in the bog,   10
the weighing stone,
the floating rods and boughs.

Under which at first
she was a barked sapling
that is dug up   15
oak-bone, brain-firkin:°

her shaved head
like a stubble of black corn,
her blindfold a soiled bandage,
her noose a ring   20

to store
the memories of love.
Little adulteress,
before they punished you

you were flaxen-haired,   25
undernourished, and your
tar-black face was beautiful.
My poor scapegoat,

I almost love you
but would have cast, I know,   30
the stones of silence.
I am the artful voyeur

of your brain's exposed
and darkened combs,
your muscles' webbing   35
and all your numbered bones:

I who have stood dumb
when your betraying sisters,
cauled in tar,
wept by the railings,   40

who would connive
in civilized outrage
yet understand the exact
and tribal, intimate revenge.

—1975

16 **firkin** a small barrel

Tom Disch   B. 1940

Science-fiction writer, author of interactive computer fiction, resident critic for magazines as diverse as *Playboy* and *The Nation*, and poet, Tom Disch is possibly the most brilliant satirist in contemporary American poetry. *Yes, Let's*, a collection of his selected poems, appeared in 1989.

Ballade of the New God

I have decided I'm divine.
Caligula and Nero knew
A godliness akin to mine,
But they are strictly hitherto.
They're dead, and what can dead gods do?   5
I'm here and now. I'm dynamite.
I'd worship me if I were you.
A new religion starts tonight!

No booze, no pot, no sex, no swine:
I have decreed them all taboo.   10
My words will be your only wine,
The thought of me your honeydew.
All other thoughts you will eschew
And call yourself a Thomasite
And hymn my praise with loud yahoo.   15
A new religion starts tonight.

But (you might think) that's asinine!
I'm just as much a god as you.
You may have built yourself a shrine
But I won't bend my knee. Who   20
Asked you to be my god? I do,
Who am, as god, divinely right.
Now you must join my retinue:
A new religion starts tonight.

All that I have said is true.   25
I'm god and you're my acolyte.
Surrender's bliss: I envy you
A new religion starts tonight

                                        —1995

Pattiann Rogers   B. 1940

Pattiann Rogers is the foremost naturalist among contemporary
American poets; her poems resound with the rich names of unfamiliar species of plants and animals, most of whom she seems to
know on intimate terms. *Firestarter*, a volume of selected poems, is
her most recent publication.

Foreplay

When it first begins, as you might expect,
the lips and thin folds are closed, the pouting
layers pressed, lapped lightly,
almost languidly, against one another
in a sealed bud.   5

However, with certain prolonged
and random strokings of care
along each binding line, with soft
intrusions traced beneath each pursed
gathering and edge, with inquiring   10
intensities of gesture—as the sun
swinging slowly from winter back
to spring, touches briefly,
between moments of moon and masking
clouds, certain stunning points   15
and inner nubs of earth—so
with such ministrations, a slight
swelling, a quiver of reaching,
a tendency toward space,
might be noticed to commence.   20

Then with dampness from the dark,
with moisture from the falling
night of morning, from hidden places
within the hills, each seal begins
to loosen, each recalcitrant clasp   25
sinks away into itself, and every tucked
grasp, every silk tack willingly relents,
releases, gives way, proclaims a turning,
declares a revolution, assumes,
in plain sight, a surging position   30
that offers, an audacious offering
that beseeches, every petal parted wide.

Remember the spiraling, blue
valerian, remember the violet, sucking
larkspur, the laurel and rosebay   35
and pea cockle flung backwards, remember
the fragrant, funnelling lily, the lifted
honeysuckle, the sweet, open pucker
of the ground ivy blossom?

Now even the darkest crease possessed,   40
the most guarded, pulsing, least drop
of pearl bead, moon grain trembling
deep within is fully revealed, fully exposed
to any penetrating wind or shaking fur
or mad hunger or searing, plunging surprise   45
the wild descending sky in delirium
has to offer.

                                        —1994

ROBERT HASS   B. 1941

Hass was born and reared in San Francisco, and teaches at Berkeley.
His first book, *Field Guide*, was chosen for the Yale Series of Younger
Poets in 1973. Recently he has collaborated with Nobel Prize-winner
Czeslaw Milosz on English translations of the latter's poetry. He was
appointed U.S. Poet Laureate in 1995.

Picking Blackberries with a Friend Who Has Been Reading Jacques Lacan°

August dust is here. Drought
stuns the road,
but juice gathers in the berries.

We pick them in the hot
slow-motion of midmorning.   5
Charlie is exclaiming:

for him it is twenty years ago
and raspberries and Vermont.
We have stopped talking

Jacques Lacan French psychoanalyst and literary theorist

about *L'Histoire de la vérité,*°   10
about subject and object
and the mediation of desire.

Our ears are stoppered
in the bee-hum. And Charlie,
laughing wonderfully,   15

beard stained purple
by the word *juice,*
goes to get a bigger pot.

                                              —1979

Simon J. Ortiz   B. 1941

Born in the Pueblo of Acoma, near Albuquerque, New Mexico,
Ortiz has explained why he writes: "Because Indians always tell a
story. The only way to continue is to tell a story." The author of collections of poetry and prose and of several children's books, Ortiz
has taught creative writing and Native American literature at many
universities.

The Serenity in Stones

I am holding this turquoise
in my hands.
My hands hold the sky
wrought in this little stone.
There is a cloud   5
at the furthest boundary.
The world is somewhere underneath.

I turn the stone, and there is more sky.
This is the serenity possible in stones,
the place of a feeling to which one belongs.   10
I am happy as I hold this sky
in my hands, in my eyes, and in myself.

                                              —1975

---

10 *L'Histoire de la vérité* The History of Truth, by Lacan

GIBBONS RUARK   B. 1941

A native of North Carolina, Ruark is the author of five collections
of poetry. He teaches at the University of Delaware.

The Visitor

Holding the arm of his helper, the blind
Piano tuner comes to our piano.
He hesitates at first, but once he finds
The keyboard, his hands glide over the slow
Keys, ringing changes finer than the eye   5
Can see. The dusty wires he touches, row
On row, quiver like bowstrings as he
Twists them one notch tighter. He runs his
Finger along a wire, touches the dry
Rust to his tongue, breaks into a pure bliss   10
And tells us, "One year more of damp weather
Would have done you in, but I've saved it this
Time. Would one of you play now, please? I hear
It better at a distance." My wife plays
Stardust. The blind man stands and smiles in her   15
Direction, then disappears into the blaze
Of new October. Now the afternoon,
The long afternoon that blurs in a haze
Of music . . . Chopin nocturnes, *Clair de Lune*,
All the old familiar, unfamiliar   20
Music-lesson pieces, *Papa's Haydn's*
Dead and gone, gently down the stream . . . Hours later,
After the latest car has doused its beams,
Has cooled down and stopped its ticking, I hear
Our cat, with the grace of animals free   25
To move in darkness, strike one key only,
And a single lucid drop of water stars my dream.

—1971

BENJAMIN ALIRE SÁENZ   B. 1941

A native of New Mexico, Sáenz spoke only Spanish as a child, a background that lies behind lines like "I want to feel words / swimming
in my throat / like fighting fish / that refuse to be hooked / on a
line." His book, *Dark and Perfect Angels*, contains poems about the
landscape of the Southwest and about Sáenz's three years as a
Roman Catholic priest.

To the Desert

I came to you one rainless August night.
You taught me how to live without the rain.
You are thirst and thirst is all I know.
You are sand, wind, sun, and burning sky,
The hottest blue. You blow a breeze and brand   5
Your breath into my mouth. You reach—then *bend*
Your force, to break, blow, burn, and make me new.
You wrap your name tight around my ribs
And keep me warm. I was born for you.
Above, below, by you, by you surrounded.   10
I wake to you at dawn. Never break your
Knot. Reach, rise, blow, *Sálvame, mi dios,*
Trágame, mi tierra. Salva, traga, Break me,
I am bread. I will be the water for your thirst.

                                              —1995

GLADYS CARDIFF   B. 1942

Gladys Cardiff is a member of the Cherokee nation. "Combing" is
taken from her first collection, *To Frighten a Storm*, which was originally published in 1976.

Combing

Bending, I bow my head
And lay my hand upon
Her hair, combing, and think
How women do this for
Each other. My daughter's hair   5
Curls against the comb,
Wet and fragrant—orange
Parings. Her face, downcast,
Is quiet for one so young.

I take her place. Beneath   10
My mother's hands I feel
The braids drawn up tight
As a piano wire and singing,
Vinegar-rinsed. Sitting
Before the oven I hear   15
The orange coils tick
The early hour before school.

She combed her grandmother
Mathilda's hair using
A comb made out of bone.   20
Mathilda rocked her oak wood
Chair, her face downcast,
Intent on tearing rags
In strips to braid a cotton
Rug from bits of orange   25
and brown. A simple act,

Preparing hair. Something
Women do for each other,
Plaiting the generations.

                                              —1976

CHARLES MARTIN   B. 1942

A lifelong resident of New York City, Martin has taught English as a
second language for many years at Queensborough College. "E.S.L."
appeared as a prefatory poem to Martin's sequence "Passages from
Friday," an ironic retelling of the Robinson Crusoe story from his
servant's point of view.

E.S.L.°

    My frowning students carve
    Me monsters out of prose:
This one——a gargoyle——thumbs its contemptuous nose
At how, in English, subject must agree
With verb——for any such agreement shows   5
    Too great a willingness to serve,
        A docility

    Which wiry Miss Choi
    Finds un-American.
She steals a hard look at me. I wink. Her grin   10
Is my reward. *In his will, our peace, our Pass:*
Gargoyle erased, subject and verb now in
    Agreement, reach object, enjoy
        Temporary truce.

E.S.L. English as a Second Language

Tonight my students must   15
    Agree or disagree:
America is still a land of opportunity.
The answer is always, uniformly, *Yes*—even though
"*It has no doubt that here were to much free,*"
    As Miss Torrico will insist.   20
        She and I both know

    That Language binds us fast,
        And those of us without
Are bound and gagged by those within. Each fledgling
Polyglot must shake old habits: tapping her sneakered feet, 25
Miss Choi exorcises incensed ancestors, flout-
        ing the ghosts of her Chinese past.
            Writhing in the seat

    Next to Miss Choi, Mister
        Fedakis, in anguish   30
Labors to express himself in a tongue which
Proves *Linear B* to me, when I attempt to read it
Later. They're here for English as a Second Language,
    Which I'm teaching this semester.
        God knows they need it,   35

    And so, thank God, do they.
        The night's made easier
By our agreement: I am here to help deliver
Them into the good life they write me papers about.
English is pre-requisite for that endeavor,   40
    Explored in their nightly essays
        Boldly setting out

    To reconnoiter the fair
        New World they would enter:
Suburban Paradise, the endless shopping center   45
Where one may browse for hours before one chooses
Some new necessity—gold-flecked magenta
    Wallpaper to re-do the spare
        Bath no one uses,

    Or a machine which can,   50
        In seven seconds, crush
A newborn calf into such seamless mush
As a *mousse* might be made of—or our true sublime:
The gleaming counters where frosted cosmeticians brush

Decades from the allotted span,   55
    Abrogating Time

    As the spring tide brushes
    A single sinister
Footprint from the otherwise unwrinkled shore
Of America the Blank. In absolute confusion   60
Poor Mister Fedakis rumbles with despair
    And puts the finishing smutches
        To his conclusion

    While Miss Choi erases:
    One more gargoyle routed.   65
Their pure, erroneous lines yield an illuminated
Map of the new found land. We will never arrive there,
Since it exists only in what we say about it,
    As all the rest of my class is
        Bound to discover.   70
                                              —1987

Sharon Olds   B. 1942

Olds's candor in dealing with the intimacies of family romance covering three generations has made her, along with Stephen Dunn, one of the chief contemporary heirs to the confessional tradition. A powerful and dramatic reader, she is much in demand on the lecture circuit. Born in San Francisco, she currently resides in New York City.

The One Girl at the Boys Party

When I take my girl to the swimming party
I set her down among the boys. They tower and
bristle, she stands there smooth and sleek,
her math scores unfolding in the air around her.
They will strip to their suits, her body hard and   5
indivisible as a prime number,
they'll plunge into the deep end, she'll subtract
her height from ten feet, divide it into
hundreds of gallons of water, the numbers
bouncing in her mind like molecules of chlorine   10
in the bright blue pool. When they climb out,
her ponytail will hang its pencil lead
down her back, her narrow silk suit
with hamburgers and french fries printed on it

will glisten in the brilliant air, and they will   15
see her sweet face, solemn and
sealed, a factor of one, and she will
see their eyes, two each,
their legs, two each, and the curves of their sexes,
one each, and in her head she'll be doing her   20
wild multiplying, as the drops
sparkle and fall to the power of a thousand from her body.

                                                        —1983

Henry Taylor   b. 1942

Many of Henry Taylor's poems reflect his experiences as a horseman
and breeder of horses, an avocation revealed by the title of his first
collection, *The Horse Show at Midnight*. Taylor's fourth collection of
poetry, *Understanding Fiction*, appeared in 1996.

Artichoke

If poetry did not exist, would you have had the
wit to invent it?—Howard Nemerov

He had studied in private years ago
the way to eat these things, and was prepared
when she set the clipped green globe before him.
He only wondered (as he always did
when he plucked from the base the first thick leaf,   5
dipped it into the sauce and caught her eye
as he deftly set the velvet curve against
the inside edges of his lower teeth
and drew the tender pulp toward his tongue
while she made some predictable remark   10
about the sensuality of this act
then sheared away the spines and ate the heart)
what mind, what hunger, first saw this as food.

                                                        —1985

James Tate   b. 1943

Tate's unique brand of comic surrealism has remained constant
throughout his career. *The Lost Pilot* won the Yale Younger Poets
Award in 1966. Tate's *Selected Poems* was the recipient of the Pulitzer
Prize in 1992.

Teaching the Ape to Write Poems

They didn't have much trouble
teaching the ape to write poems:
first they strapped him into the chair,
then tied the pencil around his hand
(the paper had already been nailed down).   5
Then Dr. Bluespire leaned over his shoulder
and whispered into his ear:
"You look like a god sitting there.
Why don't you try writing something?"

—1991

Ellen Bryant Voight   B. 1943

A native of Virginia, Voight was trained as a concert pianist before earn-
ing her creative writing degree from the University of Iowa. She has
taught poetry at a number of colleges in New England and the South.

Daughter

There is one grief worse than any other.

When your small feverish throat clogged, and quit,
I knelt beside the chair on the green rug
and shook you and shook you,
but the only sound was mine shouting you back,   5
the delicate curls at your temples,
the blue wool blanket,
your face blue,
your jaw clamped against remedy—

how could I put a knife to that white neck?   10
With you in my lap,
my hands fluttering like flags,
I bend instead over your dead weight
to administer a kiss so urgent, so ruthless,
pumping breath into your stilled body,   15
counting out the rhythm for how long until
the second birth, the second cry
oh Jesus that sudden noisy musical inhalation
that leaves me stunned
by your survival.   20

—1983

Robert Morgan   b. 1944

A native of the mountains of North Carolina, Morgan has always
retained a large degree of regional ties in his poetry. A recent collection, *Sigodlin*, takes its title from an Appalachian word for things that
are built slightly out of square.

Mountain Bride

They say Revis found a flatrock
on the ridge just
perfect for a natural hearth,
and built his cabin with a stick

and clay chimney right over it.   5
On their wedding night he lit
the fireplace to dry away the mountain
chill of late spring, and flung on

applewood to dye
the room with molten color while   10
he and Martha that was a Parrish
warmed the sheets between the tick

stuffed with leaves and its feather
cover. Under that wide hearth
a nest of rattlers,   15
they'll knot a hundred together,

had wintered and were coming awake.
The warming rock
flushed them out early.
It was she   20

who wakened to their singing near
the embers and roused him to go look.
Before he reached the fire
more than a dozen struck

and he died yelling her to stay   25
on the big four-poster.
Her uncle coming up the hollow
with a gift bearham two days later

found her shivering there
marooned above a pool   30

of hungry snakes,
and the body beginning to swell.

                                                              —1979

CRAIG RAINE   B. 1944

Raine's brand of comic surrealism was responsible for so many
imitations that critic James Fenton dubbed him the founder of
the "Martian School" of contemporary poetry. Born in Bishop
Auckland, England, and educated at Oxford, Raine is an editor with
the prestigious publishing firm of Faber & Faber.

A Martian Sends a Postcard Home

Caxtons° are mechanical birds with many wings
and some are treasured for their markings—

they cause the eyes to melt
or the body to shriek without pain.

I have never seen one fly, but   5
sometimes they perch on the hand.

Mist is when the sky is tired of flight
and rests its soft machine on ground:

then the world is dim and bookish
like engravings under tissue paper.   10

Rain is when the earth is television.
It has the property of making colours darker.

Model T is a room with the lock inside—
a key is turned to free the world

for movement, so quick there is a film   15
to watch for anything missed.

But time is tied to the wrist
or kept in a box, ticking with impatience.

---

1 **Caxtons** i.e., books; after William Caxton (1422-1491), first English printer

In homes, a haunted apparatus sleeps,
that snores when you pick it up.   20

If the ghost cries, they carry it
to their lips and soothe it to sleep

with sounds. And yet, they wake it up
deliberately, by tickling with a finger.

Only the young are allowed to suffer   25
openly. Adults go to a punishment room

with water but nothing to eat.
They lock the door and suffer the noises

alone. No one is exempt
and everyone's pain has a different smell.   30

At night, when all the colours die,
they hide in pairs

and read about themselves—
in colour, with their eyelids shut.

                                                        —1978

Enid Shomer   B. 1944

Shomer grew up in Washington, D.C., and has lived for a number
of years in Gainesville, Florida. Her first collection, *Stalking the
Florida Panther* (1987), explored both the Jewish traditions of her
childhood and her adult attachment to her adopted state. A second
book, *This Close to the Earth*, appeared in 1992.

Women Bathing at Bergen-Belsen°

April 24, 1945

Twelve hours after the Allies arrive
there is hot water, soap. Two women bathe
in a makeshift, open-air shower while nearby
fifteen thousand are flung naked into mass graves
by captured SS guards. Clearly legs and arms   5

Bergen-Belsen German concentration camp in WWII

are the natural handles of a corpse. The bathers,
taken late in the war, still have flesh
on their bones, still have breasts. Though nudity was
a death sentence here, they have undressed,
oblivious to the soldiers and the cameras.   10
The corpses push through the limed earth like upended
headstones. The bathers scrub their feet, bending
in beautiful curves, mapping the contours
of the body, that kingdom to which they've returned.

                                                    —1987

ALICE WALKER   B. 1944

> As the author of *The Color Purple* and other novels, Alice Walker is a
> leading African-American writer. Less well known as a poet, she won
> the Pulitzer Prize for fiction in 1983. Her most recent novels com-
> bine her concerns with both racial and feminist issues.

Even as I Hold You

Even as I hold you
I think of you as someone gone
far, far away. Your eyes the color
of pennies in a bowl of dark honey
bringing sweet light to someone else   5
your black hair slipping through my fingers
is the flash of your head going
around a corner
your smile, breaking before me,
the flippant last turn   10
of a revolving door,
emptying you out, changed,
away from me.

Even as I hold you
I am letting go.   15

                                                    —1979

LEON STOKESBURY   B. 1945

> Governor's Square Mall is located in Tallahassee, Florida, where the
> poet attended graduate school in the early 1980s. Stokesbury has

remarked that this poem began as his attempt to write a contemporary American version of Wordsworth's "Tintern Abbey." The author of three collections, including *Autumn Rhythm: New and Selected Poems*, Stokesbury has also edited anthologies of contemporary Southern poetry and the poetry of World War II.

Day Begins at Governor's Square Mall

Here, newness is all. Or almost all. And like
a platterful of pope's noses° at a White House dinner,
I exist apart. But these trees now—
how do you suppose they grow this high in here?
They look a little like the trees I sat beneath in 1959   5
waiting with my cheesecloth net for butterflies.
It was August and it was hot. Late summer,
yes, but already the leaves in trees were
flecked with ochers and the umbers of the dead.
I sweated there for hours, so driven,   10
so immersed in the forest's shimmering life,
that I could will my anxious self not move
for half a day—just on the imagined chance
of making some slight part of it my own.
Then they came. One perfect pair of just-hatched   15
black-and-white striped butterflies. The white
lemon-tipped with light, in shade
then out, meandering. Zebra swallowtails,
floating, drunk in the sun, so rare to find
their narrow, fragile, two-inch tails intact.   20
At that moment I could only drop my net and stare.
The last of August. 1959. But these trees, now,
climb up through air and concrete never hot or cold.
And I suspect the last lepidoptera that found
themselves in here were sprayed then swept away.   25
Everyone is waiting though, as before a storm—
anticipating something. Do these leaves never fall?

Now, and with a mild surprise, faint
music falls. But no shop breaks open yet.
The people, like myself, range aimlessly;   30
the air seems thick and still. Then, lights blink on;
the escalators jerk and hum. And in the center, at
the exact center of the mall, a jet of water spurts

---

2 **pope's noses** rumps of cooked chickens

twenty feet straight up, then drops and spatters
in a shallow pool where signs announce that none   35
may ever go. O bright communion! O new cathedral!
where the appetitious, the impure, the old, the young,
the bored, the lost, the dumb, with wide dilated eyes
advance with offerings to be absolved and be made clean.
Now, the lime-lit chainlink fronts from over one hundred   40
pleasant and convenient stalls and stores are rolled away.
Now, odors of frying won tons come wafting up from
Lucy Ho's Bamboo Garden. And this music, always
everywhere, yet also somehow strangely played as if
not to be heard, pours its soft harangue down now.   45
The people wander forward now. And the world begins.

                                                    —1986

Robert A. Fink   B. 1946

A Marine veteran who saw action in Vietnam, Fink has recently published *The Tongues of Men and Angels*, a collection of poems which
alternate autobiographical subjects with a sequence spoken in the
voice of St. Paul. He teaches at Hardin-Simmons University.

The Ex-Grunt Writes His Last Letter to His Former Professor

I'm sick of Vietnam, marginal notes
suggesting I buy the latest thriller spilling
it "like it was," sit through the movie
everyone has seen but me.

You say my poems have no life.   5
I need to show; don't tell.
Open up. Confess
the "truth" of napalm strikes—
backyard barbecues you want to taste.

I guess you mean   10
slide the reader down a garbage bag;
kick him, hands tied, from a chopper just for fun;
cut out his privates, jam them between his teeth.

How about I take you headfirst
down this tunnel tight as a cat hole?   15
Mail me the metaphor for an ice pick through the eye.

May I send you twenty ways to slit a throat?
We'll start with tin-can lids.

Pretend I haven't had a bath since Thursday
and my platoon is straggling toward a friendly village   20
when Hang Ten drops crotch first
into a pit of punji sticks tipped with shit.
Describe the shape a mouth takes before it screams.

Now imagine you live in that village
and I learn you dug the pit.   25
Look at me!
I've got a razor blade.
I've got your wife.

                                                    —1995

MARILYN NELSON   B. 1946

Nelson's book *The Homeplace* is a sequence of poems on family history, perhaps, like Rita Dove's *Thomas and Beulah*, a poetic manifestation of the *"Roots"* phenomenon in African-American literary culture. *The Homeplace* is remarkable for its sensitive exploration of the mixed white and black bloodlines in a southern family tree. Nelson, who formerly wrote as Marilyn Nelson Waniek, has recently published *Magnificat*, a collection of new poems.

The Ballad of Aunt Geneva

Geneva was the wild one.
Geneva was a tart.
Geneva met a blue-eyed boy
and gave away her heart.

Geneva ran a roadhouse.   5
Geneva wasn't sent
to college like the others:
Pomp's pride her punishment.

She cooked out on the river,
watching the shore slide by,   10
her lips pursed into hardness,
her deep-set brown eyes dry.

They say she killed a woman
over a good black man

by braining the jealous heifer   15
with an iron frying pan.

They say, when she was eighty,
she got up late at night
and sneaked her old, white lover in
to make love, and to fight.   20

First, they heard the tell-tale
singing of the springs,
then Geneva's voice rang out:
I need to buy some things,

So next time, bring more money.   25
And bring more moxie, too.
I ain't got no time to waste
on limp white mens like you.

Oh yeah? Well, Mister White Man,
it sure might be stone-white,   30
but my thing's white as it is.
And you know damn well I'm right.

Now listen: take your heart pills
and pay the doctor mind.
If you up and die on me,   35
I'll whip your white behind.

They tiptoed through the parlor
on heavy, time-slowed feet.
She watched him, from her front door,
walk down the dawnlit street.   40

Geneva was the wild one.
Geneva was a tart.
Geneva met a blue-eyed boy
and gave away her heart.

                                                                —1990

A i   B. 1947

Ai's realistic dramatic monologues often reveal the agonies of characters trapped in unfulfilling or even dangerous lives. With her gallery of social misfits, she is the contemporary heir to the tradition begun by Robert Browning.

Child Beater

Outside, the rain, pinafore of gray water, dresses the town
and I stroke the leather belt,
as she sits in the rocking chair,
holding a crushed paper cup to her lips.
I yell at her, but she keeps rocking;   5
back, her eyes open, forward, they close.
Her body, somehow fat, though I feed her only once a day,
reminds me of my own just after she was born.
It's been seven years, but I still can't forget how I felt.
How heavy it feels to look at her.   10

I lay the belt on a chair
and get her dinner bowl.
I hit the spoon against it, set it down
and watch her crawl to it,
pausing after each forward thrust of her legs   15
and when she takes her first bite,
I grab the belt and beat her across the back
until her tears, beads of salt-filled glass, falling,
shatter on the floor.

I move off. I let her eat,   20
while I get my dog's chain leash from the closet.
I whirl it around my head.
O daughter, so far, you've only had a taste of icing,
are you ready now for some cake?

                                                        —1973

JIM HALL   B. 1947

Hall, one of the most brilliantly inventive comic poets in recent
years, has also written a successful series of crime novels set in his
native south Florida, beginning with *Under Cover of Daylight* in 1987.

Maybe Dats Your Pwoblem Too

All my pwoblems,
who knows, maybe evwybody's pwoblems
is due to da fact, due to da awful twuth
dat I am SPIDERMAN.

I know, I know. All da dumb jokes: 5

No flies on you, ha ha,
and da ones about what do I do wit all
doze extwa legs in bed. Well, dat's funny yeah.
But you twy being
SPIDERMAN for a month or two. Go ahead.   10

You get doze cwazy calls fwom da
Gubbener askin you to twap some booglar who's
only twying to wip off color T.V. sets.
Now, what do I cawre about T.V. sets?
But I pull on da suit, da stinkin suit,   15
wit da sucker cups on da fingers,
and get my wopes and wittle bundle of
equipment and den I go flying like cwazy
acwoss da town fwom woof top to woof top.

Till der he is. Some poor dumb color T.V. slob   20
and I fall on him and we westle a widdle
until I get him all woped. So big deal.

You tink when you SPIDERMAN
der's sometin big going to happen to you.
Well, I tell you what. It don't happen dat way.   25
Nuttin happens. Gubbener calls, I go.
Bwing him to powice, Gubbener calls again,
like dat over and over.

I tink I twy sometin diffunt. I tink I twy
sometin excitin like wacing cawrs. Sometin to make   30
my heart beat at a difwent wate.
But den you just can't quit being sometin like
SPIDERMAN.
You SPIDERMAN for life. Fowever. I can't even
buin my suit. It won't buin. It's fwame wesistent.   35
So maybe dat's youwr pwoblem too, who knows.
Maybe dat's da whole pwoblem wif evwytin.
Nobody can buin der suits, dey all fwame wesistent.
Who knows?

                                              —1980

YUSEF KOMUNYAKAA   B. 1947

A native of Bogalusa, Louisiana, Komunyakaa has written memo-
rably on a wide range of subjects, including jazz and his service dur-

ing the Vietnam War. *Copacetic,* his first collection of poems, appeared in 1984.

Facing It

My black face fades,
hiding inside the black granite.
I said I wouldn't,
dammit: No tears.
I'm stone. I'm flesh.   5
My clouded reflection eyes me
like a bird of prey, the profile of night
slanted against morning. I turn
this way—the stone lets me go.
I turn this way—I'm inside   10
the Vietnam Veterans Memorial
again, depending on the light
to make a difference.
I go down the 58,022 names,
half-expecting to find   15
my own in letters like smoke.
I touch the name Andrew Johnson;
I see the booby trap's white flash.
Names shimmer on a woman's blouse
but when she walks away   20
the names stay on the wall.
Brushstrokes flash, a red bird's
wings cutting across my stare.
The sky. A plane in the sky.
A white vet's image floats   25
closer to me, then his pale eyes
look through mine. I'm a window.
He's lost his right arm
inside the stone. In the black mirror
a woman's trying to erase names: 30
No, she's brushing a boy's hair.

—1988

R. S. Gwynn   B. 1948

R. S. Gwynn is the editor of this collection of poetry. He teaches at
Lamar University in Beaumont, Texas.

Body Bags

I

Let's hear it for Dwayne Coburn, who was small
And mean without a single saving grace
Except for stealing—home from second base
Or out of teammates' lockers, it was all
The same to Dwayne. The Pep Club candy sale,   5
However, proved his downfall. He was held
Briefly on various charges, then expelled
And given a choice: enlist or go to jail.

He finished basic and came home from Bragg°
For Christmas on his reassignment leave   10
With one prize in his pack he thought unique,
Which went off prematurely New Year's Eve.
The student body got the folded flag
And flew it in his memory for a week.

II

Good pulling guards were scarce in high school ball.   15
The ones who had the weight were usually slow
as lumber trucks. A scaled-down wild man, though,
Like Dennis "Wampus" Peterson, could haul
His ass around right end for me to slip
Behind his blocks. Played college ball a year—   20
Red-shirted when they yanked his scholarship
Because he majored, so he claimed, in Beer.

I saw him one last time. He'd added weight
Around the neck, used words like "grunt" and "slope,"
And said he'd swap his Harley and his dope   25
And both balls for a 4-F knee like mine.
This happened in the spring of '68.
He hanged himself in 1969.

III

Jay Swinney did a great Roy Orbison
Impersonation once at Lyn-Rock Park,   30
Lip-synching to "It's Over" in his dark
Glasses beside the jukebox. He was one
Who'd want no better for an epitaph

---

9 **Bragg** Fort Bragg, N.C., a military training base

Than he was good with girls and charmed them by
Opening his billfold to a photograph: 35
Big brother. The Marine. Who didn't die.

He comes to mind, years from that summer night,
In class for no good reason while I talk
About Thoreau's remark that one injustice
Makes prisoners of us all. The piece of chalk   40
Splinters and flakes in fragments as I write,
To settle in the tray, where all the dust is.

                                                    —1990

TIMOTHY STEELE   B. 1948

Steele, who has written a successful scholarly study of the rise of free
verse, *Missing Measures*, is perhaps the most skillful craftsman of the
contemporary New Formalist poets. Born in Vermont, he has lived
for a number of years in Los Angeles, where he teaches at California
State University.

Sapphics° Against Anger

Angered, may I be near a glass of water;
May my first impulse be to think of Silence,
Its deities (who are they? do, in fact, they
            Exist? etc.).

May I recall what Aristotle says of   5
The subject: to give vent to rage is not to
Release it but to be increasingly prone
            To its incursions.

May I imagine being in the Inferno,
Hearing it asked: "Virgilio mio,° who's   10
That sulking with Achilles there?" and hearing
            Virgil say: "Dante,

That fellow, at the slightest provocation,
Slammed phone receivers down, and waved his arms like
A madman. What Attila did to Europe,   15
            What Genghis Khan did

Sapphics stanza form named after Sappho (c. 650 B.C.)   **10 Virgilio mio** Dante is addressing
Virgil, his guide through hell.

To Asia, that poor dope did to his marriage."
May I, that is, put learning to good purpose,
Mindful that melancholy is a sin, though
        Stylish at present.   20

Better than rage is the post-dinner quiet,
The sink's warm turbulence, the streaming platters,
The suds rehearsing down the drain in spirals
        In the last rinsing.

For what is, after all, the good life save that   25
Conducted thoughtfully, and what is passion
If not the holiest of powers, sustaining
        Only if mastered.

                                                  —1986

DAVID BOTTOMS   B. 1949

Born in Canton, Georgia, Bottoms is the author both of collections
of poetry and successful novels. His first book, *Shooting Rats at Bibb
County Dump*, was a winner of the Walt Whitman Award of the
Academy of American Poets. He is the co-editor, with Dave Smith,
of *The Morrow Anthology of Younger American Poets.*

Sign for My Father, Who Stressed the Bunt

On the rough diamond,
the hand-cut field below the dog lot and barn,
we rehearsed the strict technique
of bunting. I watched from the infield,
the mound, the backstop   5
as your left hand climbed the bat, your legs
and shoulders squared toward the pitcher.
You could drop it like a seed
down either base line. I admired your style,
but not enough to take my eyes off the bank   10
that served as our center-field fence.

Years passed, three leagues of organized ball,
no few lives. I could homer
into the garden beyond the bank,
into the left-field lot of Carmichael Motors,   15

and still you stressed the same technique,
the crouch and spring, the lead arm absorbing
just enough impact. That whole tiresome pitch
about basics never changing,
and I never learned what you were laying down.   20

Like a hand brushed across the bill of a cap,
let this be the sign
I'm getting a grip on the sacrifice.

—1983

JAMES FENTON   B. 1949

Born in Lincoln, England, and educated at Oxford, Fenton has
worked extensively as a book and drama critic. A brilliant satirical
poet, he has also written lyrics for *Les Misérables*, the musical version
of Victor Hugo's novel, and has served as a journalist in Asia.

God, a Poem

A nasty surprise in a sandwich,
A drawing-pin caught in your sock,
The limpest of shakes from a hand which
You'd thought would be firm as a rock,

A serious mistake in a nightie,   5
A grave disappointment all around
Is all that you'll get from th'Almighty.
Is all that you'll get underground.

Oh, he *said*: 'If you lay off the crumpet°
I'll see you alright in the end.   10
Just hang on until the last trumpet.
Have faith in me, chum—I'm your friend.'

But if you remind him, he'll tell you:
'I'm sorry, I must have been pissed—°
Though your name rings a sort of a bell. You   15
Should have guessed that I do not exist.

---

9 crumpet vulgar British slang for women   **14 pissed** drunk

'I didn't exist at Creation,
I didn't exist at the Flood.
And I won't be around for Salvation
To sort out the sheep from the cud—   20

'Or whatever the phrase is. The fact is
In soteriological° terms
I'm a crude existential malpractice
And you are a diet of worms.

'You're a nasty surprise in a sandwich.   25
You're a drawing-pin caught in my sock.
You're the limpest of shakes from a hand which
I'd have thought would be firm as a rock,

'You're a serious mistake in a nightie,
You're a grave disappointment all round—   30
'That's all that you are,' says th'Almighty,
'And that's all that you'll be underground.'

                                                   —1983

Carolyn Forché   B. 1950

Forché won the Yale Younger Poets Award for her first collection, *Gathering the Tribes* (1975). *The Country Between Us*, Forché's second collection, contains poems based on the poet's experiences in the war-torn country of El Salvador in the early 1980s.

The Colonel

What you have heard is true. I was in his house.° His wife carried a tray of coffee and sugar. His daughter filed her nails, his son went out for the night. There were daily papers, pet dogs, a pistol on the cushion beside him. The moon swung bare on its black cord over the house. On the television was a cop show. It was in English. Broken bottles were embedded in the walls around the house to scoop the kneecaps from a man's legs or cut his hands to lace. On the windows there were gratings like those in liquor stores. We had dinner, rack of lamb, good wine, a gold bell was on the table for calling the maid. The maid brought green mangoes, salt, a type of bread. I was asked how I enjoyed the country. There was a brief commercial in Spanish. His wife

---

22 **soteriological** relation to salvation
1 **his house** in El Salvador

took everything away. There was some talk then of how difficult it had become to govern. The parrot said hello on the terrace. The colonel told it to shut up, and pushed himself from the table. My friend said to me with his eyes: say nothing. The colonel returned with a sack used to bring groceries home. He spilled many human ears on the table. They were like dried peach halves. There is no other way to say this. He took one of them in his hands, shook it in our faces, dropped it into a water glass. It came alive there. I am tired of fooling around he said. As for the rights of anyone, tell your people they can go fuck themselves. He swept the ears to the floor with his arm and held the last of his wine in the air. Something for your poetry, no? he said. Some of the ears on the floor caught this scrap of his voice. Some of the ears on the floor were pressed to the ground.

—1978

D<small>ANA</small> G<small>IOIA</small>   B . 1 9 5 0

Gioia, who grew up in the suburbs of Los Angeles, took a graduate degree in English from Harvard but made a successful career in business. He is usually mentioned as one of the leading New Formalist poets and as an influential critic of contemporary poetry whose essay "Can Poetry Matter?" stimulated much discussion when it appeared in *The Atlantic* in 1991.

Cruising with the Beachboys

So strange to hear that song again tonight
Travelling on business in a rented car
Miles from anywhere I've been before.
And now a tune I haven't heard for years
Probably not since it last left the charts   5
Back in L.A. in 1969.
I can't believe I know the words by heart
And can't think of a girl to blame them on.

Every lovesick summer has its song,
And this one I pretended to despise,   10
But if I was alone when it came on,
I turned it up full-blast to sing along—
A primal scream in croaky baritone,
The notes all flat, the lyrics mostly slurred
No wonder I spent so much time alone   15
Making the rounds in Dad's old Thunderbird.

Some nights I drove down to the beach to park
And walk along the railings of the pier.
The water down below was cold and dark,
The waves monotonous against the shore.   20
The darkness and the mist, the midnight sea
The flickering lights reflected from the city—
A perfect setting for a boy like me,
The Cecil B. DeMille° of my self-pity.

I thought by now I'd left those nights behind,   25
Lost like the girls that I could never get,
Gone with the years, junked with the old T-Bird.
But one old song, a stretch of empty road,
Can open up a door and let them fall
Tumbling like boxes from a dusty shelf,   30
Tightening my throat for no reason at all
Bringing on tears shed only for myself.

                                                        —1986

Rodney Jones   B. 1950

Born in Alabama, Jones received important national attention when
Transparent Gestures won the Poets' Prize in 1990. Like many younger
southern poets, he often deals with the difficult legacy of racism and
the adjustments that a new era have forced on both whites and blacks.

Winter Retreat: Homage to Martin Luther King, Jr.

There is a hotel in Baltimore where we came together,
we black and white educated and educators,
for a week of conferences, for important counsel
sanctioned by the DOE° and the Carter administration,
to make certain difficult inquiries, to collate notes   5
on the instruction of the disabled, the deprived,
the poor, who do not score well on entrance tests,
who, failing school, must go with mop and pail
skittering across the slick floors of cafeterias,
or climb dewy girders to balance high above cities,   10
or, jobless, line up in the bone cold. We felt

---

24 **Cecil B. DeMille** American director of spectacular films like *The Ten Commandments*
4 **DOE** Department of Education

substantive burdens lighter if we stated it right.
Very delicately, we spoke in turn. We walked
together beside the still waters of behaviorism.
Armed with graphs and charts, with new strategies   15
to devise objectives and determine accountability,
we empathetic black and white shone in seminar rooms.
We enunciated every word clearly and without accent.
We moved very carefully in the valley of the shadow
of the darkest agreement error. We did not digress.   20
We ascended the trunk of that loftiest cypress
of Latin grammar the priests could never
successfully graft onto the rough green chestnut
of the English language. We extended ourselves
with that sinuous motion of the tongue that is half   25
pain and almost eloquence. We black and white
politely reprioritized the parameters of our agenda
to impact equitably on the Seminole and the Eskimo.
We praised diversity and involvement, the sacrifices
of fathers and mothers. We praised the next white   30
Gwendolyn Brooks° and the next black Robert Burns.°
We deep made friends. In that hotel we glistened
over the *pommes au gratin*° and the *poitrine de veau.*°
The morsels of lamb flamed near where we talked.
The waiters bowed and disappeared among the ferns.   35
And there is a bar there, there is a large pool.
Beyond the tables of the drinkers and raconteurs,
beyond the hot tub brimming with Lebanese tourists
and the women in expensive bathing suits doing laps,
if you dive down four feet, swim out far enough,   40
and emerge on the other side, it is sixteen degrees.
It is sudden and very beautiful and colder
than thought, though the air frightens you at first,
not because it is cold, but because it is visible,
almost palpable, in the fog that rises from difference.   45
While I stood there in the cheek-numbing snow,
all Baltimore was turning blue. And what I remember
of that week of talks is nothing the record shows,
but the revelation outside, which was the city
many came to out of the fields, then the thought   50
that we had wanted to make the world kinder,
but, in speaking proudly, we had failed a vision.

                                                        —1989

---

31 **Gwendolyn Brooks** black American poet (b. 1917)   **Robert Burns** Scottish poet (1759-1796)   33 **pommes au gratin** potatoes baked with cheese   **poitrine de veau** brisket of veal

JOY HARJO   B. 1951

A member of the Creek tribe, Harjo is one of the leading voices of contemporary Native American poetry. She is a powerful performer and was one of the poets featured on Bill Moyers's television series, *The Power of the Word.*

Song for the Deer and Myself to Return On

This morning when I looked out the roof window
before dawn and a few stars were still caught
in the fragile weft of ebony night
I was overwhelmed. I sang the song Louis taught me:
a song to call the deer in Creek,° when hunting,   5
and I am certainly hunting something as magic as deer
in this city far from the hammock of my mother's belly.
It works, of course, and deer came into this room
and wondered at finding themselves
in a house near downtown Denver.   10
Now the deer and I are trying to figure out a song
to get them back, to get all of us back,
because if it works I'm going with them.
And it's too early to call Louis
and nearly too late to go home.   15

                                                        —1990

GARRETT HONGO   B. 1951

Of Japanese ancestry, Garrett Kaoru Hongo was born in Hawaii and educated at Pomona College and the University of California at Irvine. His books include *Yellow Light* (1982) and *The River of Heaven* (1988).

Crossing Ka'ū Desert°

from under the harpstring shade of tree ferns
and the blue trumpets of morning glories
          beside the slick road,
the green creep of davallia and club moss
          (their tiny hammers   5

---

5 Creek Native American tribal language
Ka´ū Desert on the island of Hawaii

staffed quarter-notes
          and fiddlenecks on the forest floor),
spider lilies and ginger flowers like paper cranes
          furling in the tongues of overgrowth,
               in the sapphired arpeggios of rain   10

to the frozen, shale-colored sea,
          froth, swirls, bleak dithyrambs of glass,
a blizzard of cinderrock and singed amulets,
warty spires and pipelines,
          threnodies of surf whirling on the lava land—   15
our blue car the last note of color
driving a black channel
          through hymnless ground

                                                    —1988

ANDREW HUDGINS   B. 1951

Reared in Montgomery, Alabama, Hudgins has demonstrated his
poetic skills in a wide variety of poems, including a book-length
sequence of dramatic monologues, *After the Lost War*, in the voice of
Sidney Lanier, the greatest Southern poet of the late nineteenth
century.

Air View of an Industrial Scene

There is a train at the ramp, unloading people
who stumble from the cars and toward the gate.
The building's shadows tilt across the ground
and from each shadow juts a longer one
and from that shadow crawls a shadow of smoke   5
black as just-plowed earth. Inside the gate
is a small garden and someone on his knees.
Perhaps he's fingering the yellow blooms
to see which ones have set and will soon wither,
clinging to a green tomato as it swells.   10
The people hold back, but are forced to the open gate,
and when they enter they will see the garden
and some, gardeners themselves, will yearn
to fall to their knees there, untangling vines,
plucking at weeds, cooling their hands in damp earth.   15
They're going to die soon, a matter of minutes.
Even from our height, we see in the photograph
the shadow of the plane stamped dark and large

on Birkenau,° one black wing shading the garden.
We can't tell which are guards, which prisoners.   20
We're watchers. But if we had bombs we'd drop them.

—1985

Rita Dove   B. 1952

Dove won the Pulitzer Prize in 1987 for *Thomas and Beulah*, a
sequence of poems about her grandparents' lives in Ohio. She is one
of the most important voices of contemporary African-American
poetry and served as Poet Laureate of the United States from 1993
to 1995.

Adolescence—III

With Dad gone, Mom and I worked
The dusky rows of tomatoes.
As they glowed orange in sunlight
And rotted in shadow, I too
Grew orange and softer, swelling out   5
Starched cotton slips.

The texture of twilight made me think of
Lengths of Dotted Swiss.° In my room
I wrapped scarred knees in dresses
That once went to big-band dances;   10
I baptized my earlobes with rosewater.
Along the window-sill, the lipstick stubs
Glittered in their steel shells.

Looking out at the rows of clay
And chicken manure, I dreamed how it would happen: 15
He would meet me by the blue spruce,
A carnation over his heart, saying,
"I have come for you, Madam;
I have loved you in my dreams."
At his touch, the scabs would fall away.   20
Over his shoulder, I see my father coming toward us:
He carries his tears in a bowl,
And blood hangs in the pine-soaked air.

—1980

---

19 Birkenau German concentration camp in WWII
8 Dotted Swiss type of sheer fabric

Naomi Shihab Nye   B. 1952

A dedicated world traveler and humanitarian, Nye has read her poetry in Bangladesh and the Middle East. Many of her poems are informed by her Palestinian ancestry, and she has translated contemporary Arabic poetry.

The Traveling Onion

"It is believed that the onion originally came from India. In Egypt it was an object of worship—why, I haven't been able to find out. From Egypt the onion entered Greece and on to Italy, thence into all of Europe."–Better Living Cookbook

When I think how far the onion has traveled
just to enter my stew today, I c
crackly paper peeling on the drainboard,
pearly layers in smooth agreement,   5
the way knife enters onion
and onion falls apart on the chopping block,
a history revealed.

And I would never scold the onion
for causing tears.   10
It is right that tears fall
for something small and forgotten.
How at meal, we sit to eat,
commenting on texture of meat or herbal aroma
but never on the translucence of onion,   15
now limp, now divided,
or its traditionally honorable career:
For the sake of others,
disappear.

                                                      —1986

Alberto Ríos   B. 1952

Born in Nogales, Arizona, the son of a Mexican-American father and an English-born mother, Ríos won the Walt Whitman Award of the Academy of American Poets for his first book, *Whispering to Fool the Wind* (1982). He has also written a collection of short stories, *The Iguana Killer: Twelve Stories of the Heart*, which won the Western States Book Award in 1984.

The Purpose of Altar Boys

Tonio told me at catechism
the big part of the eye
admits good, and the little
black part is for seeing
evil—his mother told him   5
who was a widow and so
an authority on such things.
That's why at night
the black part gets bigger.
That's why kids can't go out   10
at night, and at night
girls take off their clothes
and walk around their
bedrooms or jump on their
beds or wear only sandals   15
and stand in their windows.
I was the altar boy
who knew about these things,
whose mission on some Sundays
was to remind people of   20
the night before as they
knelt for Holy Communion.
To keep Christ from falling
I held the metal plate under chins,
while on the thick   25
red carpet of the altar
I dragged my feet
and waited for the precise
moment: plate to chin
I delivered without expression   30
the Holy Electric Shock,
the kind that produces
a really large swallowing
and makes people think.
I thought of it as justice.   35
But on other Sundays the fire
in my eyes was different,
my mission somehow changed.
I would hold the metal plate
a little too hard   40
against those certain same
nervous chins, and I

I would look
with authority down
the tops of white dresses.   45

                                                        —1982

GARY SOTO   B. 1952

A professor of Chicano studies at the University of California at
Berkeley, Soto grew up in Fresno. His poetry collections include *The
Elements of San Joaquin* (1977) and *The Tale of Sunlight* (1978). A prose
book, *Living Up the Street* (1984), is a memoir of his urban childhood.

The Skeptics

Pyrrho of Elis and Sextus Empiricus were Skeptics,
Two big-shot thinkers who argued
Over figs, wine, and the loveliness of their sex.
I crowed to my brother about them,
And one evening, with Fig Newton crumbs in our mouths,   5
I was Pyrrho and Rick was Sextus,
Both of us skeptical about getting good jobs.
I said, "Brother Sextus, what will you render on the canvas
When you're all grown up?" He chewed
On his Fig Newton and answered, "Pyrrho,   10
My young flame, I will draw the reality
Of dead dogs with their feet in the air."
I crowed, "Wow, Rick—I mean Sextus—that's pretty good."
In sandals, we went down to the liquor store,
Each of us in our imaginary Greek robes,   15
And stole a quart of beer. Neither of us was a skeptic
When we swigged on that quart
And walked by the house with a woman hammering walnuts,
The rise and fall of her buttery hand quivering
The two hairs on my chest. We had our figs and wine,   20
And what we Skeptics needed,
Or at least I, was three strokes of that hammering.
I flowed over in my robe and said, "We're Brothers Skeptic,
Ruled by cautious truths." She smiled,
Hammer raised, and said, "Sure you are."   25
Right away we got along, a womanly skeptic
With a nice swing. I sat on the steps,
A young man with his figs, his wine,

And, with my Greek name shed,
A reverent believer in a woman with hammer in hand.   30

—1995

Julia Alvarez   B. 1953

Julia Alvarez's first collection, *Homecoming*, contained both free verse
and "33," a sequence of 33 sonnets on the occasion of the poet's
thirty-third birthday. She has recently gained acclaim for *In the Time
of the Butterflies*, a work of fiction, and *The Other Side/El Otro Lado*, a
collection of poems.

Bilingual Sestina

Some things I have to say aren't getting said
in this snowy, blond, blue-eyed, gum-chewing English:
dawn's early light sifting through *persianas* closed
the night before by dark-skinned girls whose words
evoke *cama, aposento, sueños* in *nombres*   5
from that first world I can't translate from Spanish.

Gladys, Rosario, Altagracia—the sounds of Spanish
wash over me like warm island waters as I say
your soothing names: a child again learning the *nombres*
of things you point to in the world before English   10
turned *sol, sierra, cielo, luna* to vocabulary words—
sun, earth, sky, moon. Language closed

like the touch-sensitive *moriviví* whose leaves closed
when we kids poked them, astonished. Even Spanish
failed us back then when we saw how frail a word is   15
when faced with the thing it names. How saying
its name won't always summon up in Spanish or English
the full blown genie from the bottled *nombre*.

Gladys, I summon you back by saying your *nombre*.
Open up again the house of slatted windows closed   20
since childhood, where *palabras* left behind for English
stand dusty and awkward in neglected Spanish.
Rosario, muse of *el patio*, sing in me and through me say
that world again, begin first with those first words

you put in my mouth as you pointed to the world—   25
not Adam, not God, but a country girl numbering
the stars, the blades of grass, warming the sun by saying,

¡Qué calor! as you opened up the morning closed
inside the night until you sang in Spanish,
Estas son las mañanitas, and listening in bed, no English   30

yet in my head to confuse me with translations, no English
doubling the world with synonyms, no dizzying array of words
—the world was simple and intact in Spanish—
luna, sol, casa, luz, flor, as if the nombres
were the outer skin of things, as if words were so close   35
one left a mist of breath on things by saying

their names, an intimacy I now yearn for in English—
words so close to what I mean that I almost hear my Spanish
heart beating, beating inside what I say en inglés.

—1995

Davıd Mason   B. 1954

The title poem of David Mason's The Country I Remember, a long narrative about the life of a Civil War veteran and his daughter, has
been performed in a theatrical version. Mason has recently edited,
with Mark Jarman, The Rebel Angels, an anthology of recent poetry
written in traditional forms.

Song of the Powers

Mine, said the stone,
mine is the hour.
I crush the scissors,
such is my power.
Stronger than wishes,   5
my power, alone.

Mine, said the paper,
mine are the words
that smother the stone
with imagined birds,   10
reams of them, flown
from the mind of the shaper.

Mine, said the scissors,
mine all the knives
gashing through paper's   15
ethereal lives;
nothing's so proper
as tattering wishes.

As stone crushes scissors,
as paper snuffs stone   20
and scissors cut paper,
all end alone.
So heap up your paper
and scissor your wishes
and uproot the stone   25
from the top of the hill.
They all end alone
as you will, you will.

—1996

Mary Jo Salter   B. 1954

Mary Jo Salter has traveled widely with her husband, poet and nov-
elist Brad Leithauser, and has lived in Japan, Italy, and Iceland. A
student of Elizabeth Bishop at Harvard, Salter brings to her art a
devotion to the poet's craft that mirrors that of her mentor. She has
published three collections of poetry and The Moon Comes Home, a
children's book.

Welcome to Hiroshima

is what you first see, stepping off the train:
a billboard brought to you in living English
by Toshiba Electric. While a channel
silent in the TV of the brain

projects those flickering re-runs of a cloud   5
that brims its risen columnful like beer
and, spilling over, hangs its foamy head,
you feel a thirst for history: what year

it started to be safe to breathe the air,
and when to drink the blood and scum afloat   10
on the Ohta River. But no, the water's clear,
they pour it for your morning cup of tea

in one of the countless sunny coffee shops
whose plastic dioramas advertise
mutations of cuisine behind the glass: 15
a pancake sandwich; a pizza someone tops

with a maraschino cherry. Passing by
the Peace Park's floral hypocenter (where

how bravely, or with what mistaken cheer,
humanity erased its own erasure),   20

you enter the memorial museum
and through more glass are served, as on a dish
of blistered grass, three mannequins. Like gloves
a mother clips to coatsleeves, strings of flesh

hang from their fingertips; or as if tied   25
to recall a duty for us, *Reverence*
the dead whose mourners too shall soon be dead,
but all commemoration's swallowed up

in questions of bad taste, how re-created
horror mocks the grim original,   30
and thinking at last *They should have left it all*
you stop. This is the wristwatch of a child.

Jammed on the moment's impact, resolute
to communicate some message, although mute,
it gestures with its hands at eight-fifteen   35
and eight-fifteen and eight-fifteen again

while tables of statistics on the wall
update the news by calling on a roll
of tape, death gummed on death, and in the case
adjacent, an exhibit under glass   40

is glass itself: a shard the bomb slammed in
a woman's arm at eight-fifteen, but some
three decades on——as if to make it plain
hope's only as renewable as pain,

and as if all the unsung   45
debasements of the past may one day come
rising to the surface once again——
worked its filthy way out like a tongue.

                                                        —1985

JANET HOLMES   B. 1956

Janet Holmes's first collection, *The Physicist at the Mall*, contained several poems about her work experiences as a technical writer. She lives in St. Paul, Minnesota, and teaches at Macalester College.

Cinquains for Rocky

You want
a word that means
separating two things
by bringing them closer. "What for?"
she asks.   5

"Doesn't
make sense." It does,
you tell her, when one speaks
about relationships—about
you two.   10

—1993

L i - Y o u n g   L e e   B . 1 9 5 7

Born in Indonesia to parents who emigrated to the United States,
Lee combines a rich heritage of traditional Chinese poetry with
many western influences, including Christian teachings he learned
from his father, a Presbyterian minister. *Rose*, his first collection,
appeared in 1986.

Eating Together

In the steamer is the trout
seasoned with slivers of ginger,
two sprigs of green onion, and sesame oil.
We shall eat it with rice for lunch,
brothers, sister, my mother who will   5
taste the sweetest meat of the head,
holding it between her fingers
deftly, the way my father did
weeks ago. Then he lay down
to sleep like a snow-covered road   10
winding through pines older than him,
without any travelers, and lonely for no one.

—1985

APPENDIX 1
Poems Grouped by Genre, Technique, or Subject

Since it is possible to classify the poems in the anthology in many different ways, the following appendix is not exhaustive. It should, however, provide suggestions for reading and writing about poems that share some similarities. Some poems appear in more than one category.

SATIRE
Stanzas, 99
The Ruined Maid, 151
Disillusionment of Ten O'Clock, 173
The Unknown Citizen, 211
Playboy, 233
Ballade of the New God, 299
E.S.L., 305
Teaching the Ape to Write Poems, 309
God, a Poem, 324

SEXUAL THEMES (SEE ALSO CARPE DIEM)
The Flea, 52
To His Coy Mistress, 63
The Ruined Maid, 151
The Love Song of J. Alfred Prufrock, 190
Playboy, 233
Cherrylog Road, 239
In Bertram's Garden, 248
Rape, 273
Foreplay, 300
The Purpose of Altar Boys, 333

SOLITUDE
Ode on Solitude, 70
The Soul Selects Her Own Society—, 147
The Lake Isle of Innisfree, 158
Acquainted with the Night, 167
Stopping by Woods on a Snowy Evening, 172
The Serenity in Stones, 302

SONNETS (See Appendix 2: Traditional Stanza, Fixed, and Nonce Forms)

SPORTS
The Ballad of Dead Yankees, 262
First Practice, 290

Sign for My Father, Who Stressed the Bunt, 323

SUICIDE
Bonny Barbara Allan, 37
The Mill, 163
Richard Cory, 164
Résumé, 199
Saint Judas, 261
Edge, 282

WAR
The Arsenal at Springfield, 112
A Sight in Camp in the Daybreak Gray and Dim, 130
Dreamers, 185
War Is Kind, XXI, 165
Sestina: Altaforte, 182
Dulce et Decorum Est, 198
The Fury of Aerial Bombardment, 207
The Death of the Ball Turret Gunner, 224
Mementos, I, 254
Digression on the Nuclear Age, 289
The Ex-Grunt Writes His Last Letter to His Former Professor, 315
Facing It, 320
Body Bags, 321

WOMEN'S ISSUES
Let No Charitable Hope, 183
One Perfect Rose, 199
Playboy, 233
Cinderella, 264
Aunt Jennifer's Tigers, 271
Rape, 273
Sous-Entendu, 283
to my last period, 287
Barbie Doll, 288
Siren Song, 294
Combing, 304
The One Girl at the Boys Party, 307

APPENDIX 2
Traditional Stanza, Fixed, and Nonce Forms

FOURTEENERS

Southwell, Robert: "The Burning Babe," 44

COUPLETS, HEROIC

Bradstreet, Anne: "The Author to Her Book," 62

Bradstreet, Anne: "To My Dear and Loving Husband," 62

Browning, Robert: "My Last Duchess," 127

Dryden, John: "Epigram on Milton," 66

Dryden, John: "To the Memory of Mr. Oldham," 65

Gunn, Thom: "Terminal," 268

Jonson, Ben: "On My First Son," 55

Pope, Alexander: "*from* An Essay on Criticism," 69

Rich, Adrienne: "Aunt Jennifer's Tigers," 271

Sarton, May: "A Guest," 217

Swift, Jonathan: "A Description of a City Shower," 67

Toomer, Jean: "Reapers," 202

COUPLETS, SHORT

Blake, William: "A Poison Tree," 80

Blake, William: "The Tyger," 81

Housman, A. E.: "Loveliest of Trees, the Cherry Now," 154

Housman, A. E.: "'Terence, This Is Stupid Stuff . . . ,'" 155

Marvell, Andrew: "To His Coy Mistress," 63

Whittier, John Greenleaf: "Skipper Ireson's Ride," 116

IN MEMORIAM STANZA

Tennyson, Alfred, Lord: "In Memoriam A. H. H., 54," 124

LONG MEASURE

Donne, John: "A Valediction: Forbidding Mourning," 53

Hollander, John: "Adam's Task," 268

Kizer, Carolyn: "The Ungrateful Garden," 249

Landor, Walter Savage: "Mother, I Cannot," 98

Larkin, Philip: "This Be the Verse," 238

Petersen, Donald: "The Ballad of Dead Yankees," 262

Wylie, Elinor: "Let No Charitable Hope," 183

OCTAVE

Gioia, Dana: "Cruising with the Beachboys," 326

Robinson, Edwin Arlington "Eros Turannos," 162

Robinson, Edwin Arlington: "The Mill," 163

Yeats, William Butler: "The Song of Wandering Aengus," 161

ODE, IRREGULAR

Arnold, Matthew: "Dover Beach," 143

Auden, W. H.: "The Unknown Citizen," 211

Coleridge, Samuel Taylor: "Kubla Khan," 96

Frost, Robert: "After Apple-Picking," 167

Owen, Wilfred: "Dulce et Decorum Est," 198

Wordsworth, William: "Ode: Intimations of Immortality," 82

ODE, REGULAR

Keats, John: "Ode on a Grecian Urn," 106

Keats, John: "Ode to a Nightingale," 107

OTTAVA RIMA

Yeats, William Butler: "Sailing to Byzantium," 159

PROSE POEM

Forché, Carolyn: "The Colonel," 325

QUATRAIN, ENGLISH

Causley, Charles: "Eden Rock," 226

Gray, Thomas: "Elegy Written in a Country Churchyard," 71

Hope, A. D.: "Imperial Adam," 207

Landor, Walter Savage: "Dying Speech of an Old Philosopher," 98

Longfellow, Henry Wadsworth: "The Arsenal at Springfield," 112

Robinson, Edwin Arlington: "Richard Cory," 164

QUATRAIN, ITALIAN

Eberhart, Richard: "The Fury of Aerial Bombardment," 207

ACKNOWLEDGMENTS

Betty Adcock, "Digression on the Nuclear Age" reprinted by permission of Louisiana State University Press from *Beholdings* by Betty Adcock. Copyright © 1988 by Betty Adcock.

Ai, "Child Beater" from *Cruelty*. Published by Houghton Mifflin Co. Reprinted by permission of Ai.

Margaret Walker Alexander, "For Malcolm X" from *This Is My Century: New and Collected Poems*. Reprinted by permission of The University of Georgia Press.

Julia Alvarez, "Bilingual Sestina" from *The Other Side/El Otro Lado*. Copyright © 1995 by Julia Alvarez. Published by Dutton, a division of Penguin USA. Reprinted by permission of Susan Bergholz Literary Services, New York. All rights reserved.

John Ashbery, "Farm Implements and Rutabagas in a Landscape" and "Paradoxes and Oxymorons" from *Shadow Train* (New York: Viking, 1981). Reprinted by permission of Georges Borchardt, Inc., for the author. Copyright © 1980, 1981 by John Ashbery.

Margaret Atwood, "Siren Song" from *Selected Poems 1965-1975*. Copyright © 1976, 1990 by Margaret Atwood. Reprinted by permission of Houghton Mifflin Co. and Oxford University Press Canada.

W. H. Auden, "As I Walked Out One Evening," "Musee des Beaux Arts," and "The Unknown Citizen." From *W. H. Auden: Collected Poems* by W. H. Auden, ed. by Edward Mendelson. Copyright 1940 and renewed 1968 by W. H. Auden. Reprinted by permission of Random House, Inc. and Faber and Faber Ltd.

Gerald Barrax, "I Had a Terror—Since September" from *An Audience of One*, p. 59. Reprinted by permission of University of Georgia Press.

Elizabeth Bishop, "The Fish" and "One Art" from *The Complete Poems 1927-1979* by Elizabeth Bishop. Copyright © 1979, 1983 by Alice Helen Methfessel. Reprinted by permission of Farrar, Straus & Giroux, Inc.

Louise Bogan, 'Women" from *The Blue Estuaries*. Copyright © 1968 by Louise Bogan. Copyright renewed © 1996 by Ruth Limmer. Reprinted by permission of Farrar, Straus & Giroux, Inc.

David Bottoms, "Sign for My Father, Who Stressed the Bunt" from *Armored Hearts*, © 1995 by David Bottoms. Reprinted by permission of Copper Canyon Press, PO Box 271, Port Townsend, WA 98368.

Gwendolyn Brooks, "the mother" and "We Real Cool" from *Blacks* by Gwendolyn Brooks. Copyright © 1991 by Gwendolyn Brooks. Reprinted by permission of the author.

Gladys Cardiff, "Combing." Copyright © 1971 by Gladys Cardiff. Reprinted from *To Frighten a Storm* (Copper Canyon Press, 1976) by permission of the author.

Charles Causley, "Eden Rock" from *Secret Destinations: Selected Poems 1977-1988* by Charles Causley. Copyright © 1989 by Charles Causley.

Reprinted by permission of David R. Godine, Publisher.

Fred Chappell, "Narcissus and Echo" reprinted by permission of Lousiana State University Press from *Source* by Fred Chappell. Copyright ©1985 by Fred Chappell.

Lucille Clifton, "To My Last Period," © 1991 by Lucille Clifton. Reprinted from *Quilting: Poems 1987-1990* by Lucille Clifton, with the permission of BOA Editions, Ltd., 260 East Ave., NY 14604.

Hart Crane, "Chaplinesque" from *Complete Poems of Hart Crane* by Marc Simon, editor. Copyright © 1933, © 1958, 1966 by Liveright Publishing Corporation. Copyright © 1986 by Marc Simon. Reprinted by permission of Liveright Publishing Corporation.

Robert Creeley, "I Know a Man" and "Oh No" from *Collected Poems of Robert Creeley, 1945-1975*. Copyright © 1983 by The Regents of University of California. Reprinted by permission of The Regents of the University of California.

Countee Cullen, "Incident" and "Yet Do I Marvel" from the book *Color* by Countee Cullen. Copyright © 1925 by Harper & Brothers; copyright renewed 1953 by Ida M. Cullen. Reprinted by permission of GRM Associates, Inc., as agents for the Estate of Ida M. Cullen.

E. E. Cummings, "In just-," copyright © 1923, 1951, © 1991 by the Trustees for the E. E. Cummings Trust. Copyright © 1976 by George James Firmage, "pity this busy monster, manunkind" copyright © 1944, © 1972, 1991 by the Trustees for the E. E. Cummings Trust, "r-p-o-p-h-e-s-s-a-g-r" copyright © 1935, © 1963, 1991 by the Trustees for the E. E. Cummings Trust, copyright © 1978 by George James Firmage, from *Complete Poems: 1904-1962* by E. E. Cummings, edited by George J. Firmage. Reprinted by permission of Liveright Publishing Corporation.

James Dickey, "Cherrylog Road" from *Poems 1957-1967*. Reprinted by permission of University Press of New England.

Emily Dickinson, "Because I Could Not Stop for Death," "I Died for Beauty," "I Heard a Fly Buzz—When I Died—," "My Life Closed Twice Before Its Close," "A Narrow Fellow in the Grass," and "The Soul Selects Her Own Society" from *The Poems of Emily Dickinson*. Reprinted by permission of the publishers and the Trustees of Amherst College from *The Poems of Emily Dickinson*, Thomas H. Johnson, ed., Cambridge, Mass.: The Belknap Press of Harvard University Press, copyright © 1951, © 1955, 1979, 1983 by the President and Fellows of Harvard College.

Tom Disch, "Ballade of the New God" from *The Dark Horse*, © 1966 by Tom Disch. Reprinted by permission of the author.

Hilda Doolittle, "Pear Tree" from *Collected Poems*

349

1912-1944. New Directions Publishing. No portion of this text may be reprinted without written permission of the publisher.

Rita Dove, "Adolescence . . . III" from *The Yellow House on the Corner,* Carnegie-Mellon University Press, copyright © 1980 by Rita Dove. Used by permission of the author.

Alan Dugan, "Love Song: I and Thou" from *New & Collected Poems.* Reprinted by permission of The Ecco Press.

Stephen Dunn, "The Sacred" from *Between Angels.* Copyright © 1989 by Stephen Dunn. Reprinted by permission of W. W. Norton & Company, Inc.

Richard Eberhart, "The Fury of Aerial Bombardment" from *Collected Poems 1930-1976.* Copyright © 1976 by Richard Eberhart. Used by permission of Oxford University Press, Inc.

T. S. Eliot, "Journey of the Magi" and "The Love Song of J. Alfred Prufrock" from *Collected Poems,* copyright © 1936 by Harcourt Brace & Company, copyright © 1964, 1963 by T.S. Eliot, reprinted by permission of Harcourt Brace & Company, Inc. and Faber and Faber Ltd.

James Fenton, "God: A Poem." From *Children in Exile* by James Fenton. Copyright ©1972, 1978, 1980, 1981, 1982, 1983 by James Fenton. Reprinted by permission of Random House, Inc.

Lawrence Ferlinghetti, "A Coney Island of the Mind, #15." Published by New Directions Publishing. No portion of this text may be reprinted without permission from New Directions Publishing.

Robert A. Fink, "The Ex-Grunt Writes His Last Letter to His Former Professor" from *The Tongues of Men and Angels,* copyright © Texas Tech University Press 1995. Reprinted by permission.

Carolyn Forche, "The Colonel" from *The Country Between Us* by Carolyn Forche. Copyright ©1980 by Carolyn Forche. Reprinted by permission of HarperCollins Publishers.

Robert Frost, "Acquainted With the Night," "Come In," "Design," and "Stopping By Woods on a Snowy Evening" from *The Poetry of Robert Frost,* edited by Edward Connery Lathem. Copyright © 1936, 1942 by Robert Frost. Copyright © 1964, by Leslie Frost Ballantine. Copyright © 1969 by Henry Holt & Co., Inc. Reprinted by permission of Henry Holt & Co., Inc.

Gary Gildner, "First Practice" from *First Practice* by Gary Gildner, © 1969 by University of Pittsburgh Press. Reprinted by permission of the University of Pittsburgh Press.

Allen Ginsberg, "A Supermarket in California." Copyright © 1955 by Allen Ginsberg. From *Collected Poems 1947-1980.* Reprinted by permission of HarperCollins Publishers.

Dana Gioia, "Cruising With the Beachboys" © 1986 by Dana Gioia. Reprinted from *Daily Horoscope* with the permission of Graywolf Press, Saint Paul, MN.

Thom Gunn, "From the Wave" and "Terminal" from *Collected Poems,* copyright © 1994 by Thom Gunn. Reprinted by permission of Farrar, Straus & Giroux, Inc., and Faber & Faber Ltd.

R. S. Gwynn, "Body Bags" from *Texas Poets in Concert: A Quartet,* 1990. Reprinted by permission of R. S. Gwynn.

Jim Hall, "Maybe Dats Your Pwoblem Too" from *The Mating Reflex.* By permission of Carnegie Mellon University Press, © 1980 by Jim Hall.

Joy Harjo, "Song for the Deer and Myself to Return On" from *In Mad Love and War,* reprinted by permission of University Press of New England.

Robert Hass, "Picking Blackberries with a Friend Who Has Been Reading Jacques Lacan" from *Praise.* Reprinted by permission of The Ecco Press.

Robert Hayden, "Those Winter Sundays," copyright © 1966 by Robert Hayden, from *Angle of Ascent: New and Selected Poems* by Robert Hayden. Reprinted by permission of Liveright Publishing Corporation.

Seamus Heaney, "Bogland," "Digging" and "Punishment" from *Selected Poems 1966-1987* by Seamus Heaney. Copyright © 1990 by Seamus Heaney. Reprinted by permission of Farrar, Straus & Giroux, Inc., and Faber & Faber Ltd.

Anthony Hecht, "'More Light, More Light!'." From *Collected Earlier Poems* by Anthony Hecht. Copyright © 1990 by Anthony Hecht. "In Memory of David Kalstone." From *The Transparent Man* by Anthony Hecht. Copyright © 1990 by Anthony Hecht. Reprinted by permission of Alfred A. Knopf, Inc.

John Hollander, "Adam's Task." From *Selected Poetry* by John Hollander. Copyright © 1993 by John Hollander. Reprinted by permission of Alfred A. Knopf, Inc.

Janet Holmes, "Cinquains for Rocky" from *The Physicist at the Mall,* 1993. No portion of this text may be reprinted without permission from Anhinga Press (FL).

Garrett Hongo, "Crossing Ka'ū Desert." From *The River of Heaven* by Garrett Hongo. Copyright ©1988 by Garrett Hongo. Reprinted by permission of Alfred A. Knopf, Inc.

A. D. Hope, "Imperial Adam." No portion of this text may be reprinted without permission of Collins/Angus & Robertson (Australia).

A. E. Housman, "Eight O'Clock," from *The Collected Poems of A. E. Housman,* by A. E. Houseman, copyright © 1922, 1936, 1939, 1940, © 1965 by Holt, Rinehart & Winston, copyright © 1950 by Barclays Bank Ltd., © 1964, 1968 by Robert E. Symons. Reprinted by permission of Henry Holt & Co., Inc.

Andrew Hudgins, "Air View of an Industrial Scene" from *Saints and Strangers.* Copyright © 1985 by Andrew Hudgins. Reprinted by permission of Houghton Mifflin Co. All rights reserved.

Langston Hughes, "Dream Boogie" from *Collected Poems* by Langston Hughes. Copyright © 1994 by the Estate of Langston Hughes. Reprinted by permission of Alfred A. Knopf, Inc. "The Negro Speaks of Rivers," from *Selected Poems* by Langston Hughes. Copyright 1926 by Alfred A. Knopf, Inc. and renewed 1954 by Langston Hughes. Reprinted by permission of the publisher.

Ted Hughes, "Pike" and "The Thought-Fox" from *Selected Poems 1957-1981.* Reprinted by permission of HarperCollins and Faber & Faber Ltd.

Randall Jarrell, "The Death of the Ball Turret Gunner" from *The Complete Poems.* Copyright © 1969 by Mrs. Randall Jarrell. Reprinted by permission of Farrar, Straus & Giroux, Inc.

Robinson Jeffers, "The Purse-Seine." From *The Selected Poetry of Robinson Jeffers* by Robinson Jeffers. Copyright 1937 and renewed 1965 by Donnan Jeffers and Garth Jeffers. Reprinted by permission of Random House, Inc.

Rodney Jones, "Winter Retreat: Homage to Martin Luther King, Jr." from *Transparent Gestures.* Copyright © 1989 by Rodney Jones. Reprinted by permission of Houghton Mifflin Co. All rights reserved.

Donald Justice, "In Bertram's Garden" from *New and Selected Poems* by Donald Justice, copyright © 1995 by Donald Justice. Reprinted by permission of Alfred A. Knopf, Inc.

Weldon Kees, "For My Daughter" from *The Collected Poems of Weldon Kees*, edited by Donald Justice, by permission of University of Nebraska Press. Copyright © 1975 by the University of Nebraska Press.

X. J. Kennedy, "In a Prominent Bar in Secaucus One Day" from *Nude Descending a Staircase*, 1961. Reprinted by permission of Curtis Brown Ltd. Copyright © 1961 by X. J. Kennedy, renewed.

Carolyn Kizer, "The Ungrateful Garden" from *Midnight Was My Cry: New & Selected Poems.* Copyright © 1961 by Carolyn Kizer. Reprinted by permission of the author.

Kenneth Koch, "Permanently." Copyright © 1994 by Kenneth Koch. Reprinted by permission of the author.

Yusef Komunyakaa, "Facing It" from *Dien Cai Dau*, reprinted by permission of University Press of New England.

Maxine Kumin, "Noted in The New York Times" from *Nurture* by Maxine Kumin. Copyright © 1989 by Maxine Kumin. Used by permission of Viking Penguin, a division of Penguin Books USA Inc.

Philip Larkin, "Next, Please" from *The Less Deceived.* Reprinted by permission of The Marvell Press, England and Australia. "Aubade" from *Collected Poems* by Philip Larkin. Copyright © 1988, 1989 by the Estate of Philip Larkin. Reprinted by pemission of Farrar, Straus & Giroux, Inc. "This Be The Verse" from *High Windows*. Reprinted by permission of Farrar, Straus Giroux, Inc., and Faber & Faber Ltd.

Li-Young Lee, "Eating Together," © 1986 by Li-Young Lee. Reprinted from *Rose*, by Li-Young Lee, with the permission of BOA Editions, Ltd., 260 East Ave., Rochester, NY 14604.

Denise Levertov, "The Ache of Marriage" from *Denise Levertov: Poems 1960-1967.* Copyright © 1964 by Denise Levertov Goodman. Reprinted by permission of New Directions Publishing Corporation.

Philip Levine, "Genius." From *New Selected Poems* by Philip Levine. Copyright ©1991 by Philip Levine. Reprinted by permission of Alfred A. Knopf, Inc.

Robert Lowell, "For the Union Dead" from *For The Union Dead* by Robert Lowell. Copyright © 1959 and Copyright renewed © 1987 by Harriet Lowell, Caroline Lowell, and Sheridan Lowell. Reprinted by permission of Farrar, Straus & Giroux, Inc.

Archibald MacLeish, "The End of the World" from *Collected Poems 1917-1982* by Archibald

MacLeish. Copyright © 1985 by the Estate of Archibald MacLeish. Reprinted by permission of Houghton Mifflin Co. All rights reserved.

Charles Martin, "E.S.L." From *Steal the Bacon* by Charles Martin, © 1987 The Johns Hopkins University Press. Reprinted by permission of the publisher.

David Mason, "Song of the Powers" from *The Country I Remember*, 1996. Story Line Press. No portion of this text may be reprinted without permission.

James Merrill, "Casual Wear" and "Charles on Fire" from *Selected Poems 1946-1985* by James Merrill. Copyright © 1992 by James Merrill. Reprinted by permission of Alfred A. Knopf, Inc.

W. S. Merwin, "For the Anniversary of My Death" and "The Last One" from *The Lice*, © 1963, 1964, 1965, 1966, 1967 by W. S. Merwin. No portion of this text may be reprinted without permission of Georges Borchardt, Inc.

Edna St. Vincent Millay, "Sonnet 11" from *Fatal Interview* by Edna St. Vincent Millay, "Oh, Oh, You Will Be Sorry for That Word" and "What Lips My Lips Have Kissed" from *Collected Poems*, HarperCollins. Copyright © 1923, 1931, 1951, 1958 by Edna St. Vincent Millay and Norma Millay Ellis. Reprinted by permission of Elizabeth Barnett, Literary Executor.

Vassar Miller, "Subterfuge" from *If I Had Wheels of Love: Collected Poems.* Reprinted by permission of Martha Failing & Co. (Houston, TX).

Marianne Moore, "Poetry" and "Silence" from *Collected Poems of Marianne Moore*, copyright © 1935 by Marianne Moore; copyright renewed © 1963 by Marianne Moore & T. S. Eliot. Reprinted by permission of Simon & Schuster, Inc.

Robert Morgan, the poem "Mountain Bride" by Robert Morgan from his book *Groundwork* (1979) is reprinted by permission of Gnomon Press.

Howard Nemerov, "The Goose Fish" and "A Primer of the Daily Round" from *New and Selected Poems* by Howard Nemerov, copyright © 1960 by Howard Nemerov (University of Chicago Press). Reprinted by permission of Margaret Nemerov.

Naomi Shihab Nye, "The Traveling Onion." Reprinted by permission of Naomi Shihab Nye from *Yellow Glove*, Breitenbush Books, Portland, OR. Copyright ©1986 by Naomi Shihab Nye.

Frank O' Hara, "The Day Lady Died" from *Lunch Poems.* Copyright © 1964 by Frank O' Hara. Reprinted by permission of City Lights Books.

Sharon Olds, "The One Girl at the Boys Party." From *The Dead and the Living* by Sharon Olds. Copyright ©1983 by Sharon Olds. Reprinted by permission of Alfred A. Knopf, Inc.

Mary Oliver, "The Black Walnut Tree" from *Twelve Moons: Poems* by Mary Oliver. Copyright © 1978 by Mary Oliver. First appeared in *The Ohio Review.* Reprinted by permission of Little, Brown and Company.

Simon J. Ortiz, "The Serenity in Stones." Reprinted by permission of the author, Simon J. Ortiz.

Wilfred Owen, "Dulce et Decorum Est" from *Wilfred Owen: Collected Poems of Wilfred Owen.* Copyright © 1963 by Chatto & Windus Ltd.

Gary Soto, © 1996, published by Chronicle Books, San Francisco. Reprinted by permission of Chronicle Books.

William Stafford, "Traveling through the Dark." Copyright © 1960 by William Stafford. Reprinted from *Stories That Could Be True* by permission of the author.

Timothy Steele, "Sapphics Against Anger" from *Sapphics Against Anger and Other Poems* (Random House, 1986). Copyright © 1986 by Timothy Steele. Reprinted by permission of the author.

Wallace Stevens, "The Snow Man," "Anecdote of the Jar," "Disillusionment of Ten O'Clock," and "Sunday Morning." From *Collected Poems* by Wallace Stevens. Copyright 1923 and renewed 1951 by Wallace Stevens. Reprinted by permission of Alfred A. Knopf, Inc.

Anne Stevenson, "Sous-Entendu" (1970). Reprinted from *The Collected Poems of Anne Stevenson 1955-1996* by Anne Stevenson (1996) by permission of Oxford University Press.

Leon Stokesbury, "Day Begins at Governor's Square Mall." Reprinted by permission of the University of Arkansas Press from *The Drifting Away* by Leon Stokesbury, copyright 1986.

Mark Strand, "The Tunnel" from *Selected Poems* by Mark Strand. Copyright © 1979, 1980 by Mark Strand. Reprinted by permission of Alfred A. Knopf, Inc.

Dabney Stuart, "Discovering My Daughter" from *Light Years: New and Selected Poems,* 1994. Copyright © 1990, 1991, 1992, 1993, 1994 by Dabney Stuart. Reprinted by permission of Louisiana State University Press.

May Swenson, "How Everything Happens (Based on a Study of the Wave)" from *The Complete Poems to Solve* by May Swenson. Copyright © 1993 by The Literary Estate of May Swenson. Reprinted with the permission of Simon & Schuster Books for Young Readers, an imprint of Simon & Schuster Children's Publishing Division.

James Tate, "Teaching the Ape to Write Poems." Reprinted by permission of James Tate.

Henry Taylor, "Artichoke" from *The Flying Change,* 1985. Copyright © 1985 by Henry Taylor. Reprinted by permission of Louisiana State University Press.

Dylan Thomas, "Do Not Go Gentle Into That Good Night" and "Fern Hill" from *Poems of Dylan Thomas.* Reprinted by permission of New Directions Publishing and David Higham Associates.

Jean Toomer, "Reapers" from *Cane* by Jean Toomer. Copyright © 1923 by Boni & Liveright, renewed 1951 by Jean Toomer. Reprinted by permission of Liveright Publishing Corporation.

Ellen Bryant Voigt, "Daughter" from *The Forces of Plenty.* Copyright © 1983 by Ellen Bryant Voigt.

Reprinted by permission of W. W. Norton & Company, Inc.

Derek Walcott, "Central America" from *The Arkansas Testament.* Copyright © 1987 by Derek Walcott. Reprinted by permission of Farrar, Straus & Giroux, Inc.

Alice Walker, "Even as I Hold You" from *Good Night Willie-Lee, I'll See You in the Morning* by Alice Walker. Copyright © 1979 by Alice Walker. Used by permission of Bantam Doubleday Dell Publishing Group, Inc.

Marilyn Nelson Waniek, "The Ballad of Aunt Geneva" reprinted by permission of Louisiana State University Press from *The Home Place* by Marilyn Nelson Waniek. Copyright © 1990 by Marilyn Nelson Waniek.

Richard Wilbur, "Hamlen Brook" from *The Bread Loaf Anthology,* © 1985 by Middlebury College and University Press of New England. "Playboy" from *Walking to Sleep: New Poems and Tranlsations,* copyright © 1968 by Richard Wilbur. Reprinted by permission of Harcourt Brace & Company, Inc. "The Writer" from *The Mind Reader,* copyright © 1971 by Richard Wilbur. Reprinted by permission of Harcourt Brace & Company, Inc. "Year's-End" from *Cremony and Other Poems,* copyright © 1949 and renewed 1977 by Richard Wilbur. Reprinted by permission of Harcourt Brace & Company, Inc.

Nancy Willard, "A Hardware Store as Proof of the Existence of God." From *Water Walker* by Nancy Willard. Copyright © 1989 by Nancy Willard. Reprinted by permission of Alfred A. Knopf, Inc.

William Carlos Williams, "The Red Wheelbarrow," "Spring and All," and "The Last Words of My English Grandmother" from *William Carlos Williams: The Collected Poems of William Carlos Williams 1909-1939,* Vol. I. Copyright 1938 by New Directions Publishing Cor-poration. Reprinted by permission of the publisher.

James Wright, "A Blessing" and "Saint Judas" from *Saint Judas,* reprinted by permission of University Press of New England.

Elinor Wylie, "Let No Charitable Hope" from *Collected Poems of Elinor Wylie,* copyright © 1932 by Alred A. Knopf, Inc. and renewed 1960 by Edwina C. Rubenstein. Reprinted by permission of the publisher.

William Butler Yeats, " The Lake Isle of Innisfree," "Leda and the Swan," "Sailing to Byzantium," "The Second Coming" and "The Song of Wandering Aengus" from *The Poems of W. B. Yeats: A New Edition,* edited by Richard J. Finnegan. New York: Macmillan, 1983. Reprinted by permission of Simon & Schuster. Copyright © 1928 by Macmillan Publishing Company; copyright renewed © 1956 by Georgie Yeats.

INDEX OF CRITICAL TERMS

INDEX OF POETS, TITLES, AND FIRST LINES